Praise for the "Kids Love" Guide

*On-Air Personality Comments (Tele

D1318106

"The great thing about these books is that your whole family actually lives these adventures" – (**WKRC-TV**, Cincinnati)

"Very helpful to lots of families when the kids say, I'm bored...and I don't want to go to same places again!" – (**WISH-TV**, Indianapolis)

"Dividing the state into many sections, the book has something for everyone...everywhere." – (**WLVT-TV**, Pennsylvania)

"These authors know first-hand that it's important to find hands-on activities that engage your children..." (**WBNS-TV**, Columbus)

"You spent more than 1000 hours doing this research for us, that's really great – we just have to pick up the book and it's done..." (**WTVR-TV**, Richmond)

"A family that's a great source for travel ideas..." (**WBRA-TV**, Roanoke)

"What a great idea...this book needed to be done a long time ago!" (**WKYT-TV**, Lexington)

"A fabulous idea...places to travel that your kids will enjoy" (**WOOD-TV**, Grand Rapids)

"The Zavatskys call it a dream come true, running their own business while keeping the family together. Their goal, encourage other parents to create special family travel memories." - (**WLVT-TV,** Pennsylvania)

"It's a wonderful book, and as someone who has been to a lot of these places...you hit it right on the money!" – (**WKRC-TV**, Cincinnati)

Praise for the "Kids Love" Guidebook Travel Series
Customer Comments (actual letters on file)

"I wanted to tell you how helpful all your books have been to my family of 6. I rarely find books that cater to families with kids. I have your Indiana, Ohio, Kentucky, Michigan, and Pennsylvania books. I don't want to miss any of the new books that come out. Keep up the great ideas. The books are fantastic. I have shown them to tons of my friends. They love them, too." – H.M.

"I bought the Ohio and Indiana books yesterday and what a blessing these are for us!!! We love taking our grandsons on Grammie & Papaw trips thru the year and these books are making it soooo much easier to plan. The info is complete and full of ideas. Even the layout of the book is easy to follow...I just wanted to thank you for all your work in developing these books for us..." – G.K

"I have purchased your book. My grandchildren and I have gone to many of the places listed in your book. They mark them off as we visit them. We are looking forward to seeing many more. It is their favorite thing to look at book when they come over and find new places to explore. Thank you for publishing this book!" - B.A.

"At a retail price of under $17.00, any of the books would be well worth buying even for a one-time only vacation trip. Until now, when the opportunity arose for a day or weekend trip with the kids I was often at a loss to pick a destination that I could be sure was convenient, educational, child-friendly, and above all, fun. Now I have a new problem: How in the world will we ever be able to see and do all the great ideas listed in this book? I'd better get started planning our next trip right away. At least I won't have to worry about where we're going or what to do when we get there!" – VA Homeschool Newsletter

"My family and I used this book this summer to explore our state! We lived here nearly our entire life and yet over half the book we never knew existed. These people really know what kids love! Highly recommended for all parents, grandparents, etc.." – Barnes and Noble website reviewer

KIDS ♥ LOVE OHIO

WITHDRAWN

A Family Travel Guide for Exploring "Kid-Tested" Places in Ohio

George & Michele Zavatsky

Dedicated to the Families of Ohio

In a Hundred Years...It will not matter, The size of my bank account...The kind of house that I lived in, the kind of car that I drove...But what will matter is...That the world may be different Because I was important in the life of a child.

- author unknown

For the latest major updates corresponding to the pages in this book visit our website:

www.KidsLoveTravel.com

- **REMEMBER**: *Museum exhibits change frequently. Check the site's website before you visit to note any changes. Also, HOURS and ADMISSIONS are subject to change at the owner's discretion. If you are tight on time or money, check the attraction's website or call before you visit.*

- **INTERNET PRECAUTION**: *All websites mentioned in KIDS LOVE OHIO have been checked for appropriate content. However, due to the fast-changing nature of the Internet, we strongly urge parents to preview any recommended sites and to always supervise their children when on-line.*

- **EDUCATORS**: *There are suggestions for finding FREE lessons plans embedded in many listings as helpful notes for educators.*

ISBN-13: 978-0-9774434-8-2

KIDS ♥ OHIO ™   Kids Love Publications, LLC

TABLE OF CONTENTS

State Detail Map

(With Major Routes and Cities Marked)

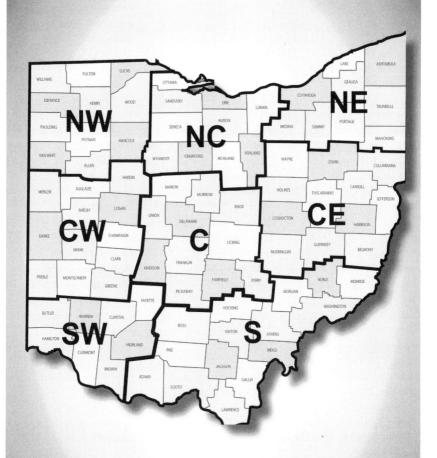

Chapter Area Map

(Chapters arranged alphabetically by chapter name)

CITY INDEX *(Listed by City, Area, Page Numbers)*

CITY INDEX *(Listed by City, Area, Page Numbers)*

HOW TO USE THIS BOOK

(a few hints to make your adventures run smoothly:)

BEFORE YOU LEAVE:

- Each chapter represents a two hour radius area of the state or a Day Trip. The chapter begins with an introduction and Quick Tour of favorites within the chapter. The listings are by City and then alphabetical by name, numeric by zip code. Each listing has tons of important details (pricing, hours, website, etc.) and a review noting the most engaging aspects of the place. Our popular Activity Index in back is helpful if you want to focus on a particular type of attraction (i.e. History, Tours, Outdoor Exploring, Animals & Farms, etc.).

- Begin by assigning each family member a different colored highlighter (for example: Daniel gets blue, Jenny gets pink, Mommy gets yellow and Daddy gets green). At your leisure, begin to read each review and put a highlighter "check" mark next to the sites that most interest each family member or highlight the features you most want to see. Now, when you go to plan a quick trip - or a long van ride - you can easily choose different stops in one day to please everyone.

- Know directions and parking. Use a GPS system or print off directions from websites.

- Most attractions are closed major holidays unless noted.

- When children are in tow, it is better to make your lodging reservations ahead of time. Every time we've tried to "wing it", we've always ended up at a place that was overpriced, in a unsafe area, or not super clean. We've never been satisfied when we didn't make a reservation ahead of time.

- If you have a large family, or are traveling with extended family or friends, most places offer group discounts. Check out the company's website for details.

- For the latest critical updates corresponding to the pages in this book, visit our website: www.kidslovetravel.com. Click on *Updates*.

ON THE ROAD:

- Consider the child's age before you stop at an exit. Some attractions and restaurants, even hotels, are too formal for young ones or not enough adventure for teens. Read our trusted reviews first.

- Estimate the duration of the trip and how many stops you can afford to make. From our experience, it is best to stop every two hours to stretch your legs or eat/snack or maybe visit an inexpensive attraction.

- Bring along travel books and games for "quiet time" in the van. (see tested travel products on www.kidslovetravel.com) As an added bonus, these "enriching" games also stimulate conversation - you may get to know your family better and create memorable life lessons.

ON THE ROAD: *(cont.)*

- In between meals, we offer the family snacks like: pretzels, whole grain chips, nuts, water bottles, bite-size (dark) chocolates, grapes and apples. None of these are messy and all are healthy.
- Plan picnics along the way. Many Historical sites and State Parks are scattered along the highway. Allow time for a rest stop or a scenic byway to take advantage of these free picnic facilities.

WHEN YOU GET HOME:

- Make a family "treasure chest". Decorate a big box or use an old popcorn tin. Store memorabilia from a fun outing, journals, pictures, brochures and souvenirs. Once a year, look through the "treasure chest" and reminisce. "Kids Love Travel Memories!" is an excellent travel journal and scrapbook template that your family can create (available on www.kidslovetravel.com).

WAYS TO SAVE MONEY:

- Memberships - many children's museums, science centers, zoos and aquariums are members of associations that provide FREE or Discounted reciprocity to other such museums across the country. AAA Auto Club cards offer discounts to many of the activities and hotels in this book. If grandparents are along for the ride, they can use their AARP card and get discounts. Be sure to carry your member cards with you as proof to receive the discounts.
- Supermarket Customer Cards - national and local supermarkets often offer good discounted tickets to major attractions in the area.
- Internet Hotel Reservations - if you're traveling with kids, don't take the risk of being spontaneous with lodging. Make reservations ahead of time. We don't use non-refundable, deep discount hotel "scouting" websites (ex. Hotwire) unless we're traveling on business - just adults. You can't cancel your reservation, or change them, and you can't be guaranteed the type of room you want (ex. non-smoking, two beds). Instead, stick with a national hotel chain you trust and join their rewards program (ex. Choice Privileges) to accumulate points towards FREE night stays.
- State Travel Centers - as you enter a new state, their welcome centers offer many current promotions.
- Hotel Lobbies - often have a display of discount coupons to area shops and restaurants. When you check in, ask the clerk for discount pizza coupons they may have at the front desk.
- Attraction Online Coupons - check the websites listed with each review for possible printable coupons or discounted online tickets good towards the attraction.

MISSION STATEMENT

At first glance, you may think that this is a book that just lists hundreds of places to travel. While it is true that we've invested thousands of hours of exhaustive research (*and drove over 3000 miles in Ohio*) to prepare this travel resource…just listing places to travel is <u>not</u> the mission statement of these projects.

As children, Michele and I were able to travel extensively throughout the United States. We consider these family times some of the greatest memories we cherish today. We, quite frankly, felt that most children had this opportunity to travel with their family as we did. However, as we became adults and started our own family, we found that this wasn't necessarily the case. We continually heard friends express several concerns when deciding how to spend "quality" and "quantity" family time. 1) What to do? 2) Where to do it? 3) How much will it cost? 4) How do I know that my kids will enjoy it?

Interestingly enough, as we compare our experiences with our families when we were kids, many of our fondest memories were not made at an expensive attraction, but rather when it was least expected.

It is our belief and mission statement that if you as a family will study and <u>use</u> the contained information <u>to create family memories</u>, these memories will grow a stronger, tighter family. Our ultimate mission statement is, that your children will develop a love and a passion for quality family experiences that they can pass to another generation of family travelers.

We thank you for purchasing this book, and we hope to see you on the road (*and hear your travel stories!*) God bless your journeys and Happy Exploring!

EXTRA SPECIAL THANKS TO:

We are most thankful to be blessed with our parents, Barbara (Darrall) Callahan and George & Catherine Zavatsky who help us every way they can – researching, proofing and baby-sitting. More importantly, they are great sounding boards and offer unconditional support. So many places around Ohio remind us of family vacations years ago…

We also want to express our thanks to the many Convention & Visitor Bureaus' staff for providing the attention to detail that helps to complete a project. We felt very welcome during our travels in Ohio and are proud to call it home!

Our own kids, Jenny and Daniel, were delightful and fun children during our trips across the state. What a joy it is to be their parents…we couldn't do it without them as our "kid-testers"!

We both sincerely thank each other – our partnership has created an even greater business/personal "marriage" with lots of exciting moments, laughs, and new adventures in life woven throughout. Above all, we praise the Lord for His so many blessings through the last few years.

We think Ohio is a wonderful, friendly area of the country with more activities than you could imagine. Our sincere wish is that this book will help everyone "fall in love" with all of Ohio.

General State Agency & Recreational Information

Call *(or visit websites)* for the services of interest. Request to be added to their mailing lists.

- Ohio Department of Natural Resources, (877) 4BOATER. (800) WILDLIFE. www.dnr.state.oh.us/odnr
- Ohio Campground Owner's Association (614) 764-0279 or www.ohiocamper.com
- National Camping Information www.gocampingamerica.com
- Ohio State Parks (614) 466-0652 or www.dnr.state.oh.us/parks
- Ohio State Park Lodges & Resorts (800) 282-7275 or www.dnr.state.oh.us/parks/overnightfacilities
- Ohio's Agricultural Fairs, www.ohioagriculture.gov. (614) 728-6200. Schedules available.
- Muskingum Watershed Conservancy District (877) 363-8500 or www.mwcdlakes.com. Well-maintained boating, swimming and fishing lakes in CE Ohio.

- Ohio Division of Travel & Tourism (800) BUCKEYE or www.discoverohio.com
- **C** - Greater Columbus CVB (800) 345-4FUN or www.experiencecolumbus.org
- **CE** - Carroll County CVB (877) 727-0103 or www.carrollcountyohio.com
- **CE** - Tuscarawas County CVB (800) 527-3387 or www.neohiotravel.com
- **CE** - Wayne County CVB (800) 362-6474 or www.wooster-wayne.com/wccvb
- **CW** - Greene County CVB (800) 733-9109 or www.greenecountyohio.org
- **CW** - Greene County Parks (937) 562-7440 or www.co.greene.oh.us/parks.htm

- **NC** - Lorain County Metroparks (440) 458-5121 or www.loraincountymetroparks.com
- **NC** - Ottawa County Visitors Bureau (800) 441-1271 or www.lake-erie.com
- **NC** - Sandusky/Erie County VCB (800) 255-ERIE or www.buckeyenorth.com
- **NE** - Convention & Visitors Bureau of Greater Cleveland (800) 321-1001 or www.positivelycleveland.com
- **SC** - Ross County-Chillicothe CVB (800) 413-4118
- **SW** - Cincinnati CVB (800) CINCYUSA or www.cincyusa.com

Skiing / Tobogganing - Usually December – early March. Ski Conditions, (800) BUCKEYE. Or contact local MetroParks or Ohio Department of Natural Resources for cross-country skiing.

- **C** - Clearfork – (800) 237-5673, Butler. www.skiclearfork.com.
- **C** - Snow Trails – (800) DEC-SNOW or (800) OHIO-SKI, Mansfield. www.snowtrails.com.
- **CW** - Mad River Mountain – (937) 599-1015 or (800) 231-7669, Bellefontaine. www.skimadriver.com
- **NE** - Alpine Valley - (440) 729-9775, Chesterland. www.alpinevalleyohio.com.
- **NE** - Boston Mills/Brandywine – (800) USKI241, Peninsula or Northfield. www.bmbw.com.
- **SC** - Spicy Run - (740) 493-2599, Latham. www.spicyrun.com
- **CE** - Bear Creek Resort Ranch KOA, 3232 Downing St. S.W., East Sparta. (330) 484-3901. Ohio's longest, fastest, and safest way to toboggan. Newly rebuilt twin half-mile-long refrigerated toboggan chutes operate 40 degrees or colder, snow or no snow. A bus takes riders and toboggans back to the top so there's no walking and hauling the toboggan back up the hill.
- **NE** – Cleveland Metroparks Chalet in Mill Stream Run Reservation, Strongsville. (440) 572-9990. Toboggan chutes 1000 feet long and 42 feet tall.

College Athletics
- **SW** - University of Cincinnati - (513) 556-CATS. www.ucbearcats.com. 18 sports. Fall, Winter, Spring.
- **SW** - Xavier University, Cintas Center - (513) 745-3900 or www.xu.edu. Volleyball, basketball.

Canoeing - **SW**- Morgan's Canoe - SR 350, Oregonia. - (800) WECANOE. www.morgancanoe.com

AIRPORTS - All children love to visit the airport! Why not take a tour and understand all the jobs it takes to run an airport? Tour the terminal, baggage claim, gates and security / currency exchange. Maybe you'll even get to board a plane.

ANIMAL SHELTERS - Great for the would-be pet owner. Not only will you see many cats and dogs available for adoption, but a guide will show you the clinic and explain the needs of a pet. Be prepared to have the children "fall in love" with one of the animals while they are there!

BANKS - Take a "behind the scenes" look at automated teller machines, bank vaults and drive-thru window chutes. You may want to take this tour and then open a savings account for your child.

CITY HALLS - Halls of Fame, City Council Chambers & Meeting Room, Mayor's Office and famous statues.

ELECTRIC COMPANY / POWER PLANTS - Modern science has created many ways to generate electricity today, but what really goes on with the "flip of a switch". Because coal can be dirty, wear old, comfortable clothes. Coal furnaces heat water, which produces steam, that propels turbines, that drives generators, that make electricity.

FIRE STATIONS - Many Open Houses in October, Fire Prevention Month. Take a look into the life of the firefighters servicing your area and try on their gear. See where they hang out, sleep and eat. Hop aboard a real-life fire engine truck and learn fire safety too.

HOSPITALS - Some Children's Hospitals offer pre-surgery and general tours.

NEWSPAPERS - You'll be amazed at all the new technology. See monster printers and robotics. See samples in the layout department and maybe try to put together your own page. After seeing a newspaper made, most companies give you a free copy (dated that day) as your souvenir. National Newspaper Week is in October.

PETCO - Various stores. Contact each store manager to see if they participate. The Fur, Feathers & Fins™ program allows children to learn about the characteristics and habitats of fish, reptiles, birds, and small animals. At your local Petco, lessons in science, math and geography come to life through this hands-on field trip. As students develop a respect for animals, they will also develop a greater sense of responsibility.

PIZZA HUT & PAPA JOHN'S - Participating locations. Telephone the store manager. Best days are Monday, Tuesday and Wednesday mid-afternoon. Minimum of 10 people. Small charge per person. All children love pizza – especially when they can create their own! As the children tour the kitchen, they learn how to make a pizza, bake it, and then eat it. The admission charge generally includes lots of creatively made pizzas, beverage and coloring book.

KRISPY KREME DONUTS - Participating locations. Get an "inside look" and learn the techniques that make these donuts some of our favorites! Watch the dough being made in "giant" mixers, being formed into donuts and taking a "trip" through the fryer. Seeing them being iced and topped with colorful sprinkles is always a favorite with the kids. Contact your local store manager. They prefer Monday or Tuesday. Free.

SUPERMARKETS - Kids are fascinated to go behind the scenes of the same store where Mom and Dad shop. Usually you will see them grind meat, walk into large freezer rooms, watch cakes and bread bake and receive free samples along the way. Maybe you'll even get to pet a live lobster!

TV / RADIO STATIONS - Studios, newsrooms, Fox kids clubs. Why do weathermen never wear blue/green clothes on TV? What makes a "DJ's" voice sound so deep and smooth?

WATER TREATMENT PLANTS - A giant science experiment! You can watch seven stages of water treatment. The favorite is usually the wall of bright buttons flashing as workers monitor the different processes.

U.S. MAIN POST OFFICES - Did you know Ben Franklin was the first Postmaster General (over 200 years ago)? Most interesting is the high-speed automated mail processing equipment. Learn how to address envelopes so they will be sent quicker (there are secrets). To make your tour more interesting, have your children write a letter to themselves and address it with colorful markers. Mail it earlier that day and they will stay interested trying to locate their letter in all the high-speed machinery.

GEOCACHING AND LETTERBOXING

Geocaching and Letterboxing are the ultimate treasure hunt and can add excitement and fun to your driving, camping and hiking experiences. Geocaching employs the use of a GPS device (global positioning device) to find the cache.

Letterboxing uses clues from one location to the next to find the letterbox; sometimes a compass is needed. Both methods use the Internet advertising the cache, providing basic maps and creating a forum for cache hunters.

GEOCACHING

The object of Geocaching is to find the hidden container filled with a logbook, pencil and sometimes prizes! Where are Caches? Everywhere! But to be safe, be sure you're treading on Public Property. When you find the cache, write your name and the date you found it in the logbook. Larger caches might contain maps, books, toys, even money! When you take something from the cache you are honor-bound to leave something else in its place. Usually cache hunters will report their individual cache experiences on the Internet. (www.geocaching.com)

GPS RECEIVER

You'll need a GPS receiver that will determine your position on the planet in relation to the cache's "waypoint," its longitude/latitude coordinates. You can buy a decent GPS receiver for around $100. More expensive ones have built-in electronic compasses and topographical maps, but you don't need all the extras to have fun geocaching.

LETTERBOXING

The object is similar to geocaching — find the Letterbox — but instead of just signing and dating the logbook, use a personalized rubber stamp. Most letterboxes include another rubber stamp for your own logbook. The creator of the letterbox provides clues to its location. Finding solutions to clues might require a compass, map and solving puzzles and riddles! This activity is great fun for the entire family! (www.letterboxing.org)

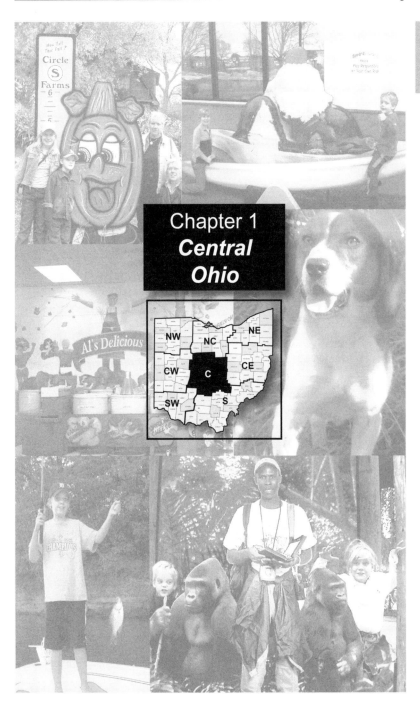

Chapter 1
*Central
Ohio*

C Area

Ashville
- Slate Run Historical Farm

Buckeye Lake
- Buckeye Lake State Park
- Cranberry Bog Annual Open House

Canal Winchester
- Mid-Ohio Historical Doll And Toy Museum

Circleville
- A.W. Marion State Park
- Circleville Pumpkin Show

Columbus
- All American Quarterhorse Congress
- Al's Delicious Popcorn (The Popcorn Outlet)
- Anthony Thomas Candy Company
- Balletmet
- Central Ohio Fire Museum & Learning Center
- Columbus Children's Theatre
- Columbus International Festival
- Columbus Motor Speedway
- Columbus Museum Of Art
- Columbus Sports
- Columbus Symphony Orchestra
- Cosi
- Davis Discovery Center
- Festival Latino
- First Night Columbus
- Fort Rapids Indoor Waterpark Resort
- Franklin Park Conservatory And Botanical Gardens
- Graeter's Ice Cream Factory
- Greek Festival
- Ohio Historical Center
- Ohio State Fair
- Ohio State University Museums
- Ohio Statehouse
- Red, White And Boom
- Santa Maria
- Schakolad Chocolate Factory
- Thurber House
- Topiary Garden

Columbus (Dublin)
- Irish Festival

Columbus (Groveport)
- Motts Military Museum

Columbus (Hilliard)
- Franklin County Fair

Columbus (Pickerington)
- Motorcycle Hall Of Fame Museum

Columbus (Powell)
- Columbus Zoo And Aquarium
- Zoombezi Bay

Columbus (Reynoldsburg)
- Tomato Festival

Columbus (Westerville)
- Hanby House

Columbus (Worthington)
- American Whistle Corporation
- Ohio Railway Museum
- Orange Johnson House

Delaware
- Alum Creek State Park
- Delaware State Park
- Harvest Festival, Stratford Ecological
- Little Brown Jug & All Horse Parade
- Maple Syrup Festival
- Olentangy Indian Caverns
- Perkins Observatory

Glenford
- Flint Ridge

Grove City
- Fall Fun Days

Heath
- Great Circle Earthworks
- Jurassic Journey Dinosaur Museum

Hebron
- Pumpkin Maze Playland (S)
- Zanesville & Western Scenic Railroad

Lancaster
- Aha! A Hands-On Adventure Children's Museum
- Sherman House Museum
- Wahkeena Nature Preserve

Lithopolis
- Wagnalls Memorial Library

London
- Madison Lake State Park

Marion
- Apple Festival
- Christmas By Candlelight
- Harding Home
- Marion County Fair
- Mysterious Revolving Ball
- Popcorn Pop-N-Drop
- Wyandot Popcorn Museum

Milford Center
- The Maize At Little Darby Creek

Mt. Gilead
- Mt. Gilead State Park

Mt. Sterling
- Deer Creek State Park Resort

Mt. Vernon
- Knox County Fair
- Knox County Historical Society Museum

Newark
- Coco Key Water Resort
- Dawes Arboretum
- The Works - Ohio Center Of History, Art & Technology

Ostrander
- Pumpkin Maze Playland

Sugar Grove
- Pumpkin Maze Playland

Sunbury
- Hartman Aviary

Utica
- Pumpkin Maze Playland
- Velvet Ice Cream: Ye Olde Mill Ice Cream Museum

A Quick Tour of our Hand-Picked Favorites Around...

Central Ohio

Pack your most comfortable walking shoes and be ready for everything that central Ohio has to offer. An early morning hike on the trails at the Columbus Metro Parks will prepare you for an afternoon at **COSI Science Center** (voted the #1 Science Museum in the nation). Right across the Scioto River is the mooring of a replica **Santa Maria** – the same size ship Columbus sailed the ocean blue – and you are welcome to come aboard and tour. All of that walking works up an appetite, so plan to don your scarlet and gray to watch the Buckeyes at **Ohio State** or the Buckeye Hall of Fame Café and Games. Go Bucks!

How about a visit to the snack food capital of Ohio! What do ducks, a mill and ice cream have in common? Ye Olde Mill at **Velvet Ice Cream**. Learn some history, watch it being made, try some and then feed what's left of your cone to the ducks! On the north end of Columbus sits a small factory and retail store home to the Popcorn Outlet and **Al's Delicious Popcorn**. Meet the Popcorn people while watching a video tour of large poppers spilling out mounds of popped corn. Try some bubble gum flavor or savory pizza popcorn. Right down the street is another ice cream factory – **Graeter's Ice Cream Factory**! Arrange a tour or just show up and take your own self-guided tour of the French Pot method of the creamiest ice cream. How do they get those big dark chocolate chunks in there anyway? There's an ice cream store and soft play area on the premises, too. And, I know you're probably full from snacking on samples already, but you have to see the giant Buckeye candy and the silver foil wrapped pipes of molten chocolate flowing through the **Anthony Thomas Candy Company Factory** (west side of Columbus). Walk the "cat-walk" above a giant chemistry cooking lesson below. And, even though it's not a food, what kid could resist a tour of the **American Whistle** factory (north of town in Worthington). They make the whistles that coaches and referees use – the loudest whistles in the world!

Now, weave in a visit to the **Columbus Zoo and Aquarium** and its new additions, the polar bears, Alaskan brown bears, Arctic Fox and reindeer as part of the Polar Frontier. To experience the fun of the zoo combined with the thrill of an outdoor waterpark, visit **Zoombezi Bay** Water Park (on the same campus), with six waterslides, a wave pool, kiddie areas and more. And as part of the waterpark admission, entrance to the zoo is free (seasonally).

Finally, head out of town a little ways to the quaint town of Newark. Here you'll find an indoor waterpark, a science museum and even Indian mounds. The **Great Circle Earthworks** are fun to get outside and run around but the small museum that explains the culture of natives who lived there during biblical times gives this place a spiritual tone to just how ancient it is.

Sites and attractions are listed in order by City, Zip Code, and Name. Symbols indicated represent:

 Festivals   Restaurants   Lodging

Ashville

SLATE RUN HISTORICAL FARM

Ashville - 1375 SR 674 North (in Slate Run Park on SR 674, off US 33 east) 43103. www.metroparks.net/ParksSlateRunFarm.aspx. Phone: (614) 508-8000 or (614) 833-1880. Hours: Tuesday, Wednesday, Thursday 9:00am-4:00pm, Friday and Saturday 9:00am-6:00pm, Sunday 11:00am-6:00pm (June-August). Closes earlier rest of year. Wednesday – Saturday 9:00 am – 4:00pm, Sunday 11:00am – 4:00pm (September – May). Memorial and Labor Day, Noon – 6:00 pm Admission: FREE to browse around. Small admission for special programs - mostly held on weekends. Tours: Available by appointment (special prices). Metro Park open 6:30am-dusk.

This historic farm depicts life on a working family farm of the 1880's. Visitors may join in with the barnyard and household chores. All the work is done using equipment and methods of the time (some horse-powered machinery). Some of the specially scheduled programs may be: maple syrup demonstrations and production, toy making, fishing, ice cream socials, making root beer, rope making and pretend old-fashioned school. Kids love getting involved and doing chores at Slate Run. They offer nature trails, picnic grounds, and children's play facilities at the adjoining Slate Run Metro Park.

C Area

Buckeye Lake

BUCKEYE LAKE STATE PARK

Buckeye Lake - *2905 Liebs Island Road (9 miles South of Newark off State Route 13) 43046. Phone: (740) 467-2690. www.dnr.state.oh.us.*

Buckeye Lake, constructed as a canal feeder lake in 1826, is Ohio's oldest state park. The park has long been a popular vacation spot and today offers endless water-related recreational opportunities including swimming, skiing, boating

> In the 1930's, as many as 1,000 boats a day were crappie fishing on the lake.

(unlimited hp) and fishing. Public swimming areas with parking facilities, change booths and latrines are located at Fairfield Beach and at Brooks Park on the south side of the lake. Permanent & rental properties are available around the lake.

CRANBERRY BOG ANNUAL OPEN HOUSE

Buckeye Lake - *Cranberry Bog State Nature Preserve. (800) 589-8224. Take a tour of the island's rare and fascinating plants by pontoon boat. Admission. (last Saturday in June)*

Canal Winchester

MID-OHIO HISTORICAL DOLL AND TOY MUSEUM

Canal Winchester - *700 Winchester Pike (off US 33 at Gender Road, east side of Columbus) 43110. Phone: (614) 837-5573. www.dollmuseumohio.org. Hours: Wednesday-Saturday 11:00am-5:00pm (Spring - Mid December). Admission $3.00 (under 6 free) Miscellaneous: Gift Shop, Old and New Collectibles.*

As you step in the door, you will see a train display in the lobby. To your left, you will go through a door into the magical world of dolls. The collection includes rare antique dolls and toys dating from the 1700's to contemporary. Barbie fans of all ages will love the extensive Barbie collection. Boys will love the GI Joe, Disney and Lionel trains.

Circleville

A.W. MARION STATE PARK

Circleville - *(5 miles East of Circleville off SR 23 to SR 22) 43113. Phone: (740) 869-3124. www.dnr.state.oh.us.*

454 acres of camping, hiking trails, boating and rentals, fishing, and winter sports. Electric motors only are permitted. The nearby floodplains of the Scioto River are adorned with a variety of wildflowers. The Hargus Lake Trail offers five miles of scenic pleasure, providing access to the entire shoreline of the lake. Wildlife indigenous to the area includes fox squirrel, ring-necked pheasant, a variety of songbirds, red fox and white-tailed deer.

CIRCLEVILLE PUMPKIN SHOW

Circleville - Downtown. www.pumpkinshow.com. (740) 474-7000. Ohio's largest and oldest harvest celebration has seven parades, lots of pumpkin, squash and gourds, pumpkin foods (cotton candy, burgers, chips and ice cream), rides and entertainment. See some of the largest pumpkins and the world's largest pumpkin pie (approximately 350 lbs. and 5 feet in diameter). Contests galore like hog calling, egg toss, pie eating and carved pumpkins. FREE. (mid-October, Wednesday-Saturday)

Columbus

COLUMBUS SPORTS

COLUMBUS BLUE JACKETS HOCKEY - (614) 246-PUCK or (800) NHL-COLS or www.bluejackets.com. Nationwide Arena. NHL Hockey in Ohio. Look for their mascot, Stinger here and at special events. Season runs October-early April. Tickets range from $20-$185.

COLUMBUS CLIPPERS BASEBALL - www.clippersbaseball.com or (614) 462-5250. Huntington Park (Arena District). Semi-professional AAA farm team for the Cleveland Indians. LouSeal is the official mascot for the Columbus Clippers. Krash is the crazy parrot who has taken the position as LouSeal's First Mate. Many post game concerts and occasional fireworks. Tickets: $3.00-$10.00. (April – Labor Day weekend)

COLUMBUS CREW SOCCER - Major League Soccer (Mid April – Late September). (614) 221-CREW or www.thecrew.com. Crew stadium (near Ohio State Fairgrounds). Prices start as low as $10.

COLUMBUS SPORTS *(cont.)*

COLUMBUS DESTROYERS ARENA FOOTBALL - (614) 246-4252.
Enjoy all of the hard-hitting, fast-paced action of the Columbus Destroyers
Arena Football League at Nationwide Arena. www.columbusdestroyers.com.
Season runs March-June. (Note: AFL Season was cancelled for 2009.)

OHIO STATE UNIVERSITY BUCKEYES - www.ohiostatebuckeyes.com.
(614) 292-2524. Big 10 College sports: Football, Basketball (Men's &
Women's), Hockey, OSU Ice Skating, Golf, Swimming, Tennis & Volleyball.

OHIO STATE UNIVERSITY MUSEUMS

Columbus - *Woody Hayes Dr. & High Street (most facilities between High St. &
Olentangy River - off SR 315) 43201. Phone: (614) 292-3030. http://undergrad.osu.
edu/pdf/WalkingTour.pdf & www.osu.edu/visitors/museums.php. Miscellaneous:
The Buckeye Hall of Fame Café (casual restaurant & gameroom) is down the road
1412 Olentangy River Rd. http://www.halloffamecafes.com/prod/buckeye/. (614)
291-2233.*

The Student Visitors Center (Room 132 Enarson Hall) provides a packet
to chaperones. The self-guided tour (with tour brochure for kids) includes
information about ten specific locations on campus, is interactive and suggests
activities that the kids can do as they move through campus. It asks questions
at each stop geared towards kids in order to get them more acquainted with
the university. A completed tour should take about 1 - 1½ hours.

Many other "add-on" Tour Options are available:

ATHLETIC FACILITY TOURS – Value City Arena, Monday - Friday on non-
event days between 9:00am-3:30pm. 60 minutes. (614) 292-3231. Ohio
Stadium, Monday-Friday between 8:00am-5:00pm. (614) 292-9748. Athletic
Facility Tours are for groups of students ages 12+.

JACK NICKLAUS MUSEUM - 2355 Olentangy River Road. Tuesday-
Saturday 9:00am-5:00pm. www.nicklausmuseum.org. Admission: $5.00-
$10.00. Shows the long history of the game, Mr. Nicklaus' place in that
history, famous OSU golfers and a prototype of the Nicklaus family's den
with personal stories narrated by his wife.

WEXNER CENTER FOR THE ARTS – Family days and guided tours. (614)
292-3535 or www.wexarts.org/ctr/gen/overview.shtml.

ASTRONOMY – www.astronomy. mps.ohio-state.edu/events/star.html. (614)
292-1773. Perkins Observatory Lectures or monthly Star Talks.

BIOLOGICAL SCIENCES GREENHOUSE FACILITY – Insectary, a quarantine facility, two research labs, a growth chamber area and prep room. www.biosci.ohio-state.edu/ ~plantbio/greenhouse/index.html. Monday - Friday 8:30am-4:30pm, except holidays.

FOOD SCIENCE BUILDING – tours of miniature pilot plant, OSU Dairy Store (ice cream treats, breakfast, lunch items), Parker Building, 2015 Fyffe Road (off Woody Hayes Dr) (614) 292-6281.

ORTON GEOLOGICAL MUSEUM – skeleton of a giant sloth, fossils, fluorescent minerals, and rocks. The museum is also home to the fossil skeleton of a 7-foot-tall giant ground sloth, Megalonyx Jeffersonian. 9:00am-5:00pm. On the oval, open free to the public. http://library.osu.edu/sites/geology/museum/index.php.

HISTORIC COSTUME & TEXTILES COLLECTION – (614) 292-3090. Historic textiles from the 15th century to 20th century in costume pieces including men's, women's, and children's garments and accessories. www.hec.ohio-state.edu/cts/collect/bucket/geninfo.htm. 175 Campbell Hall.

OHIO STATEHOUSE

Columbus - *Broad and High Streets (10 acre square in downtown) 43201. Phone: (614) 728-6350 or (888) OHIO-123. www.ohiochannel.org/your_state/ohio_ statehouse/information/about_the_statehouse/index.cfm. Hours: Weekdays 7:00am-6:00pm, Weekends 11:00am-5:00pm. Admission: FREE. Tours: For groups of fewer than 10, free guided tours are offered Monday through Friday on the hour from 10:00am until 3:00pm, and on Saturdays and Sundays from noon until 3:00pm. Self-Guided & Audio Wand Tours. Visitors may wander on their own anytime during Statehouse hours with a self-guided tour brochure or borrow a tour wand with pre-recorded information to follow at your own pace. Self guided tour brochures and tour wands are available at the 3rd Street Information Desk. Miscellaneous: Museum shop has clever and unique Ohio gifts and souvenirs.*

Learn about Ohio's Statehouse history, its architecture and the legislative process. Visit the place where Abraham Lincoln made speeches in 1859 and 1861. Inside you'll see the rotunda with the state seal and historic paintings and documents. The sweeping grand staircase of the Senate Building was modeled after the Paris Opera House. Restored to its original grandeur in 1996, the Statehouse is filled with priceless historic art, including a marble bust of Abraham Lincoln – the only one the President posed for during his lifetime. Even the Statehouse's expansive grounds have a history, as Civil War Union soldiers frequently camped there. If the Ohio House or Senate is in session, you'll be able to listen to the debates. Outside is home to several war memorials and statues including the new Veterans Plaza where visitors read the letters sent home from enlisted men and women. Educational displays and touch-screen kiosks (ex. Pass through all 88 counties in the Map Room) along with a great Museum shop are found in the basement. The basement is all white painted brick and stone. Why are the formal walls painted light shades of pink or peach? The Atrium used to be called Pigeon Alley - why?

NEW for 2009

OHIO STATEHOUSE MUSEUM: (scheduled to open spring 2009) Interactive, hands-on exhibits will challenge visitors' knowledge about Ohio history and the workings of state government and equip them to more fully participate as citizens. Historical artifacts and images will tell the stories of those who designed and built the Statehouse and those who have come here to serve. Audiovisual media and theatrical effects will transport visitors to historical events and invite them to imagine themselves governor, legislator or judge.

HOLIDAY TOURS ON CAPITOL SQUARE

Columbus - *Ohio Statehouse. Step back in time with a guided tour of the 1861 Statehouse and see holiday decorations as they were in Victorian times. Holiday concerts and occasional activities for kids. Candy Cane sale at store. (monthlong in December)*

COLUMBUS CHILDREN'S THEATRE

Columbus - *775 East Long Street 43203. http://colschildrenstheatre.org. Phone: (614) 224-6672.*

Theatre activities for youth of all ages, backgrounds and cultures. Do you remember your first magical theatrical moment? That moment when your heart flew into your mouth, you caught your breath and you were transferred to a new magical world? One of the greatest joys of theatre is witnessing a child's Wide-Eyed-Wonder when they really connect to a play. Many lessons to be learned watching plays like Oliver, Emperors New Clothes or the seasonal the Best Christmas Pageant Ever. Tickets run $10.00-$20.00 per person, per show. Children's theatre classes are held at different campuses (downtown, Grove City, Gahanna, Westerville, Dublin and Pickerington). (July-May)

FRANKLIN PARK CONSERVATORY AND BOTANICAL GARDENS

Columbus - *1777 East Broad Street (off I-71) 43203. Phone: (614) 645-TREE or (800) 214-PARK. www.fpconservatory.org. Hours: Tuesday-Sunday & Holiday Mondays 10:00am-5:00pm. Wednesday evenings 5:00-8:00 pm. Admission: $7.50 adult, $6.00 senior/student, $4.00 child (2-12). Miscellaneous: Café and gift shop. Family activities each season including Blooms & Butterflies, Holidays, and the Orchid Forest. Educators: click their online icon for school tours, then lesson plans for some suggestions.*

A place where you can learn where coffee comes from or watch the careful pruning of Bonsai trees. The kid-friendly ants, iguanas, and lories are becoming permanent enhancements to the conservatory. The large 1895 glass structure resembles the style of London's Crystal Palace. The Conservatory is the only public botanical garden in the world to own a signature collection of Chihuly's artworks, which represents more than 3,000 pieces of glass. Flowers and mushrooms and vines - all made from glass - this color and art really engages the imagination. Chihuly's work is modern art but never "out there" and even more special when presented amongst greenery and natural light. Walk through a simulated tropical rain forest, a desert, a tree fern forest, a Pacific Island water garden and then on to the Himalayan Mountains. Outside is a sculpture garden.

HOLIDAYS AT THE CONSERVATORY

Columbus - Franklin Park Conservatory. *A tradition each year with a poinsettia tree and annual gingerbread house competition. Admission. (Thanksgiving weekend thru first weekend in January)*

COLUMBUS MOTOR SPEEDWAY

Columbus - *1845 Williams Road 43207. www.columbusspeedway.com. Phone: (614) 491-1047.*

Stock car racing. Kids Day (late August or September). Climb into a real race car! 7:00 pm race starts Saturdays.

OHIO HISTORICAL CENTER

Columbus - *1982 Velma Avenue (I-71 to 17th Avenue Exit) 43211. Phone: (614) 297-2300 or (800) 646-5184. http://ohsweb.ohiohistory.org/places/c09/. Hours: Thursday-Saturday 9:00am-5:00pm, Sunday and Holidays Noon-5:00pm. Closed*

Christmastime, Thanksgiving & New Years. Admission: $8.00 adult, $4.00 student. Parking fee $4.00 per vehicle. Includes Ohio Village entrance (if open). Tours: Summer Kids Kamps and Discovery Days bring out the hands-on fun. Educators: ohiohistoryteachers.org is the OHS website with state history lesson plans and activities. Case History or Educational Kit trunks that contain artifacts, documents,

on a wide range of specific topics that can be rented for a week. Pick up Educational Resource scavenger hunt game flyers near many area entrances. School groups can reserve a tour of the Center and the adjoining Ohio Village. Miscellaneous: Gift Shop, food and picnic tables. The adjacent Ohio Village is now open to the public for signature events only. Ohio Village is designed to recreate the appearance of a typical county-seat town in Ohio during the mid 19th century, about the time of the Civil War.

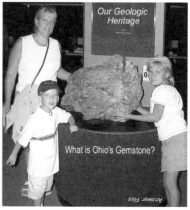

Our Geologic Heritage

What is Ohio's Gemstone?

Answer: Flint

This is a museum and a whole lot more. There are exhibits and artifacts covering the history of Ohio from archaeology to natural history and the history of Ohio. There are many historical collections from early fossils and Indian tribes (large dioramas and artifact study of prehistoric Indians), original accounts from early explorers, and papers from political leaders such as General Meigs and Thomas Worthington. Other highlights of this history gallery are 1920s children's activities, including a log cabin and pioneer kitchen, where young people can try on pioneer clothes, operate a spinning wheel and "cook" pioneer food. The newly renovated Battelle Discovery Park and Theater provide modern audiovisual technology, and an interactive

No illusion here...see a real two-headed cow!

science park for children makes learning about Ohio's natural history fun. The Center's permanent natural history exhibit features Ohio's plants, animals, geology, geography, and climate and weather. "The Nature of Ohio" exhibit is guarded by a huge mastodon found in a swamp in Clark County. See the quirky 2-headed calf and Egyptian mummy, too. Continuous early 1900s newsreels, an operating 1880s carriage shop, vintage automobiles, Adena Pipe and Hopewell mica cutouts are here, too.

DICKENS OF A CHRISTMAS

Columbus - *Ohio Historical Center - Ohio Village. Step into the world of Charles Dickens as Ohio Village revisits the Victorian Christmas made famous in his stories. From plum pudding to that pretty little German toy, the Christmas tree, Dickens created a festive and enduring vision of Christmas. Join others in the village as the spirit of Dickens comes to life through interactions with characters from his writings, cooking demonstrations, hands-on crafts, decorations, caroling, readings by candlelight, street vendors, and many more Victorian holiday traditions. Refreshments are available for purchase. Admission. (second and third weekend evenings in December)*

BALLETMET

Columbus - *322 Mt. Vernon Ave. 43215. www.balletmet.org. Phone: (614) 229-4860. Educators: Fun and Games, links to sample lessons, etc. on the Education icon online.*

Classic to contemporary ballet including the famous Nutcracker. Sneak Peeks - spend time with dancers or Morning at the Ballet (mini programs like Cinderella) seem to engage the younger kids the most.

CENTRAL OHIO FIRE MUSEUM & LEARNING CENTER

Columbus - *240 N. 4th Street, No. 16 Engine House 43215. Phone: (614) 464-4099. www.centralohiofiremuseum.com. Hours: Tuesday-Saturday, 10:00am-4:00pm. Group tours by appointment only. Admission: $5.00 adult, $4.00 senior, $3.00 student, Under 6 FREE.*

Visually, the hand-drawn, horse-drawn, & motorized fire vehicles will initially interest the kids. Curiosity will have them asking firefighters about the day-to-day lives in an engine house. Then, kids can climb on board a fire engine and video drive through a smoke-filled bedroom. Walk through a kitchen to see what dangers may lurk. A child paramedic can sit in the back of an ambulance, access a patient and listen to the radio calls coming in. On a group tour? Look for Boots the Fire Mouse as your escort.

COLUMBUS MUSEUM OF ART

Columbus - *480 East Broad Street (four blocks east of the Capitol) 43215. Phone: (614) 221-4848 info line. www.columbusmuseum.org. Hours: Tuesday-Sunday 10:00am-5:30pm. Thursday until 8:30pm. Admission: $8.00 adult, $5.00 senior and student (age 6+). FREE on Sunday. Parking is free. Educators: We highly recommend that you prepare students for their Museum visit by borrowing the* *classroom resource packets or requesting a Docent-in-the-School to present a classroom packet. Click on Teachers and Schools and Lesson Plans for printable pages.*

American and European art from 1850-1950. See the life-size horse of welded steel or the works of Columbus realist George Bellows and folk artist Elijah Pierce (go inside a barber shop with radio broadcast of the times). Doodles and Wow Art! are weekly programs for families. Its My Museum Gallery/Sculpture Guide, Art Speaks audio tour $3.00 - is where art talks. EYE SPY adventure offers art-interactive docent-led creative, colorful weekday mornings where kids learn how works of art are created and preserved. Maybe dress up like figures in a 17th century Dutch painting. Café & gift shop.

COLUMBUS SYMPHONY ORCHESTRA

Columbus - *55 East State Street (most performances at Ohio Theatre)   43215. Phone: (614) 228-8600.   www.columbussymphony.org.*

The orchestra closed and is now re-opened with a more limited budget and staff - but still here! Enjoy several family performances with pre-concert activities. Average $10.00 or more for tickets.

COSI

Columbus - *333 West Broad Street (I-71 exit Broad or Front St. or I-70 exit Broad or Fourth St. to downtown riverfront) 43215. Phone: (614) 228-COSI or (888) 819-COSI.   www.cosi.org.   Hours: Wednesday-Friday 10:00am-5:00pm, Saturday 9:00am-5:00pm, Sunday Noon-6:00pm. Open holiday Mondays. Closed most major winter holidays and first two weeks of September. Admission: $12.50 adult, $10.50 senior, (60+), $7.50 child (2-12). Special exhibits and movies add on $5.00-$6.00. Miscellaneous: Science 2 Go Store, AtomiCafé. Educators: go to this site: www.cosi.org/educators/activities/   to find games, puzzles and test standards met study guides.*

Parents Magazine voted COSI the #1 Science Center in the Country !

Explore hands-on exhibits focusing on science, technology, health and history. Take your preschool-aged children to Kid-Space. They pretend they are a doctor or nurse, paint their faces, do a puppet show, water play, ride in a boat, and just have a good active time there. Other favorite areas are Big Science Park (outdoor), where older kids conquer their fears and ride the high wire cycle. Ocean Learning World features a simulated shipwreck with dive tanks and a yellow submarine you can climb inside. Progress is where you travel through time and interact with people in a small Midwestern town. Gadgets is a giant "erector set". The Life area has an Echo

Free room, Hot/Cold Coils and Rat Basketball (plus some mature displays that make this area PG). In Space, you get dizzy in a tunnel and see a great space 3D movie. The idea of "learning worlds" really makes visitors feel like they are someplace else.

DAVIS DISCOVERY CENTER

Columbus - *549 Franklin Avenue 43215. www.davisprograms.com. Phone: (614) 645-SHOW.*

The Children's Drama Company for 8 to 12-year-olds are held at the center. At the Davis Youth Complex, classes for children ages 4 through 19 include magic, piano, ballet, acting, puppetry and more. Children who are home-schooled may take advantage of theater and dance classes offered in the daytime at both locations. Shows like Treasure Island and Scrooge are performed during the school year. Tickets only run $3.00-$5.00 per person.

SANTA MARIA

Columbus - *Battelle Riverfront Park Scioto River (Downtown – Northeast of Broad Street Bridge at Marconi) 43215. www.santamaria.org. Phone: (614) 645-8760. Hours: Wednesday-Friday 10:00am-3:00pm. Weekends & Holidays Noon-5:00pm. (April-October). Early evenings in Summer. Admission: $3.50 adult,*

$3.00 senior (60+), $2.00 student (5-17). Tours: depart frequently during the Santa Maria's hours of operation. Tours last approximately 45 minutes and explore every part of this working wooden tall ship. Educators: wonderful pdf of lesson plans, games and crafts (click on Group Programs, then Teacher's guide). Miscellaneous: The Santa Maria Seeds of Change Visitor Education Center is now the home of the world's first multimedia exhibit on successful invisibility research, featuring the Santa Maria herself!

In 1492, Columbus sailed the ocean blue!

Can you make her disappear? River Jam summer weekend evenings and the annual October "Dueling at the Dock" or Discover Columbus Days.

The world was forever changed when, in 1492, Christopher Columbus set sail searching for a direct trade route to the Indies. Carrying him was the Santa Maria. The Columbus Santa Maria is the world's most authentic, museum quality representation of Christopher Columbus'

flagship. Climb aboard and return to 1492 as costumed guides share facts about the ship and the famous voyage. Feel the challenges and hardships

faced by Columbus and his crew. Hear the wood structure creak as you hear stories about what they ate (no wonder they got sick a lot!) or how they managed through rough waters. Most everything is touchable - something we like in historical tours. You better be on your best behavior or you'll have to "walk the gang plank"! Sleeping quarters available for campouts.

Learning about how important ropes and knots are on a sailing ship...

THURBER HOUSE

Columbus - *77 Jefferson Avenue (Downtown) (I-71 exit Broad Street, head west one block and turn north on Jefferson) 43215. www.thurberhouse.org. Phone: (614) 464-1032. Hours: Daily 1:00-4:00pm except major holidays. Admission: FREE. Tours: Self-guided tours are free Monday through Saturday. Visitors have the option of taking a guided tour every Sunday for a small fee of $2.50 for adults and $2.00 for students and seniors. Group tours by reservation.*

James Thurber, the well-known humorist and cartoonist, grew up in Columbus. The restored home is where James lived during his college years. Thurber House is a living museum. They allow visitors to experience Thurber's life by becoming a guest of the Thurber family. While in the house

museum, visitors are invited to sit on the chairs, play a tune on the downstairs piano, or, touch the typewriter that was Thurber's while he was at the New Yorker. The house is featured in several of Thurber's stories. (Stories about the time Thurber lived in this house are included in his My Life and Hard Times and The Thurber Carnival.) Be sure to read some of Thurber's works before you visit or purchase some of his books at the bookstore in Thurber House.

TOPIARY GARDEN

Columbus - *480 East Town Street (Old Deaf School Park, NW corner of E. Town & Washington, downtown, east of the Main Library) 43215. Phone: (614) 645-0197. www.topiarygarden.org. Hours: Visitor Center open Tuesday, Saturday, Sunday 11:00am-3:00pm (April-December). Educators: Be sure to print off the online "Tour Guide" handout to orient yourself before and during the visit.*

C
Area

The topiary (greenery shaped like people, boats, animals, etc.) garden and pond depicts the theme "A Sunday Afternoon on the Island of La Grande Jaffe". FREE (open daily dawn to dusk).

AL'S DELICIOUS POPCORN (THE POPCORN OUTLET)

Columbus - 1500 Bethel Road (SR 315 to Bethel Road exit west) 43220. Phone: (614) 451-7677 or (800) 396-7010. www.thepopcornoutlet.com. Hours: Monday-Saturday 11:00am-7:00pm. Admission: FREE. Tours: By Appointment, Approximately 20-30 minutes. No minimum or maximum number of people.

This wonderfully enthusiastic staff will answer every question you've ever had about popcorn. Kids love watching the 2-minute video tour of the large poppers and closely watch the popped corn flow out. They have a tremendous assortment of 60 spicy and sweet flavors to coat the popcorn. They have a

challenge presented with the Bubble Gum flavor: If you can blow a bubble from it (it tastes that real!), you get loads of free popcorn. You won't leave without trying lots of favorite flavors like Pizza, Buckeye Mix or Jelly Bean. Kids and parents will want to bring their allowance to spend on these treats! Their huge

Fun Fact: How high can popcorn kernels pop? Up to 3 feet in the air.

selection of colorful tins will fill many of your gift needs. A great "quick stop" as part of an inexpensive day trip.

GRAETER'S ICE CREAM FACTORY

Columbus - 2555 Bethel Road (near intersection of Sawmill Road) 43220. Phone: (614) 442-0622. www.graeters.com. Tours: Group tours by appointment.

You can be guided through the factory by an experienced tour leader who can answer your questions or just look through the observation windows. You'll enjoy an informative video and see their unique French Pot process that makes only two gallons of ice cream at a time. Gourmet ice cream is made in small batches in French Pots (old-fashioned, no air whipped in as in modern, commercial brands). The tour

Famous ice cream cones, Jenny & Daniel...

lasts about 20 minutes and is appropriate for all ages. Guided Tours can be scheduled on any week day when they are making ice cream (minimum of 10 people). Self-guided tours are available anytime. There is no charge for the

tour, only for whatever ice cream you choose to buy! Try a dip of the signature chocolate-chipped flavors. Specially made liquid chocolate is poured into the ice cream, frozen and then broken by paddles, creating planks of dark chocolate within the ice cream. The Soft Play Area may be just the place (indoors) to let the kids expend some of their sugar energy.

The play area was so "yummy"!

ANTHONY THOMAS CANDY COMPANY

Columbus - 1777 Arlingate Lane (I-270W to Roberts Road Exit) 43228. Phone: (614) 274-8405 or (877)Candy-21. www.anthony-thomas.com. Admission: FREE. Tours: Tuesdays and Thursdays from 9:30am to 2:30pm. You don't need to make an appointment and there is no size limit on the group. Free sample at end of tours. Approximately 60 minutes. Factory Candy Shop Miscellaneous: Gift shop open during tour times. You finish your tour in the retail store.

Have you seen "Willy Wonka's Chocolate Factory?" This tour will remind you of that movie, especially when you first see the clean, bright white equipment, near spotless floors and dozens of silver insulated pipes running to several production lines. View chocolate and fillings being prepared and molded in rooms remaining at a constant 90 degrees F. with 0% humidity (so workers and chocolate don't sweat!) Walk along the comfortable, glass-enclosed suspended "Cat-Walk" and observe eight lines producing 25,000 pounds of chocolates per shift. A couple of wrapping machines are exclusively for fundraisers and airline chocolates, but most of the production line packers can be seen hand packing chocolates for stores. A giant physics and chemistry cooking lesson!

FORT RAPIDS INDOOR WATERPARK RESORT

Columbus - 4560 Hilton Corporate Drive (I-70 exit 107) 43232. Phone: (877) 33-splash. www.fortrapids.com. Hours: Basically 9:00am-10:00pm peak seasons and weekends. Restricted hours during school year weekdays and closed most Tuesdays and Wednesdays during School year. Admission: Day Pass Rate $26.95 per person; After 4:00pm - $21.95; Spectator Pass - $9.95 per person. Available after 10:00am until capacity reached.

Every Season Is SUMMER here. Get ready for wet and wild fun 365 days a year in a climate controlled, 84 degree indoor water park. Zip around all 12 of Fort Rapids indoor water slides and water activity areas with names like Rattlesnake Falls, Raging Bull, and Cowboy Creek Lazy River. Also Trading Post gift shop, Gold Rush arcade and a fitness center. The contemporary western theme is tastefully carried throughout the waterpark and the resort itself. Waterpark passes around $19-$24 each person. Overnight rooms are booked thru Holiday Inn rates.

SCHAKOLAD CHOCOLATE FACTORY

Columbus - *1500 Polaris Parkway, LifeStyle Center part of Mall, 43240. Phone: (614) 846-8053. www.schakolad.com. Tours: Call a couple of days in advance to reserve the store for a Sweet tour. The store is closed and you can make your own chocolate item (s). These are only done with call ahead reservations.*

A world of sweet possibilities: Handmade Fine Chocolates. Molds of all kinds wait along a chocolate-brown wall, chocolate novelties line shelves, then there are the gleaming glass cases full of chocolate truffles and filled chocolates of every description. You get to learn about the history of chocolate, how they make everything and make your own treat to package and eat. They even make Buckeyes! In cold weather, ask for a cup of hot cocoa. Great place for family time or small birthday parties.

FESTIVAL LATINO

Columbus - *Downtown Riverfront. (614) 645-7995. www.musicintheair.org. Celebrate Latin culture, food (contemporary and traditional) and music (Mambo, Salsa, Conjunto, Flamenco). Children's workshops. FREE (third weekend in June)*

RED, WHITE AND BOOM

Columbus - *Downtown. www.redwhiteandboom.org. Full day of parades, rides, entertainment and the largest fireworks display synchronized to music and lights in the Midwest. (July 3rd)*

OHIO STATE FAIR

Columbus - *Ohio Expo Center, I-71 & 17th Avenue. www.ohiostatefair.com. (614) 644-4000. Includes the largest junior fair in the nation, puppet shows, laser light shows, petting zoo, rodeo, tractor pulls, horse shows, fishing and lumberjack shows, exhibitors from agriculture to the arts, rides and big name entertainment. Favorite family areas* *include: the Natural Resources area (live wildlife, log cabin, butterfly house); the Nursery; and the Butter Cow sculpture and ice cream. Admission. Family Value Days on Mondays. (twelve days beginning the middle of the first week of August)*

GREEK FESTIVAL

Columbus - *Greek Orthodox Cathedral, Short North Area, 555 N. High Street. (614) 224-9020. www.greekcathedral.com. Gyros, baklava, music, dance, tours of the church, cooking demos and videos about Greece. Admission. (Labor Day Weekend)*

ALL AMERICAN QUARTERHORSE CONGRESS

Columbus - *Ohio Expo Center, I-71 & 17th Avenue. (614) 943-2346 before October, (614) 294-7469 (during show). www.oqha.com. The world's largest single breed horse show with seven acres of commercial exhibits and demos. Fee per vehicle. (two weeks long during mid-to-late October)*

COLUMBUS INTERNATIONAL FESTIVAL

Columbus - *Veterans Memorial, 300 West Broad Street. (614) 228-4010. More than 60 nationalities and cultures will participate in a mix of dance, music, foods and crafts. Educational interactive activities for kids. Admission. (first weekend in November)*

FIRST NIGHT COLUMBUS

Columbus - *Ohio Statehouse Square & downtown locations. A family oriented non-alcoholic event with indoor and outdoor activities such as kid's/parent's food, entertainment and crafts, and a countdown to midnight. www.firstnightcolumbus.com. Admission. (New Years Eve)*

IRISH FESTIVAL

Columbus (Dublin) - *Coffman Park, 6665 Coffman Road. (614) 410-4545 or (877) 67-GREEN or www.dublinirishfestival.org. A weekend of all things Irish, from entertainment, dance competitions and sports demos to the very best in Irish foods. Admission. (first weekend each August)*

MOTTS MILITARY MUSEUM

Columbus (Groveport) - *5075 South Hamilton Road (I-270 exit Rte 33/SR 317) 43125. Phone: (614) 836-1500. www.mottsmilitarymuseum.org. Hours: Tuesday-Saturday 9:00am-5:00pm, Sunday 1:00-5:00pm. Admission: $5.00 adult, $4.00 senior, $3.00 student.*

Its purpose is to bring military history into perspective by collecting and preserving memorabilia. Secondly, it educates the public on the importance of past, present and new military events that impact our lives (good way to "tie-in" current events). Best on a group tour with a specific theme in mind.

FRANKLIN COUNTY FAIR

Columbus (Hilliard) - *Franklin County Fairgrounds. Open during the fair is Northwest Village including the church, 1850's log cabin, outhouse, caboose, train station, granary, barn and museum with vintage household equipment. (mid-July for 7 days)*

MOTORCYCLE HALL OF FAME MUSEUM

Columbus (Pickerington) - *13515 Yarmouth Drive (I-70 east exit 112A, left on SR 204) 43147. Phone: (614) 856-2222. www.motorcyclemuseum.org. Hours: Daily 9:00am-5:00pm. Closed winter holidays. Open summer holidays Noon-4:00pm. Admission: $10.00 adult, $5.00 AMA members, $8.00 senior, $3.00 student (12-17). FREE child (under 12).*

The Museum is more than just a wide range of motorcycles on display. Its goal is to tell the stories and history of motorcycling. A self-guided tour features a wall mural, the history of motorcycles, and the Glory Days. Themed "sets" (some permanent - some traveling) add to the presentation. Be sure to visit their website for current exhibits - For example through June 2009, you can see "Awesome-Ness," the Hall of Legends exhibit, features 11 custom motorcycles built by the king of choppers, Arlen Ness, a 1992 Hall of Fame inductee. This exhibit chronicles the life of Arlen Ness and highlights motorcycles from his career that will inspire you. You'll see Top Banana, Smooth-Ness, Jet Bike, Untouchable, and the ever-popular '57 Chevy inspired Ness-Stalgia. If you're a custom bike lover, this exhibit is for you; lots of chrome, lots of heavy metal, and exotic paint schemes. Kids are most attracted to the 50 motorcycles on display. Motocross, BMW, and Harley abound here.

C Area

COLUMBUS ZOO AND AQUARIUM

Columbus (Powell) - *9990 Riverside Drive (Route 257, I-270 to Sawmill Road exit, follow signs) 43065. Phone: (614) 645-3550. www.columbuszoo.org. Hours: Daily 9:00am-6:00pm (Summer), Daily 9:00am-5:00pm (September-May), 9:00am-8:00pm (Wednesday Family Night, mid-June to mid-August). Open 365 days a*

year. Admission: $10.00 adult, $7.00 senior (60+),$5.00 child (2-11). Tuesday is Senior Day and Wednesday is half off admission for Franklin County residents. Family Membership available. Parking fee. Miscellaneous: Gift Shops and Concessions. Food Court similar to a mall. Pony, boat, train and carousel rides (small additional fee). Play gym. Picnic facilities.

Two "ferocious" animals that escaped from the zoo...

The famous Director Emeritus of the zoo, Jack Hanna, is a regular on national talk shows. Highlights of the naturally landscaped zoo include cheetahs, black rhinos, lowland gorillas, Habitat Hollow (what makes human/animal habitats home- play & pet area), and North American Bald Eagles (named George and Barbara). A 100,000-gallon coral reef exhibit and one of the largest reptile collections in the United States are also featured. The habitat "Manatee Coast" is modeled after the famous Island Refuge in Florida with a 190,000 gallon pool and floor to ceiling glass viewing walls! The expanded African Forest exhibit offers a walk-through rainforest-themed area with incredible interaction with all kinds of monkeys. Newer exhibits include the Islands of Southeast Asia (primitive ruins, Indonesian buildings and music, komodo dragons, orangutans and otters) and an Australia area. A

A fun safari photo op!

waterway allows narrated boat rides through the exhibit to give visitors a different view while still providing more room for the animals to roam freely. Polar Frontier became part of the North American Region at the Zoo in 2008. Home to polar bears, brown bears, arctic foxes, reindeer and mountain goats in a 13-acre exhibit space. It just keeps getting better!

EGGS, PAWS & CLAWS

Columbus (Powell) - *Columbus Zoo and Aquarium*. *Ages 2-12. Admission. Easter Bunny appearance, treat stations, egg hunts, and kids' entertainment and crafts. (Usually held the Saturday before Easter).*

WILDLIGHT WONDERLAND

Columbus (Powell) - *Columbus Zoo and Aquarium. Something for everyone, millions of lights, zoo animals of all kinds, and when we visited we even saw an underwater "Santa in a diving suit" - What fun! Great hot chocolate, too! Ice skating, carolers, delicious treats and wagon/train rides. Walk-thru. Daily, evenings. Admission. (Thanksgiving - January 1)*

ZOOMBEZI BAY

Columbus (Powell) - 9990 Riverside Drive (Route 257, I-270 to Sawmill Road exit, follow signs) 43065. Phone: (614) 645-3550. www.zoombezibay.com. Hours: Typically 11:00am-6:00pm (Memorial Day weekend thru Labor Day). Extended summer break hours. Admission: Average $25.00 per person.

The new park right next to the Columbus Zoo opened in 2008 with 15 contemporary water slides with names such as Cyclone, Sea Snakes and Tahitian Twister. Wave pool fanatics like us love the 4 foot waves created in Wild Tides, while Katoomba Lagoon provides safe water fun for younger kids with 12 marine animal play structures and another giant pool that is only about a foot deep. Although the park is smaller than waterparks in resort areas, this park is very manageable for parents. Families can "base" from ample chairs and tables available at central locations by the wave pool or the kiddie lagoon. We also liked their menu selection and pricing. Fried food, modest entrees and even a dozen healthy (and yummy, try the grilled caesar chicken salad wrap) choices are offered at fair prices with generous portions.

TOMATO FESTIVAL

Columbus (Reynoldsburg) - *Civic Park, 6800 Daugherty Drive. (614) 866-2861. www.reynoldsburgtomatofestival.org. Ohio's tomato harvest is celebrated with things like free tomato juice, fried green tomatoes, tomato pies, tomato fudge, tomato cakes & cookies, Tiny Tim Tomatoland, crafts, parade and The Largest Tomato Contest ($100 per pound). Fee for parking. (September - Wednesday through Sunday)*

HANBY HOUSE

Columbus (Westerville) - *160 West Main Street (across from Otterbein College, between SR 3 & Cleveland Ave.) 43081. www.ohiohistory.org/places/hanby. Phone: (614) 891-6289. Hours: Saturday and Sunday 1:00-4:00pm (May-September). Groups by appointment. Admission: $0.75 - $2.00 per person.*

"Up on the Housetop reindeer pause, Out Jumps dear ol' Santa Claus. " Hanby played many roles in his life; student, abolitionist, father, teacher, minister. But it was as a composer that we remember him. Benjamin Hanby was the composer of over 80 folk songs and hymns including "Sweet Nelly Gray" and "Up On the Housetop". Children will enjoy seeing Ben's original instruments and musical scores. This home was part of the Underground Railroad. Be sure to notice and ask about the roses in a vase by the front window. The tour also includes viewing a short introduction movie.

OHIO RAILWAY MUSEUM

Columbus (Worthington) - *990 Proprietors Road (Off State Route 161, just past railroad tracks, head north) 43085. http://dev.ohiorailwaymuseum.net/. Phone: (614) 885-7345. Hours: Sunday 1:00-5:00 pm (Memorial Day-September). Admission: $4.00-$6.00 (age 4+).*

They have displayed approximately 30 pieces of Ohio Railway History dating from 1897 – 1950. The guide explains that steam engines have their own personality. Get close to one under steam and hear it talk! Try a hand truck or catch a one mile trolley. Special seasonal train excursions take you on a steam train day-trip. See website for details. Small admission for museum.

ORANGE JOHNSON HOUSE

Columbus (Worthington) - *956 North High Street (just north of State Route 161) 43085. Phone: (614) 885-1247. www.worthington.org/about/orangejohnson.cfm. Hours: (Open House) Sunday 2:00-5:00pm (April-December). Closed holidays. Admission: $2.00-$3.00 which includes a tour.*

This place is best known by locals for cooking and combs! The Orange Johnson House is a restored early 1800's home. This property offers a unique view of both the pioneer and antebellum periods in Worthington. Part of it is Federal style, the back part is pioneer. There are many authentic objects and toys that children can pick up and pretend to use. In 1816 Orange Johnson, a hornsmith, who specialized in comb-making bought the property. Visitors will learn about the comb making trade and see a collection of 19th century women's hair combs and comb making tools. The guide will describe chores children were given in those days (your own children will think they have it made!). A good time to visit is when they have cooking demonstrations. The smell in the air engages everyone to explore early settler's kitchen tools and techniques. The Old Rectory in downtown Worthington has a doll museum with changing exhibits.

CHRISTMAS OPEN HOUSE

Columbus (Worthington) - *Orange Johnson House. You are invited to stroll through the beautifully decorated 19th century house, sample holiday treats in front of the keeping room fireplace and listen to traditional music in the drawing room. Open house is free. Programs have fee. (first and third Sunday in December)*

AMERICAN WHISTLE CORPORATION

Columbus (Worthington) - *6540 Huntley Road (I-71 to Route 161 west, turn right on Huntley-look for small sign) 43229. www.americanwhistle.com. Phone:*

(800) 876-2918. Admission: $4.00 per person (15 person minimum) and $5.00 per person for whistle and lanyard included.   Tours: Monday-Friday 10:00am-4:00pm. One hour long, 15-40 people, appointment necessary. Don't have at least 15 people? They can add your group onto an already existing tour. Miscellaneous: Gift shop where you'll want to buy a lanyard to go with your new whistle or a gold plated whistle! Educators: the Ohio Grade 4 curriculum includes learning about what is involved in the production of goods and services that people use. The factors of production include land, labor, capital and entrepreneurship...all covered at the factory tour.

See whistles made from solid brass, the same metal that musical instruments are made from. No wonder they sound so sweetly loud!

Do you know what a lanyard is? Do you know what makes a whistle louder? See and hear the only metal whistle manufactured in the United States (used by police, referees, coaches, etc.). These "American Classics" are the loudest whistles in the world - 4 decibels higher pitch than the competitors! You'll learn everything you ever wanted to know about whistles and really get to see a small manufacturing operation up close. See mechanical engineering at work - in one-of-a-kind machines designed to perform specific tasks. Learn how a whistle works - and how sciences like aerodynamics and chemistry contribute. Learn how a whistle can be an effective safety tool for people of all ages. These people know how to give great tours! Each person gets to take home a whistle they just watched being made!

Delaware

ALUM CREEK STATE PARK

Delaware - *3615 South Old State Road (7 miles Southeast of Delaware off State Route 36/37, 1 mile West of I-71) 43015. www.dnr.state.oh.us. Phone: (740) 548-4631.*

8,600 acres with a great sandy beach! Food service is available at the marina.

Camping (tent, RV, and cabin rentals), hiking trails, lots of good boating, boaters swimming holes, boat rentals, fishing, a Nature Center and winter sports. Over forty miles of trail wind along the lakeshore through mature beech-maple forests and across deep ravines. The forest is home to the fox squirrel, woodchuck, rabbit, white-tail deer and many other species of wildlife. And, they have a great Dog Park and Beach area just for dogs of all sizes (separate areas) to play by

Daniel and his catch...

the water, too. Snowshoes, our beagle, loves this place best. Because they're so close to metro Columbus, they host many well-attended seasonal events on and off the water (ex. Fall Fest, Fishing Tournaments).

I "wuv" this place...

ALUM CREEK HOLIDAY FANTASY OF LIGHTS

Delaware - Alum Creek State Park. Hundreds of thousands of lights and holiday/ storybook characters. Entrance is on Hollenback Road, at Alum Creek Marina. Drive thru. Free cookies and cocoa with Santa.Daily, evenings (unless noted). Admission. (Thanksgiving - January 1)

DELAWARE STATE PARK

Delaware - *(6 miles North of Delaware on US 23) 43015. Phone: (740) 369-2761. www.dnr.state.oh.us.*

Dense woodlands, expansive meadows and a reservoir blend to create Delaware State Park. Once home to the Delaware Indians, this recreational area offers 3,145 acres of camping, hiking trails, boating and rentals, fishing, swimming, and winter sports. The trails connect the lakeshore with each of the four camping areas, transecting meadows, woodlands and wetlands. Eat at the nearby Hamburger Inn, (740) 369-3850, 16 N. Sandusky St, 50's theme.

OLENTANGY INDIAN CAVERNS

Delaware - *1779 Home Road (US 23 North to Home Road, follow signs, 6 miles north of I-270) 43015. Phone: (740) 548-7917. www.olentangyindiancaverns.com. Hours: Daily 9:30am-5:00pm (April-October). Admission: $8.50 adult, $5.00 child (7-15). Miscellaneous: Large picnic facilities. Frontierland (cute western village) with gem mining, rock climbing wall and mini-golf $5.00 extra. Gift shop, playground. The caverns are not wheelchair or stroller accessible.*

A historic Indian meeting room...

Wyandot Indians used these underground caves until 1810 for protection from the weather and their enemies. The caves were formed by an underground river that flows to the Olentangy River hundreds of feet below the surface. The caves were originally discovered during a search for oxen that broke loose from a wagon train. Their owner, J. M. Adam's name and date can be seen on the entrance wall. The tour lasts 30 minutes and takes you through winding passages and coves underground. Then, you visit the museum where Indian artifacts found in the caves are displayed. If you're still in an adventurous mood, play a game of miniature golf, climb a rock wall, mine for gems or go on a nature hike past teepees and longhouses. Something for every size adventurer here.

PERKINS OBSERVATORY

Delaware - *State Route 23 (2 miles south of Delaware, 1 miles south of US 23/SR 315) 43015. Phone: (740) 363-1257. www.perkins-observatory.org. Hours: Friday nights. Schedule online. Admission: $6.00 adult, $4.00 senior/child. $1.00 more if purchased day of program. Highly recommended to order in advance, by phone or mail-in order form.*

Gaze at the galaxies, count the craters on the moon, and enjoy an entertaining astronomy lesson along with a historical tour of this unique observatory built in 1923. Children who have studied astronomy will especially enjoy this. The stars naturally fascinate them at night so this is a real treat to see them this close. The program includes a tour of the observatory, an amusing talk on astronomy, and then telescope observation if it is a clear night (otherwise, maybe a planetarium show). There's also Mind & Space games in the Kids Zone area. Occasional lawn telescope observation and rocket launches.

MAPLE SYRUP FESTIVAL

Delaware - Camp Lazarus. 4422 Columbus Pike. www.camplazarus.org. (740) 548-5502. Syrup making demos. Pancake dinners/breakfasts. Sugarbush tours by foot or by wagon or by train. (weekends in March)

HARVEST FESTIVAL, STRATFORD ECOLOGICAL

Delaware - Stratford Ecological Center. www.stratfordecologicalcenter.org. 3083 Liberty Road. Puppet shows, entertainers and storytellers take over the picnic area on the main stage. Big kids are occupied as the pasture becomes "Kid's World" and is active with kites, stilts, face painting, and a giant earth ball. Little tykes are kept active in the hay bale toddler area with farm toys. Kids of all ages can climb on a tractor, make apple cider, ride on a horse-drawn wagon, make paper, grind grain, and so much more! Stratford sells home-grown food for lunch and volunteers provide a great array of baked goods for sale. Admission. (third Saturday in September)

LITTLE BROWN JUG & ALL HORSE PARADE

Delaware - Delaware County Fairgrounds, 236 Pennsylvania Avenue. (800) 335-3247 or www.littlebrownjug.com. The most coveted horse race for three-year old pacers held on the fastest half-mile track in the world. Kick off parade with the largest all-horse, mule and donkey parade east of the Mississippi. Admission. (mid-September - Saturdays only)

Glenford

FLINT RIDGE

Glenford - 7091 Brownsville Road SE (SR 16 east to SR 668 south) 43739. Phone: (740) 787-2476 or (800) 283-8707.   www.ohiohistory.org/places/flint. Hours: Saturday & Sunday Noon-5:00pm (Memorial Day-Labor Day). Admission: Donations. Miscellaneous: Flint Preserve open April - October, 9:30am to Dusk.

Because of flint's features, it has been respected throughout the ages and used in the making of tools, weapons, ceremonial objects of native cultures, and in modern times in the production of jewelry. Indians came to see this

C Area

stretch of hills for flint stone (official gemstone of the State of Ohio). Displays show how flint is formed from silica and what objects can be made today with flint (like sparks that start flames when flint is rubbed against steel). Outdoors you can explore the trails past ancient quarry pits. Several quarry pits may be seen in the park today, and the museum is built over one of them. There are several hiking trails and a paved nature trail with Braille and regular text for visitors looking for a beautiful hiking area. How else can we use flint?

Grove City

FALL FUN DAYS

Grove City - Circle S Farms. 9015 London Groveport Rd. www.circlesfarm.com. Pumpkin Patches/ Hayrides/ Corn Mazes/ Fall Playland - Admission (average $6.00). 2 mazes, entertainment on weekends, snack bar & autumn treats. Plan on at least two hours playtime. Open weekends, some weekdays (by appointment) and weeknights. (late September - late October).

Heath

GREAT CIRCLE EARTHWORKS

Heath - *455 Hebron Road (I-70 to SR 79 north, follow signs to Convention & Visitors Bureau) 43056. http://ohsweb.ohiohistory.org/places/c08/greatcircle.shtml. Phone: (740) 344-1920 or (800) 600-7174. Hours: Park open daylight hours all year. Museum open Monday-Friday 8:30am-5:00pm, Saturday 10:00am-5:00pm, and Sunday 1:00-5:00pm. Holidays Noon-5:00pm. (mid-April to mid-October). Miscellaneous: The Great Circle Earthworks are part of the Newark Earthworks consisting of the nearby Octagon Earthworks and Wright Earthworks. The Great Circle Museum is also the new home of the Licking County Convention and Visitors Bureau. This re-opening comes as a delight to those of us who really missed the museum part of the earthworks that explained, so well, the unusual nature of this mysterious people. Support them and the CVB and townspeople who worked hard to get this "back on the map." Educators: Lesson Plans, Vocabulary and Worksheets Online under Lesson Plans.*

The Moundbuilders is a circular mound 1200 feet in diameter with walls 8 to 14 feet high. The Hopewell Indians were believed to exist between 100BC and 500AD - around the same time as the New Testament. Visitors to the Great Circle Museum are invited to watch an interactive video explaining the significance of the site and tour a 1,000-square-foot exhibit that includes a timeline of Ohio's ancient cultures and an explanation of why American Indians regard the Newark Earthworks as a sacred site. The exhibit also details how the earthworks align with the rising and setting of the moon. Following the museum tour, visitors can take self-guided tours of the grounds during daylight hours. As you walk outside, you walk right into the mouth opening of a

> The Newark Earthworks State Memorial is the largest system of connected geometric earthworks built anywhere in the world!

circular mound. Once inside, just imagine the Hopewell Indian ceremonies that occurred many years ago. Research has concluded that the central Eagle shaped mound was the site of a grand ceremonial site. Octagon Earthworks and Wright Earthworks are both additional local sites that preserve other features of prehistoric Ohio. Admission is free, donations accepted.

JURASSIC JOURNEY DINOSAUR MUSEUM

Heath - *4600 Ridgely Tract Road (Burning Tree Golf Course, off SR 79 south of Heath) 43056. www.jurassicjourneyexhibits.com. Phone: (740) 522-3464 or (888) 37-DINOS. Hours: Daily 7:00am-9:00pm (when the course is open). Closed when golf course is closed due to weather. Admission: $3.00-$4.00.*

About 100 individual, full-size cast replicas of dinosaurs are made and on display here. Also, an Ice Age exhibit featuring the Burning Tree Mastodon, which was discovered on the golf course in 1989 while forming the back 9 holes.

Hebron

ZANESVILLE & WESTERN SCENIC RAILROAD

Hebron - *US 40 (3 miles East of Hebron – I-70 to Route 79 North Exit to US 40) 43025. Phone: (740) 928-3827 or (800) 579-7521. www.zwsr.org. Hours: Call or visit website for details.*

As of December 31, 2007, Buckeye Central Scenic Railroad has ceased operations. However, a new scenic railroad is forming- hoping to open in 2009. What this might look like once they're running: Take a trip through Ohio farmland for a 90 minute ride on the same route the train traveled in the mid-1800's on the Shawnee line (important line for pioneers heading west). They offer a scenic, 1½ hour round trip excursion through the rolling countryside of central Ohio on historic rail in vintage passenger coaches powered by a classic diesel locomotive.

PUMPKIN MAZE PLAYLAND

Hebron - Devine Farms, 672 National Road. Pumpkin Patches/ Hayrides/ Corn Mazes/ Fall Playland - Admission (average $6.00). Plan on at least two hours playtime. Open weekends, some weekdays (by appointment) and weeknights. Pumpkin painting, make a scarecrow, pumpkin egg hunt. www.devinefarms.com. (late September - late October).

PUMPKIN MAZE PLAYLAND

Hebron - Pigeon Roost Farm, (I-70 exit 122 to Rte. 40). Pumpkin Patches / Hayrides / Corn Mazes / Fall Playland - Admission (average $6.00). Plan on at least two hours playtime. Open weekends, some weekdays (by appointment) and weeknights. www.pigeonroostfarm.com. (late September - late October).

Lancaster

AHA! A HANDS-ON ADVENTURE CHILDREN'S MUSEUM

Lancaster - 315 S. Broad Street, Broadway Center 43130. Phone: (740) 653-1010. www.aha4kids.org. Hours: Thursday-Saturday 9:30am-4:30pm, Sunday 12:30-3:30pm. Open late until 6:30pm on Friday. Admission: $5.00 per person. Miscellaneous: Outdoor picnic tables.

AHA! the liveliest, convenient, and educational, place for children (especially those age 0-7) in town. Schools are going to like it. You are going to like it. There's Lego Play, Sand Play, Train Play, Water Play, Craft areas, Pretend Theater, Market, Pizza Shop, Vet Office and Garden areas…even music play with flowers.

SHERMAN HOUSE MUSEUM

Lancaster - 137 East Main Street 43130. Phone: (740) 654-9923. Hours: Tuesday-Sunday 1:00-4:00pm (April - mid-December). Guided tours last 45 minutes for each home. www.fairfieldheritage.org/shermanhouse.htm. Admission: $6.00 adult, $1.00 students under 18.

The Sherman House Museum was the birthplace of General William Tecumseh Sherman and his brother, U.S. Senator John Sherman, and home to the remarkable Sherman Family. One upstairs bedroom houses family memorabilia, and another offers a re-creation of General Sherman's Civil War field tent including several items he used during the war, and a sound and light presentation depicting his passion for the Union. The last room houses an excellent exhibit, "Sherman at War," explaining his war story with artifacts, paintings, prints, maps, weapons, and GAR memorabilia. Imagine how life must have been in the "Little Brown House on the Hill," the Sherman House, with eleven children and four adults as you visit the wooden structure in which one of the most famous / infamous Civil War Generals was born.

WAHKEENA NATURE PRESERVE

Lancaster - *2200 Pump Station Road (US 33 to County Road 86 west, follow signs) 43155. www.ohiohistory.org/places/. Phone: (740) 746-8695 or (800) 297-1883. Hours: Saturday-Sunday 8:00am-4:30pm (April -October). Admission: $7.00 per vehicle.*

Wahkeena, named with an Indian word meaning "most beautiful" is a located on the edge of the Hocking Hills. Trees, ferns, mountain laurels, wildflowers, orchids, and sandstone cliffs. All that beauty plus 70 species of birds and 15 species of mammals including woodpeckers and white-tailed deer. At the lodge, tour groups may view nature study exhibits. There are two trails available for hiking.

Lithopolis

WAGNALLS MEMORIAL LIBRARY

Lithopolis - *150 East Columbus Street 43136. www.wagnallslibrary.org. Phone: (614) 837-7003.*

Series of musical concerts and dramatic events in Wagnalls Memorial (Adam Wagnall was the co-founder of the Funk and Wagnalls Publishing Co.). The series programs and workshops have included light and serious drama, dance groups, mime, a puppeteer and a wide variety of musical events ranging from the classical to bluegrass. Tickets $8.00-$12.00. Tours of the library are available by appointment and include a description of the unusual architectural features and history of the Memorial and Wagnalls family.

London

MADISON LAKE STATE PARK

London - *(3 miles East of London off State Route 665) 43140. Phone: (740) 869-3124.. www.dnr.state.oh.us.*

One of the best examples of existing prairie in Ohio is within the Darby Plains of Madison County. Bigelow Cemetery State Nature Preserve near Chuckery contains prairie plants including big bluestem, Indian grass and purple coneflower. Smith Cemetery Prairie contains stiff goldenrod, gray willow and wild petunia. The 106-acre lake is ideal for sailboats, row boats and canoes. A 300-foot sand beach provides enjoyment for swimmers and sunbathers. Changing booths and latrines are provided. A scenic ½-mile hiking trail takes visitors through woodlands and along the lakeshore.

Marion

HARDING HOME

Marion - *380 Mount Vernon Avenue (2 miles west of State Route 23 on State Route 95) 43302. www.ohiohistory.org/places/harding. Phone: (740) 387-9630 or (800) 600-6894. Hours: Thursday-Saturday 9:30am-5:00pm, Sunday and Holidays Noon-5:00pm (Summer). Weekends Only (April, May, September and October). By appointment in Spring. Admission: $6.00 adult, $3.00 student (all ages). Educators: Bio online. www.ohiohistoryteachers.org has several themed lesson plans online. Miscellaneous: Memorial is a circular monument (with columns of white marble) containing the tombs of Mr. and Mrs. Harding on Delaware Avenue.*

A great way to learn Presidential history without a fuss from the kids. Do you know what the fancy pot is in the guestroom - the one lying on the floor? They have displayed a podium used at Harding's inauguration in 1920 as our 29th President. See the porch where Harding campaigned what was later called the "Front Porch Campaign", speaking to over 600,000 people overall. The original porch collapsed and a new one had to be built during the campaign. A special small house was built behind the main house for the press associates visiting the area to cover the campaign. Look for the ornate collar worn by their dog "Laddie Boy".

MYSTERIOUS REVOLVING BALL

Marion - *Marion Cemetery 43302. Hours: Dawn-Dusk.*

Can you scientifically solve the "Marion Unsolved Mystery"? Here's the scoop! The ball is a grave monument for the Merchant family (located in the northeast corner of the cemetery) erected in 1896. The 5200-pound granite ball turns mysteriously with continuous movement. There has been no scientific explanation for this revolution and the phenomenon is featured in many newspapers including "Ripley's Believe It or Not"!

WYANDOT POPCORN MUSEUM

Marion - *169 East Church Street (Heritage Hall – Marion County Museum of History) 43302. www.wyandotpopcornmus.com. Phone: (740) 387-HALL or (800) WYANDOT. Hours: Wednesday-Sunday 1:00-4:00pm (May-October). Weekends Only (November-April). Closed most holidays. Admission: $1.00-$3.00 (age 6+).*

Before you enter the Popcorn Museum, see the hand-made miniature, working carousel and Prince Imperial (a stuffed 25 year old horse from France). You won't believe how they braided his mane! As you enter the large, colorful tent, you'll be enchanted by the antique popcorn poppers and concession wagons. See the first automated popper and the first all electric popper – all in pristine condition. It's the only museum like it in the world. Free popcorn is served daily - the smell wafting in the air adds to the atmosphere.

POPCORN FESTIVAL

Marion - Downtown. (740) 387-FEST or www.popcornfestival.com. Highlights include a parade, tours of the Popcorn Museum, popcorn sculptures and nationally known entertainment nightly. Free. (weekend after Labor Day)

MARION COUNTY FAIR

Marion - Marion County Fairgrounds, 220 E. Fairground Street. (740) 382-2558. Huber Machinery Museum open (steam & gas tractors, threshers and road-building equipment, plus Marion steam shovel #6). (first week of July)

APPLE FESTIVAL

Marion - *Lawrence Orchards. 2634 Smeltzer Road. Apples & cider. Apple pie eating contests. Apple peeling contests. Apple butter. Candy apples. Wagon/hayrides. Apple Dumplings, Fritters, Donuts, etc. Parades. Pioneer crafts. Petting Zoo. www.lawrenceorchards.com. (September weekend)*

CHRISTMAS BY CANDLELIGHT

Marion - *Marion County Fairgrounds, 220 E. Fairground St. www.marioncounty.com. Hundreds of thousands of lights & holiday / storybook characters. Daily, evenings. Drive thru. Admission. (Thanksgiving - January 1)*

POPCORN POP-N-DROP

Marion - *Downtown, Busby Park (corner of Center & Prospect). (740) 244-9567. A family oriented non-alcoholic event with indoor and outdoor activities such as kid's/ parent's food, entertainment and crafts, and a countdown to midnight. At midnight, watch the Popcorn Ball drop. Admission. (New Years Eve)*

Milford Center

THE MAIZE AT LITTLE DARBY CREEK

Milford Center - *Little Darby Creek, 8657 Axe Handle Rd. Pumpkin Patches / Hayrides / Corn Mazes / Fall Playland - Admission (average $6.00). Plan on at least two hours playtime. Open weekends, some weekdays (by appointment) and weeknights. Cow train, rubber duck races, corn cannon. www.cornfieldmaze.com. (late September - late October).*

Mt. Gilead

MT. GILEAD STATE PARK

Mt. Gilead - *4119 State Route 95 (1 mile East of Mt. Gilead on State Route 95) 43338. Phone: (419) 946-1961. www.dnr.state.oh.us.*

Mt. Gilead State Park is a quiet, small park centrally located in the state of Ohio. Picnicking, fishing and hiking can be enjoyed year-round. Six and a half miles of trails, including a two-mile multipurpose trail for hikers and horseback riders, traverse Mt. Gilead State Park. 172 acres of camping, hiking trails, boating, fishing & some winter sports.

Mt. Sterling

DEER CREEK STATE PARK RESORT

Mt. Sterling - *20635 Waterloo Road (I-71 to SR 56 to SR 207, 7 miles south of town) 43143. Phone: (740) 869-3124 Park or (740) 869-2020 Lodge or (877) 678-3337 Reservations. www.visitdeercreek.com. Admission: FREE.*

A collage of meadows and woodlands surround the scenic reservoir. This resort park features a modern lodge, cottages, campground, golf course, swimming beach and boating for outdoor enthusiasts. Nature Programs, bike rentals, hiking trails, boating and rentals, fishing, golf, and winter sports are available throughout park. The

> The first campers at Deer Creek were here around 2000 BC! Historians believe that a nomadic Indian tribe of hunters and gatherers used this area as a camp periodically throughout the year.

Resort has over 100 guest rooms (some with bunk beds, some with lofts), 25 fully furnished two-bedroom cottages (screened porch, many with gas

fireplaces, fire ring and grills), indoor/outdoor pools, whirlpool/sauna, gamerooms, sport courts, fitness center, full service restaurant and plenty of activities. Great to plan a group/family get-together here as there are things to do and places everywhere to gather for games (cards, board games) or crafts (Shrinky Dink, buttons, sand art, etc) or evening family videos or hayrides or campfires. They have short hiking trails that are "kid-friendly" (we loved "tracking" the paw prints on the trails early morning) and their Holiday or Theme Weekends are well-planned with entertainment and special guests (i.e. astronauts). Be careful, this place could be habit forming!

Mt. Vernon

KNOX COUNTY HISTORICAL SOCIETY MUSEUM

Mt. Vernon - *875 Harcourt Road (routes 3 and 36) 43050. Phone: (740) 393-KCHS. www.knoxhistory.org. Hours: Thursday-Sunday 2:00-4:00pm, Wednesday 6:00-8:00pm (February-mid December).*

Exhibits portray the life and travels of Johnny Appleseed, the story of educational institutions, the postal service and radio stations history, toys and dolls, business and industry collections (Cooper Heritage Collection 19th century steam farm engines- became Rolls Royce), Bridge Company exhibit and the musical heritage of the county (Dan Emmett-composer, musician "Turkey in the Straw" and "Old Dan Tucker" - festival in town mid-August).

KNOX COUNTY FAIR

Mt. Vernon - Fairgrounds (SR 3). (740) 397-0484 or www.visitknoxohio.org. Check out the traditional favorites plus rodeo, bull-riding, tractor pulls, and Safety Day. The Agricultural Museum that houses hundreds of old-fashioned pieces of equipment and tools is open. (last week of July)

Newark

COCO KEY WATER RESORT

Newark *- 2299 Cherry Valley Road (Cherry Valley Lodge, I-70 exit 126. OH37 NE to OH16 E.) 43055. www.cocokeyresort.com. Phone: (740) 788-1200 or (800) 788-8008. Hours: Generally opens at 11:00am weekdays, 10:00am weekends until 7:00 to 10:00pm in the evening. Admission: Waterpark access is included with the purchase of a waterpark package room. Lodging and waterpark passes start at $159.00. Packages include CoCo Key Indoor Water Resort access for up to 4 people per room. They are valid the day you check in, as well as the day you check out (until 4:00pm). DayPass, when available is $19.95 online. Regular rates run $25.00-$35.00 per person. Children UNDER the age of 2 years are free of charge. Miscellaneous: In addition to CoCo Key Water Resort, Cherry Valley Lodge has a traditional recreational pool located inside the hotel. A fitness center is also available for those wishing to exercise during their visit. Restaurants and snack bars located throughout the property. All rooms feature refrigerators.*

Inspired with a Key West theme, every day is a sunny 84 degrees and full of water excitement. Little ones can make a splash at Parrot's Perch zero depth entry slide and bucket area. Big-kid thrills await on the River tube ride or the Shark Slam, Gator Gush and Barracuda Blast body-and raft-water slides. Key Quest Arcade features over 40 state-of-the-art electronic games and a full-service ticket redemption center.

DAWES ARBORETUM

Newark - *7770 Jacksontown Road (SR 13, I-70 exit 132) 43056. Phone: (740) 323-2355 or (800) 44-DAWES. www.dawesarb.org. Hours: Grounds open daily dawn to dusk. Visitors Center open: Monday-Saturday, 8:00am-5:00pm, Sundays & holidays, 1:00pm-5:00pm. Closed Thanksgiving, Christmas and New Years. Admission: FREE.*

The Dawes Arboretum features plants tolerant of central Ohio's climate. Azaleas, crab apples, hollies, oaks and conifers are a few of the collections accessible from the 4.5 mile Auto Tour and more than 8 miles of hiking trails. There's also meadows, woods, gardens, cypress swamp, holly, and a Bird-Watching garden. Try a free visit each season to see the new colors.

LUMINARY TOUR

Newark - Dawes Arboretum. North End Auto Tour and Visitors Center. The Dawes Arboretum brings you an evening of illumination with 1,500 candle luminaries. Join others inside the Visitors Center after the drive for a cup of hot cocoa, a holiday treat and some activities for the whole family. All proceeds will benefit the Licking County Food Pantry. (first Friday night in December)

THE WORKS - OHIO CENTER OF HISTORY, ART & TECHNOLOGY

Newark - *55 South First Street (I-70 to SR 13 north to between 1st & 2nd streets) 43058. Phone: (740) 349-9277. www.attheworks.org. Hours: Tuesday-Saturday 9:00am-5:00pm. Open Sundays Noon-5:00pm (October-April only). Some Labs only open when staffed from 11:00am-2:00pm. Admission: $7.00 adult, $5.00 senior (55+), $3.00 child (2-17).*

"The Works" is a reoccurring theme. The art gallery and studio have the name, "Art Works." Pottery and ceramics are the central theme of the studio; you decide how you want to experience them, whether creating your own Bisque Studio (fired pottery), or throwing on the wheel in the mud room. The newly refurbished glass studio has become "Glass Works". Watch workshop glass blowers demonstrate their craft as they create artistic pieces of glassware including intricate vases, bowls, paperweights and seasonal items. Also found in the complex is the Digital Works (web design and TV studio). The original 1880s machine shop complex houses The Works traces the development of industry in central Ohio from prehistoric Indians to the 21st century. Learn methods of transportation thru the years or which products were made here (ex. Mason jars and engines for farm machines). See where local raw materials are used in manufacturing, farming and fuel production. Interactive touch displays educate kids on what, where, and how materials are extracted (raw and finished forms). INVENT Lab and TYKE Lab are new theme areas to check out.

Ostrander

PUMPKIN MAZE PLAYLAND

Ostrander - *Leeds Farm, 8738 Marysville Road. Pumpkin Patches / Hayrides / Corn Mazes / Fall Playland - Admission (average $6.00). Plan on at least two hours playtime. Open weekends, some weekdays (by appointment) and weeknights. www.leedsfarm.com. (late September - late October).*

Sugar Grove

PUMPKIN MAZE PLAYLAND

Sugar Grove - *Sharp Farms, (off US 33). Pumpkin Patches / Hayrides / Corn Mazes / Fall Playland - Admission (average $6.00). Plan on at least two hours playtime. Open weekends, some weekdays (by appointment) and weeknights. www.sharpfarms.com. (late September - late October).*

Sunbury

HARTMAN AVIARY

Sunbury - *9000 Cheshire Road (I-71 Sunbury exit - Rtes. 36.37 east. Right on Golf Course Rd. towards Sunbury Golf Course) 43074. http://hartmanaviary.com. Phone: (740) 965-9464. Hours: From mid-April until mid-October Hartman Aviary opens it outside facilities to the public on Saturdays. The hours are from 12:00 to 4:00pm.*

The owner has painstakingly committed to breeding high quality and well-socialized parrots for private sale. During open house, visitors are able to see hundreds of parrots in large outdoor flights. Visitors are able to get inches away from the smaller conjures and lories to the largest hyacinth macaws. In most cases you will be able to hand-feed fruit, nuts and seeds to these birds. There is no cost, as it is a service to the aviary to help socialize the young birds. You don't have to purchase anything – unless you want a baby parrot to take home and love...

C Area

Utica

VELVET ICE CREAM: YE OLDE MILL ICE CREAM MUSEUM

Utica - Velvet Ice Cream (State Route 13) 43080. Phone: (740) 892-3921 or (800) 589-5000. www.velveticecream.com. Hours: Daily 11:00am-7:00pm (May-October). Extended evening summer hours. Weekend entertainment during summer. Admission: FREE. Tours: Public Tours Monday - Friday 11:00am-3:00pm only.

Did you know that the ice cream cone originated by mistake at the St. Louis World's Fair when a waffle vendor rolled waffles into cones for an ice cream vendor who ran out of serving cups? Learn all sorts of ice cream trivia at the

Ice Cream Museum located in the restored 1817 mill and water wheel which is surrounded by 20 acres of wooded parklands with ducks and picnic areas. While you are at the mill, stop by the NEW viewing gallery to watch ice cream being made and packaged and learn what it takes to produce more than 6 million gallons of velvety smooth ice cream every year. Then, come into the 18th century ice cream counter and try Velvet's newest creations such as Raspberry Fudge Cordial or an old favorite like Mint Chocolate Chip.

ICE CREAM FESTIVAL

Utica - Velvet Ice Cream hosts a tribute to our national dessert, ice cream, with family entertainment and lots of food made from ice cream. Kids can watch sheep herding with border collies, catch the kiddie tractor pull and wheelbarrow races, or watch the parade or magic circus. Admission. (Memorial Day Weekend)

HARVEST FESTIVAL

Utica - Velvet Ice Cream hosts Hay rides, petting zoo, pumpkins, live entertainment. (every Sunday afternoon in October)

PUMPKIN MAZE PLAYLAND

Utica - L & M Family Farm, 20750 Bell Church Road (SR 13 & SR 62). Pumpkin Patches / Hayrides / Corn Mazes / Fall Playland - Admission (average $6.00). Plan on at least two hours playtime. Open weekends, some weekdays (by appointment) and weeknights. www.lmfamilyfarm.com. (late September - late October).

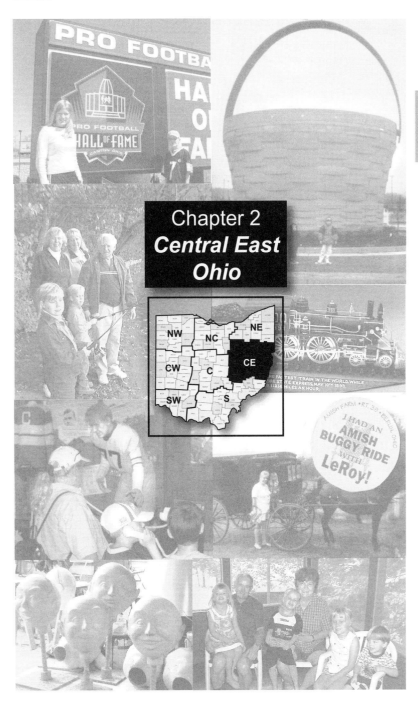

Chapter 2
*Central East
Ohio*

Barnesville
- Barnesville Pumpkin Festival
- Dickson Cattle Company

Bellaire
- Toy & Plastic Brick Museum

Belmont
- Barkcamp State Park

Berlin
- Behalt, Amish & Mennonite Ctr.
- Christmas In Berlin
- Schrock's Amish Farm & Village
- Wendell August Forge Gift Tour

Blue Rock
- Blue Rock State Forest
- Muskingum River State Park

Bolivar
- Fort Laurens

Cambridge
- Boyd's Crystal Art Glass Co.
- Living Word Passion Play
- Mosser Glass
- Salt Fork State Park
- Salt Fork State Park Resort

Canal Fulton
- St Helena Iii Canal Boat
- Yankee Peddler Festival

Canton
- Canton Classic Car MuSeum
- Canton Symphony Orchestra
- Hoover Historical Center
- Italian American Festival
- Mckinley Museum & Discover World
- Players Guild Theatre
- Pro Football Hall Of Fame
- Sippo Lake Park

Canton, North
- Harry London Chocolate Factory
- Maps Air Museum

Carrollton
- Bluebird Farm Toy Museum And Restaurant
- Holiday Lights
- McCook House

Columbiana
- Pumpkin Maze Playland

Coshocton
- Hot Air Balloon Festival
- Roscoe Village

Cumberland
- The Wilds

Dellroy
- Atwood Lake Resort

Dennison
- Dennison Railroad Depot Museum

Dover
- Broad Run CheeseHouse
- Victorian Home Open House, J.E. Reeves
- Warther Carvings

East Liverpool
- Beaver Creek State Park
- Museum Of Ceramics
- Tri-State Pottery Festival

Frazeysburg
- Longaberger Museum And Factory Tour

Gnadenhutten
- Gnadenhutten

Hartville
- Pumpkin Maze Playland
- Quail Hollow State Park

Kidron
- Lehman's Hardware

Lisbon
- Guilford Lake State Park

Magnolia
- Elson Flouring Mill

Millersburg
- Guggisberg Cheese Factory
- Holidays At The Mansion
- Rolling Ridge Ranch
- Yoder's Amish Home

Minerva
- Minerva Cheese Factory

Nashport
- Dillon State Park

New Concord
- John & Annie Glenn Historic Site

New Philadelphia
- Muskingum Watershed Lakes
- Shoenbrunn
- Trumpet In The Land
- Tuscora Park

Norwich
- Nat'l Road / Zane Grey Museum

Orrville
- Jumpin Pumpkin Special
- Smuckers Company Store & Café

Shreve
- Apple Festivals

Steubenville
- Creegan Company Animation
- Fort Steuben, Historic
- Jefferson Lake State Park

Sugarcreek
- Alpine Hills Museum
- Ohio Swiss Festival

Walnut Creek
- Coblentz Chocolate Company

Wilmot
- Amish Door Dinner Theatre
- Grandma's Alpine Homestead

Wooster
- Amerihost Inn Wooster East
- Amish Door Restaurant
- Cat's Meow Village
- Hartzler Family Dairy
- Melvins
- Ohio Agricultural R & D Center
- Pumpkin Maze Playland
- Wayne County Historical Museum

Zanesville
- Apple Festival
- Lorena Sternwheeler
- Stars & Stripes on the River

Zoar
- Zoar Village

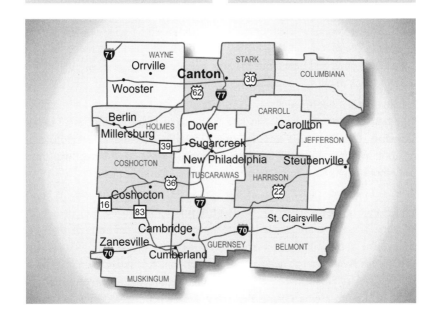

A Quick Tour of our Hand-Picked Favorites Around...

Central East Ohio

If you're longing to experience a back-to-the-basics lifestyle, a trip to Ohio's Amish country is the place! The world's largest Amish community exists in Ohio. Look for attractions in Amish communities like: Berlin, Millersburg, Walnut Creek, Dover, Wilmot, and Sugarcreek. A good first stop for a crash course in the history of the Amish is the Amish and Mennonite Heritage Center near Berlin. This is where "**Behalt**", a giant cyclorama, depicts the people of this area. Kids are curious how the artist "scratched" paint to create the mural. Enjoy beautiful scenery, visit an **Amish Farm**, savor homemade foods and listen for the clip-clop of a buggy. Say Cheese! Cause there's lots of **Cheese Factories** to view and sample around here.

At **Warther Carvings**, the Warther Family guides visitors through the life of Ernest "Mooney" Warther, declared the "World's Master Carver" for his ingenious interpretation of the history of trains. If any place is labeled "seeing is believing," this is it! (hint: have the kids sit in front for the demo portion of the tour and they might win something).

Like more modern settings? How about mixing chocolate and football together for a day trip? Within just a few exits of each other are **Harry London Chocolate Factory** (try a melt in your-mouth London mint or London buckeye!) AND the **Pro Football Hall of Fame** (take their scavenger hunt and then throw some passes) in North Canton.

Want to mix old-fashioned craft into a modern or a historical setting? Start with a tour of **Longaberger Basket Factory** in Frazeysburg, south of Newark. The one-quarter mile long factory is home to hundreds of weavers who make about 100,000 baskets per week – by hand. Your kids will be mesmerized when you go upstairs to the mezzanine to view the crafters at their station using a "horse!" Another craft that takes years for tradesmen to perfect is glass blowing. Some **Glass Factory Tours** are "heated" places to visit in Cambridge. We'd recommend overnighting nearby at **Salt Fork State Park Resort** which has accommodations for every style. Or, try your hand at pounding a hammer on metal to see if you can create art. The folks at **Wendell August Forge** (Berlin) can – with hammering (or hammering machines) you can watch art being created. **Creegan Company Animation Factory** (Steubenville) purely lights all your senses as "puppets" are created and automated. You have to see it to believe it! Then, go to a really authentic canal town at **Roscoe Village** in Coshocton. You might even get roped into doing some chores or crafts! After midday lunch, take a lesson in a one-room schoolhouse - but beware of the dunce cap!

Sites and attractions are listed in order by City, Zip Code, and Name. Symbols indicated represent:

 Festivals   Restaurants   Lodging

Barnesville

DICKSON CATTLE COMPANY

Barnesville - 35000 Muskrat Road (I-70 exit 202 south, then west) 43713. Phone: (740) 758-5050. www.texaslonghorn.com. Hours (Store): Monday-Saturday 10:00am-5:00pm, Sunday 1:00-6:00pm (June-Labor Day). Tours: One hour. Tours for adults are $10.00 with special rates for youth $4.00 (4-12). Miscellaneous: Cattle, steaks, smoked longhorn and a wide selection of longhorn related products available at the Longhorn Head to Tail Store.

Largest herd of registered quality Texas Longhorn Cattle east of San Francisco this large, family-owned ranch offers narrated tours on an adorable purple with white polka-dotted cow bus. See up to 1000 Texas Longhorns grazing the fields, hand-feed the cattle and clear water fish. Gizmo is an International Champion Sire that is on the tour route. What shape do they use for branding?

BARNESVILLE PUMPKIN FESTIVAL

Barnesville - Downtown. www.barnesvillepumpkinfestival.com. All kinds of pumpkin contests (largest pumpkin, pumpkin rolling and pie eating), parade, foods, fiddle contest, rides, crafts and entertainment. Free. (Thursday – Sunday - last full weekend of September)

Bellaire

TOY & PLASTIC BRICK MUSEUM

Bellaire - 4597 Noble Street (I-70 to Rte. 7 south to Noble Street exit) 43906. Phone: (740) 671-8890. www.brickmuseum.net. Hours: Monday-Sunday Noon-5:00pm, Saturday 10:00am-7:00pm (Summer hours). Friday-Sunday Noon-5:00pm (Winter hours). Admission: $8.00 adult, $6.00 senior and student (5+).

This museum is housed in a former school and the rooms are full of over 4 million bricks, over 500 statues, over 1000 Lego creations, some animatronics and some robotics. Look for themes like Space, TV cartoons and animals. Want a preview? Take a look thru the website of pictures of over 300 creations, then write down which ones you want to search for when you visit.

Belmont

BARKCAMP STATE PARK

Belmont - 65330 Barkcamp Park Road (I-70 exit 208, off SR 149) 43718. Phone: (740) 484-4064.. www.dnr.state.oh.us.

Belmont County's rugged hills provide the backdrop for picturesque Barkcamp State Park. Miles of hiking trails invite visitors to enjoy the solitude of the forest. The Lakeview Trail, Woodchuck Nature Trail, Hawthorn Trail and Hawk Trail lead to natural treasures and provide opportunities for nature study, bird watching and wildlife observation. Barkcamp's bridle trail meanders along the entire lakeshore affording a pleasant day's ride. A special paved trail winds through the pioneer village, enters the adjoining mature woodlands and provides access to the Antique Barn. Interpretive signs are placed along the route explaining the cultural and natural history of the park. 1,232 acres of camping, hiking trails through rolling hills and woodlands, boating, fishing, swimming and winter sports.

Berlin

BEHALT, AMISH & MENNONITE HERITAGE CENTER

Berlin - 5798 County Road 77 (north of State Route 39, follow signs) 44610. Phone: (330) 893-3192. www.behalt.com. Hours: Monday-Saturday 9:00am-5:00pm. Friday-Saturday 9:00am-8:00pm (June-October). Admission: $6.50 adult, $3.00 child (6-12). Tours: 30 minute guided or video (15 minute background to Amish area). Miscellaneous: Pioneer Barn will house an original Conestoga Wagon that *brought early settlers to Holmes County. Restored one-room school, dating from 1856 used to tell story of Amish education.*

Behalt means "to keep or remember". Behalt offers a fascinating and enjoyable way to learn about the Amish and Mennonite people. Besides a free 15-minute video presentation, visitors may take a 30-minute interpretive tour (paid admission) of a colorful, stunning 265-ft x 10-ft original oil painting depicting Amish and Mennonite history. This 10' x 265' cyclorama mural by artist Heinz

Gaugel clearly explains the heritage of Amish and Mennonite people from the beginnings of their faith to the present day. The circular mural took four years to paint using superimposing layers

of oil paint to create a sense of many events occurring in a small space and time. This makes the mural almost 3D when viewing. The exterior of the building is painted with an old technique called "sgraffito" which means scratched. Mr. Gaugel applied five layers of plaster to the wall (green, dark red, dark yellow, white and black). The artist starts scratching through the layers to expose the colors he wants. The tour is narrated with stories so vivid that you feel as if you are a part of the scene. We were fortunate to meet Heinz Gaugel in the gift shop and it was amazing to meet such a humble man with such apparent, unique artistic talent.

SCHROCK'S AMISH FARM AND VILLAGE

Berlin - *4363 State Route 39 (1 mile East of Downtown) 44610. Phone: (330) 893-3232. www.amishfarmmarketing.com. Hours: Monday-Friday 10:00am-5:00pm, Saturday 10:00am-6:00pm (April-October). Tours and Admission: Discount*

combo prices. $5.50-$7.50 is best as it includes the Farm & Home Tour and 1 ride, which every kid will enjoy. Miscellaneous: Gifts shops (many). Enjoy a 1.2 mile train ride through the farm grounds. This 16 gauge train ride is great for the entire family. Pony rides are for ages 3-12.

We started with a buggy ride driven by an Amish man and his horse named "Leroy". After our ride, we were given a sticker to wear that says, "I rode my first Amish buggy ride with Leroy". Next, your family can take the new horse-drawn wagon rides (30 minute narrated ride through the entire farm). We then stopped at the farm to pet animals, watched a slide show about Amish lifestyles, and received a tour through the home. Kids, even adults, were surprised to see that all appliances were gas fueled including the lamps (the gas generated light source was hidden in the table under the lamp). We learned why there are no faces on Amish dolls and why only pins and occasional buttons are used in clothing.

WENDELL AUGUST FORGE GIFT TOUR

Berlin - 7007 Dutch Country Lane (3 miles West of Berlin - Route 62) 44610. Phone: (330) 893-3713 or (866) 354-5192. www.wendell.com. Admission: FREE. Tours: Tuesday-Saturday 9:00am-4:00pm.

Free tour of the production workshop as metal giftware is taken through a fascinating eleven step process. The gift metal is hammered over a pre-designed template with random hand, or machine operated

> The showroom has the World's Largest Amish Buggy – over 1200 pounds, and each wheel is over 5 feet tall!

hammer motions. It was interesting to think someone close to the craft had to design the machine operated hammer for this specific purpose – probably a craftsman who's hands got tired! The impression is now set in one side and the signature hammer marks will stay on the other side. The artist stamps his seal and then the item is forged (put in a log fire) to get smoke marks that bring out the detail of the design. After the item cools, it is cleaned to remove most of the dark smoke color and the metal object is then thinned by hand hammering. The facility also features a video highlighting the company's history.

CHRISTMAS IN BERLIN

Berlin - Downtown & Schrocks Amish Farm, (330) 893-3467. Sleigh rides, buggy rides, hayrides and crafts. Live Nativity Parade. Luminaries, shopping. The live nativity parade and candle-lighting ceremony occurs on the town square. Live animals like sheep, donkey and even camels are paraded by shepherds. Actors as Mary, Joseph, too. FREE (Friday after Thanksgiving in November)

Blue Rock

BLUE ROCK STATE FOREST

Blue Rock - *6665 Cutler Lake Road (located 12 miles southeast of Zanesville off SR 60) 43720. Phone: (740) 674-4035. www.dnr.state.oh.us. Hours: Daily 6:00am - 11:00pm.*

4,579 acres in Muskinghum County. 26 miles of bridle trails and fishing are offered. Former fire lookout tower. Blue Rock State Park is adjacent. A public beach is located on the north end of the lake. Several miles of hiking trails begin near the campground and picnic areas of the park. Additional hiking trails are in the adjacent forest lands. Horsemen can enjoy more than 26 miles of bridle trails through the Blue Rock State Forest. No overnight facilities are available. You must provide your own horse as no rentals are available.

MUSKINGUM RIVER PARKWAY STATE PARK

Blue Rock - *(120 acres along 80 miles of the Muskingum River extending from Devola to Ellis Locks) 43720. Phone: (740) 452-3820. www.dnr.state.oh.us.*

The Muskingum River is formed by the confluence of the Walhonding and Tuscarawas rivers in Coshocton flowing south through Zanesville where it joins the Licking River. The river travels 112 miles in all and its 10 locks are still hand-operated in the same manner as 150 years ago. A trip on the Muskingum River Parkway is not complete without going through one of the ten locks. These manually-operated locks are similar to those built throughout the United States before the turn of the century and are now recognized as one of America's great engineering accomplishments. Contact the park office for current fee rates when planning your trip. Visitors are offered camping, hiking trails, boating, and fishing.

Bolivar

FORT LAURENS

Bolivar - *11067 Fort Laurens Rd. NW (I-77 and State Route 212 - Follow Signs) 44612. www.ohiohistory.org/places/ftlauren. Phone: (800) 283-8914 or (330) 874-2059. Hours: Saturday 9:30am-5:00pm, Sunday and Holidays Noon-5:00pm (Summer only). Admission: $3.00-$4.00 per student or adult.*

Visit the site of the only U.S. Military fort in Ohio during the American Revolution. This fort was built in 1778 in an ill-fated campaign to attack the

British at Detroit. Supplying this wilderness outpost was its downfall, as its starving garrison survived on boiled moccasins and withstood a month-long siege by British-led Indians. The fort was abandoned in 1779. Today, only the outline of the fort remains, but a small museum commemorates the frontier soldier, housing a video giving the fort's history and action packed audiovisual displays from the fort's excavation. Re-enactment weekends are the best time to visit to help visualize the horrible conditions of the short-lived fort.

SIEGE OF FORT LAURENS LANTERN TOUR

Bolivar - Fort Laurens - Experience the Siege at Fort Laurens in this interactive lantern tour where your guide helps you escape the fort under siege. You are guided through the woods by lantern light to safety at the nearby military camp. Guests enjoy warm drinks and snacks as they participate in campfire stories told by reenactor soldiers. Not recommended for those with mobility problems or for the very young. Pre-paid reservations required. Admission. (third Saturday in October)

Cambridge

BOYD'S CRYSTAL ART GLASS COMPANY

Cambridge - 1203 Morton Avenue (off State Route 209 North) 43725. Phone: (740) 439-2077. www.boydglass.com. Tours: Monday – Friday 8:00am – 11:00am, 15 minutes. (September – May).

The Cambridge area became popular for glass manufacturing because of good sand and abundant wells of natural gas. Boyd Glass still manufactures collectibles the old-fashioned way, to the delight of visitors and collectors, with a man and a mould and not with an automated machine. Typical shapes made are trains, airplanes, cars, small animals and Teddy the Tugboat. Watch molten glass being poured into one of 300 molds and put in a furnace. When they cool, they are hand-painted.

LIVING WORD PASSION PLAY

Cambridge - 6010 College Hill Road (2 miles west of State Route 209) 43725. Phone: (740) 439-2761. http://visitguernseycounty.com/outdoor.html. Hours: Friday – Saturday 8:00 pm (Mid-June – Labor Day). Saturday Only 7:00 pm (September) Admission: $16.00 adult, $13.00 senior (60+), $5.00 child (under 12). Free Set Tours 7:15pm. Miscellaneous: Concessions, Gift Shop, Rain Checks, Free Parking.

Bible stories come to life before your eyes. Experience an evening back in the Holy Land, in 30 AD with an authentic representation of Old Jerusalem.

Beginning with the Sermon on the Mount, The Living Word reflects on the last three years of the life of Christ, with dramatic depictions of Palm Sunday, the last supper, Gethsemane, Pilate's court, the crucifixion and the resurrection. The play is full of biblical animals and costumes, even chariots.

MOSSER GLASS

Cambridge - *9279 Cadiz Road (I-77 exit 47. US 22 West) 43725. Phone: (740) 439-1827. www.mosserglass.com. Tours: Monday-Friday 8:30am-10:00am and 11:00am - 2:30pm. No tours first 2 weeks in July and last 2 weeks in December. Best not to tour if it's hot outside as the plant is not air conditioned. FREE.*

Mosser is a glass manufacturer that's been around for 30+ years. Mosser makes glass pitchers, goblets, lamps, figurines, auto parts (headlights),

 and paper weights. Your guide starts the tour explaining the glassmaking process from the beginning when glass powder (sand and cullet-broken glass) are heated to 2000 degrees F. in a furnace. Once melted, the molten glass is pulled on a stick and then iron molded or pressed, fire glazed and finally cooled in a Lehr which uniformly reduces the temperature of the object to prevent shattering. We saw them make old Ford car headlight covers and red heart shaped paperweights. They add selenium to make red glass. A little toothpick holder or doll's glass is typical of the free souvenir of this great tour!

SALT FORK STATE PARK

Cambridge - *14755 Cadiz Road (7 miles Northeast of Cambridge on US 22) 43755. www.dnr.state.oh.us/parks/. Phone: (740) 439-3521 park or (800) 282-7275 reservations. Admission: FREE. Miscellaneous: The cabins are where memories are made! Best for grade-schoolers and up (bunk beds) because they're right in the woods. Educators: The Park Pals online link has nature activity sheets you can print off.*

What a great, family-friendly outdoor resort with many hotel comforts! As Ohio's largest state park, Salt Fork boasts recreational facilities to suit nearly every taste. Everyone seems to spend at least a couple of hours each day at the Lodge area with overnight rooms, gift shops, indoor and outdoor pools & spa, fitness center, volleyball, basketball and tennis. The dining room serves breakfast, lunch and dinner in a rustic overlook setting (also, seasonal snack bars are available). The gameroom, with multiple ping-pong and air hockey tables, is downstairs. Fun family activities are planned seasonally (i.e. crafts, pool games, kid's bingo, family movies, bonfires, plus Parent's Night Out (once or twice a week). The Nature Center is open with planned activities (seasonally, Wednesday-Sunday) and explorations. Bring your own boat to this beautiful lake (or rent one at Sugartree Marina 740-439-5833 - Kids love the pontoon or speed/ski boats). Another option, if you didn't bring your own boat, is the Salt Fork Activity Center which operates pontoon tours. The tours include the Stone House or cane pole fishing with snacks and picture for only $5.00/ person. Lots of camping, fishing, golfing, and well- marked hiking trails too. A great place to kick back and create family memories!

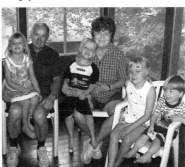

Quality time with our cousins and grandparents...what fun!

SALT FORK STATE PARK RESORT LODGE

Cambridge - *14755 Cadiz Road (7 miles Northeast of Cambridge on US 22) 43755. www.saltforkresort.com. Phone: (740) 439-2751 lodge or (800) 282-7275 reservations.*

This massive pine beam and stone lodge captures the atmosphere and flavor of the grand park lodges built at the turn of the century. Salt Fork Resort & Conference Center is tucked away in the rolling hills of southeastern Ohio, in Ohio's largest state park. The lush wooded surroundings contain miles of hiking and horseback riding trails, large and healthy populations of deer (you'll see them around most every turn), turkey, flowers, song and water birds. Salt Fork State Park Resort has created the "Family Fun Package" with four hours of geocaching. Increasingly popular with families, geocaching involves use of a hand-held global positioning system (GPS) and clues for finding hidden "treasures" throughout the park. In addition to use of the GPS, the package includes one night of lodging in a bunk room with two double beds plus a bunk bed; two movie rentals; popcorn and candy. The package is available starting at $149 per night for Sunday through Thursday stays. Families can choose to stay a second night for about $79 (room only). Bunk Rooms - These cozy, newly freshened rooms, which are great for families, include two double beds and one set of bunk beds. This room also features a refrigerator, small table and chairs, cable television, and Bunkrooms adjoin to king rooms. Views include either the woods or pool areas. We were extremely impressed with the staff and the amount of activities offered: bonfires, create-a-bear, make your own t-shirt, paint ball, sports, etc. Staying for a few days? Try to become a member of Salty's Club. Complete nature and family activities around the park with a parent and win a prize and membership. It's a clever way to bring back goal-oriented fun with parents AND children together.

Canal Fulton

ST HELENA III CANAL BOAT

Canal Fulton - 103 Tuscarawas Village Park (I-77 to Exit 111 Portage Street West, follow signs) 44614. www.discovercanalfulton.com/heritage_society/st_helena_iii.html. Phone: (330) 854-3808 or (800) HELENA-3. Admission: $5.00-$7.00 (age 5+). Tours: Daily 1:00 – 3:00pm (Summer, except Mondays when closed). Weekends 1:00 – 3:00pm (May, early June)

The St. Helena III docks and departs from the Canal Fulton Canalway Center and can carry up to sixty passengers down an original section of the Ohio-Erie Canal. The canal trip is an one-hour horse drawn canal boat freighter ride with a narrative history of the canal system and the local area. Appearing as it did in the 1800's, the view also includes Lock IV, one of the few remaining working locks on old canal routes. Included in the tour is a Canal Museum with pictorial stories of colorful local history and canal memorabilia including tools used to build and repair canal boats.

OLDE CANAL DAYS

Canal Fulton - St. Helena III Canal Boat. (330) 854-6295. Along the Ohio/Erie canal see a water float parade, fireworks, music contests, saw carving and concerts. (last weekend in August)

YANKEE PEDDLER FESTIVAL

Canal Fulton - Clay's Park. www.yankeepeddlerfestival.com. 13190 Patterson St. NW. Step back in time 200 years and visit pioneer America. See master artists and crafters setting up rustic shops along streams and amid lovely wooded dales, with foods and snacks cooked over open fires, and with non-stop entertainment across the 75-acre grounds. Keep up to the hour and follow events with the Town Criers, visit with the militia and mountain men, or learn drills with hands-on instruction. Visit with the master crafters and artists while they demonstrate the way they transform nature into something unique for you and yours. Admission. (last three weekends in September)

Canton

CANTON CLASSIC CAR MUSEUM

Canton - Market Avenue at 6th Street entrance 44702. Phone: (330) 455-3603. www.cantonclassiccar.org. Hours: Daily 10:00am-5:00pm. Admission: $5.00-$7.50 (age 6+).

Housed in Ohio's earliest Ford-Lincoln dealership, this museum offers over 45 antique, classic and special interest cars displayed in the motif of flapper era Roaring 20's. Favorite exhibits are the Rolls Royce, the Bullet Proof Police Car, the Amphicar (car and boat) and famous movie cars or Amelia Earhart's 1916 Pierce Arrow.

CANTON SYMPHONY ORCHESTRA

Canton - 2323 17th Street NW 44702. www.cantonsymphony.org. Phone: (330) 452-2094.

Presents classical, holiday, pops, family and youth concerts/symphony. Especially for the younger set: Kinder Concerts, mini-operas and Young People's Concerts. Online Teacher's Guides are available each season.

PLAYERS GUILD THEATRE

Canton - 1001 North Market Avenue 44702. www.playersguildtheatre.com. Phone: (330) 453-7619.

Family series presents plays based on award winning children's stories like The Hobbit and a Christmas Carol. Performances Thursday-Sunday. Tickets run $8.00-$15.00 per seat.

MCKINLEY MUSEUM & DISCOVER WORLD

Canton - 800 McKinley Monument Drive, NW (I-77 south exit 106, I-77 north exit 105, follow signs) 44708. Phone: (330) 455-7043. www.mckinleymuseum.org.

Hours: Monday-Saturday 9:00am-4:00pm, Sunday Noon-4:00 pm. Closed major holidays. Admission: $7.00 adult, $6.00 senior, $5.00 child (3-18). Miscellaneous: Planetarium. Museum Shop.

After you park, take the 108 steps leading up to the bronze doors of the stunning McKinley Memorial where President William McKinley and his wife and children were laid to rest. A few steps away is the McKinley Museum where you can visit McKinley Hall, Historical

Hall and the Street of Shops. Walk along the 19th Century Street of homes, general store, print shop, and doctor's office – all indoors on exhibit. Kid's eyes sparkle at the model trains and pioneer toys such as paper dolls and or mini cast-iron kitchen appliances. Last, but even more exciting for kids, is Discover World. A large dinosaur robot named "Alice" greets you and a real

Stark County mastodon Bondo Betty is around the corner. Find hidden fossil drawers, make a fossil, look for the queen bee in a living beehive, touch a chinchilla, play a tune on tone pipes, visit Space Station Earth or be a weather forecaster – All in one afternoon!

PRO FOOTBALL HALL OF FAME

Canton - *2121 George Halas Drive NW (I-77 and US 62) 44708. Phone: (330) 456-*

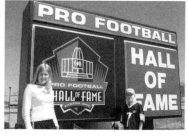

8207. www.profootballhof.com. Hours: Daily 9:00am-8:00pm (Memorial Day-Labor Day). Daily 9:00am-5:00pm (Rest of Year). Closed. Christmas Only. Admission: $18.00 adult , $15.00 senior (62+), $12.00 youth (14 & under), $32.00 family. Look for Packages or Discounts on their website. Miscellaneous: Tailgating Snack Bar – over the counter / vending with Top Twenty

Tele-trivia and QBI Call-the-Play Game. Special video presentations in the center of each room. "Located a football field away from the Hall of Fame" is The Stables Sports Restaurant (330-452-1230 or www.thestables.com). Educators: Be sure to have the kids ask for their Investigative Reporter Scavenger Hunt. Kids pretend

they are sports reporters looking for "the scoop" story about pro football history.

If you're an NFL Football Fan, the anticipation builds as you enter the grounds of the sprawling Hall of Fame. At the top of the curving ramp upstairs you view the first 100 years of football with Pro Football's Birth Certificate and

Getting to be the coach and "Call the Play"

the oldest football (1895) available for display. Then, hit some Astroturf and browse through Pro Football today and Photo Art Gallery (award winning, some amazing, photographs of football heroes in action). Older children look forward to the Enshrinement Galleries and Super Bowl Room. A newer addition to the Hall is Game Day Stadium. A 100-Yard film is shown in a two-sided rotating theater. Start at the Locker Room Show. Then the entire seating area rotates 180 degrees to the Stadium Show where you become part of a NFL game with a 2 story Cinemascope presentation. You see, hear and almost make contact with the

players! What a rush! The Hall of Fame's newest galleries, Moments, Memories & Mementos Gallery and the Pro Football Today Gallery were

officially opened in 2008 and feature new and old artifacts in the collection. This place is just full of shoes and jerseys galore from famous players old and new. What did the first helmet look like? Who's your favorite team? What are their stats? By the way, there are action activity stations around every corner and especially downstairs. What fun!

Learning about football's early days...

PROFESSIONAL FOOTBALL HALL OF FAME FESTIVAL

Canton - *(800) 533-4302. www.profootballhoffestival.com. Check out the 9 days of celebrating football greats including a parade, hot air balloon show, enshrinement ceremony and a televised professional game. Some fees. (first week of August)*

SIPPO LAKE PARK

Canton - 5712 12th Street NW (I-77 exit 106) 44708. www.starkparks.com. Phone: (330) 477-3552.

Sippo Lake Park is open daily 7:00am-11:00pm and features an enclosed Clubhouse and open picnic shelters for rent. Other on-site amenities include boat rentals, fishing, nature programming, and short hiking trails. Motor boats, row boats and paddle boats available for rental or bring your own boat (10 hp limit). Nearby marina offers food and beverages for sale as well as bait, fishing tackle, and fishing licenses. The Exploration Gateway is on the north shore of the 300-acre Sippo Lake Park. In this new two-story "edutainment" facility you can explore nature, history, and the culture of the Ohio & Erie Canalway "then and now." A large Canalway Adventure Center with 11 interactive exhibits, and FeLeap's Lily Pad Gift Shop opened in 2008. (open weekdays 8:30am-4:30pm and Saturday 10:00am-4:00pm or Sunday 1:00-5:00pm). FREE.

HOOVER HISTORICAL CENTER

Canton - *1875 Easton Street NW (I-77 Portage Street/North Canton Exit to Walsh University campus) 44720. www.walsh.edu/hooverhistoricalcent.htm. Phone: (330) 499-0287. Tours: Wednesday-Saturday at 1:00, 2:00, 3:00 and 4:00pm (March-December). Closed holidays. Admission: $3.00 (age 13+). Miscellaneous: Only known vacuum cleaner museum in the world.*

See the Hoover Industry beginnings as a leather tannery. When automobiles came on the scene, W. H. Hoover searched for a new product. He bought the rights to inventor Murray Spangler's upright vacuum player cleaner and introduced it in 1908 - The Hoover Suction Sweeper Model O (On display). A short video details the history of the company. Guided tours of the farmhouse include a display of antique vacuums. A favorite is the Kotten Suction Cleaner (1910) that requires a person to rock a bellows with their feet to create suction. An early 1900's electric vacuum weighed 100 pounds (and they advertised it as a portable!).

CHRISTMAS OPEN HOUSE

Canton – *Hoover Historical Center. Includes Santa & Mrs. Claus, live holiday music and a Christmas tree in every room. Horse-drawn wagon rides and homemade cookies and warm cider complement the festivities. (usually first weekend in December)*

ITALIAN AMERICAN FESTIVAL

Canton - *Stark County Fairgrounds, 305 Wertz Avenue. www.cantonitalianfesta.org. Italy in Ohio with entertainment, foods, dancing, exhibits, rides and a bocce tournament. Thursday - Sunday. Admission. (long weekend late June)*

Canton, North

HARRY LONDON CHOCOLATE FACTORY

Canton, North - *5353 Lauby Road (I-77 Exit 113 Airport) 44720. Phone: (330) 494-0833 or (800) 321-0444. www.harrylondon.com. Tours: Monday-Friday 10:00am-3:00pm. No tours Fridays from April thru mid-June. Admission: $2.00-$3.00 (age 3+). Tour: 45 minutes. Reservations required. Tours leave about every half hour. School tours follow Ohio Proficiency guidelines. Miscellaneous: Chocolate Hall of Fame, Largest Chocolate Store in the Midwest. They may not be as pretty, but BooBoos candies are discounted at the store. Look for them and maybe try some samples of perfect product before you buy some gifts to take home.*

London's has produced quality gourmet chocolates since 1922 using original family recipes. Live the fantasy of making, molding, wrapping, and boxing chocolate candy, fudge, and butterscotch. Oh, it smells so good here! Did you know cacao beans were once used as money and medicine? Learn this and more as you view a video and then walk near warm tanks full of chocolate (80,000 lbs. of chocolate inside each tank). Upstairs, along the mezzanine, watch as fillings are enrobed in chocolate – all over. Workers here can't wear jewelry or perfume but they get free samples all work day! Be sure to try a London Mint (money wrapped candy) or a London Buckeye.

MAPS AIR MUSEUM

Canton, North - *5359 Massillon Road, Akron-Canton Airport (I-77 to Exit 113) 44720. Phone: (330) 896-6332. www.mapsairmuseum.org. Hours: Tuesday-Saturday 10:00am-4:00pm and Wednesday evenings until 8:00pm. Sundays 11:30am-4:00pm. Admission: $5.00-$8.00 per person.*

The staff here are pilots, mechanics, officers, and crew who desire to preserve the legacy of America's aviation heritage. Their slogan "Rebuilding History – One Rivet At a Time" really describes their dedication to acquire and renovate some of the world's greatest military aircraft. MAPS offers not just displays of mint condition aircraft, but also a truly unique "hands on" view of the restoration of some of the world's greatest aircraft by people who may have flown them years ago.

Carrollton

BLUEBIRD FARM TOY MUSEUM AND RESTAURANT

Carrollton - *190 Alamo Road (at the bottom of the Square, take 332 south for two blocks, turn left on 3rd Street S.E.) 44615. www.bluebird-farm.com. Phone: (330) 627-7980. Hours: Tuesday-Sunday 11:00am-4:00pm (April-December). Lunch or Tea served in restaurant. Admission: Museum $2.00 adult, FREE child. Miscellaneous: Great reasonable gift ideas in the gift shop barn. Christmastime is magical here.*

A century old farmhouse restaurant featuring a fresh, daily menu of family-priced, old-fashioned dishes like ham loaf, Swiss steak, and chicken casserole cooked only as Grandma could. Walk off your homemade dessert on the nature trail. The Toy Museum features playthings available to American children from the 1800's to the present (brightly, cleverly displayed). Look for some popular dolls like Raggedy Ann and Andy, Shirley Temple, Mickey and Minnie Mouse, and the beloved Teddy Bear…many made abroad. Ask for the scavenger hunt pages to play a game in the museum. This entire property is a wonderful haven for families…don't miss it when in Amish / Swiss area of Ohio!

MCCOOK HOUSE

Carrollton - *Downtown Square (west side of square) 44615. Phone: (330) 627-3345 or (800) 600-7172. www.ohiohistory.org/places/mccookhse. Hours: Friday-Saturday 10:00am - 5:00pm, Sunday 1:00 - 5:00pm (Summers); Weekends only (Labor Day to mid- October). Admission: $3.00 adults, $1.00 child (6-12). Miscellaneous: History of Carroll County lifestyles and industry portrayed upstairs - the clothing will appeal to girls.*

The family earned the name of "Fighting McCooks" due to their extensive military service in the Civil War. Daniel McCook built this home and his family lived here until 1853. During the Civil War, Daniel's family contributed nine soldiers to the Union cause including 5 generals. Four of Daniel's family including Daniel himself died in the conflict. You're greeted by the painting in the front room. Each son and their father are portrayed. What's unique about the one son, John James I? In the hallway, you'll find an 1838 large map of Ohio. Can you find your home town or was it even around then? Look for the real tree trunk with cannon balls stuck in it from the Civil War.

HOLIDAY LIGHTS

Carrollton - *County Fairgrounds, SR 9. Hundreds of thousands of lights & holiday / storybook characters. Thursday-Sunday evenings. www.carrollcountyohio.com/lights. Admission. (Thanksgiving - January 1)*

Columbiana

PUMPKIN MAZE PLAYLAND

Columbiana - *Detwiler Farm. 4520 Renkenberger Road. www.detwilerfarms.com. Pumpkin Patches / Hayrides / Corn Mazes / Fall Playland - Admission (average $6.00). Plan on at least two hours playtime. Open weekends, some weekdays (by appointment) and weeknights. (late September - late October).*

Coshocton

ROSCOE VILLAGE

Coshocton - 311 Hill Street (State Route 16 and 83, near US 36 - I-77 exit 65) 43812. Phone: (740) 622-9310 or (800) 877-1830. www.roscoevillage.com. Hours: Daily, Most village shops open at 10:00am Special events May-December. History Tour Buildings Closed (January-February) for cleaning. Visitor Center daily 10:00am-5:00pm. Shops and Center closed major winter holidays. Admission: "Living History Tour" $5.00-$10.00 (ages 5+). Visitors Center exhibit hall & movie $3.00-$4.00. Just Browsing is FREE! Additional charge $4-$7.00 for canal boat ride. Tours: Guided 11:00am and 2:00pm. Summer tours are called Leisure Tours and are more self-guided. Miscellaneous: Monticello III Canal Boat-A horse drawn replica of a 1800's canal boat, offers narrated trips on the 1 1/2 mile restored

section of the original Ohio-Erie Canal. 1:00pm-5:00pm daily from Memorial Day - Labor Day. Weekends only Labor Day to mid-October. Part of the Coshocton Park District (740) 622-7528. Educators: click on "Just for Kids" link and ask Capt. Nye questions, download coloring pages or complete a maze.

CE Area

Historic buildings offer a glimpse into the daily life of these craftsmen and their families. Maybe take a lesson in the one-room school or see the trappings of

the 1800's daily life in the doctor's house.   Watch craftsmen practice their trades of broom making, weaving, pottery, bucket making and more. Kids can try their hand at candle dipping, tin punching or rope making in the Hands-On facility. They can "discover" the sights and sounds of the canal era with games, puzzles, music and activities in the Discovery Room. Look over the realistic dioramas and

Learning the art of making a broom

working lock models in the Visitor Center complex. Spend gobs of time in the General Store where you can play with and buy old-fashioned toys like harmonicas, paper dolls and wooden toys. Plan to have the kids bring their allowance (and you can too) because you won't be able to resist! The Johnson-Humrickhouse Museum is full of prehistoric American Indian tools and pottery, an Ohio Pioneer house and Oriental decorative arts (Samurai swords). During the summer, visit the Hillside where demonstrations of brick-making and woodworking take place. Grab baked goods or a light lunch at Captain Nye's Sweet Shop.

APPLE BUTTER STIRRIN FESTIVAL

Coshocton - *Roscoe Village. With over 100 crafters, this invitational craft festival celebrates the sights, sounds and scents of autumn. Smell the fresh apple butter simmering over an open fire as you stroll through the street to the tunes of bluegrass and old-time music. Watch cooking demonstrations, participate in a craft auction, a hog-calling contest or sign up for a quilt raffle. Events throughout the week-end will include living history tours, canal boat rides, musical entertainment and children's activities. $3.00 admission charge. (mid-October weekend)*

CHRISTMAS CANDLELIGHTINGS

Coshocton - *Roscoe Village. Shop all day for holiday gifts in a 19th century holiday setting and then stay for the candlelighting ceremony each night at 6:00pm. Strolling carolers, visits with Santa, live arctic reindeer, chestnuts roasting over open fire, free hot-mulled cider & cookies, and carriage rides. Also see display of decorated trees and gingerbread houses on Main Street, downtown. Parking fee. (first three Saturdays in December)*

HOT AIR BALLOON FESTIVAL

Coshocton - *County Fairgrounds, 707 Kenilworth Avenue. (740) 622-5411. Balloon launches at dawn and dusk, Nightglow (Saturday), entertainment and rides. FREE. (second weekend in June). www.coshoctoncounty.net/agency/chamber/Balloon%20Festival.php*

CE Area

Cumberland

THE WILDS

Cumberland - **14000 International Road (I-70 exit 155, Zanesville or exit 169, SR 83 - follow signs) 43732. Phone: (740) 638-5030. www.thewilds.org. Hours: Daily 10:00am-4:00pm (June - August). Weekends only in May, September & October. Hours vary, call first (November-April). Admission: $18.00 adult, $17.00 senior(60+), $13.00 child (4-12). Parking fee $3.00. Discounts to local residents and reciprocal zoo members. Visits to the Butterfly Habitat and the Birding Station at Jeffrey Point are free. Tours: Safari Transports depart regularly from the Visitor Center approximately every 10 to 20 minutes on open days beginning at 10:00am. The last Safari Transport departs at 4:00pm. Safari Transport vehicles feature large windows and are air conditioned. Strollers and coolers are not allowed on Safari Transport vehicles. Reservations Not Required. School and Group Tours available almost any day (May-October), with reservation. Miscellaneous: You can also visit the Wilds Gift Market, Overlook Cafe, Butterfly Habitat, and Birding Station without admission ticket.**

Once a strip mine (donated by American Electric Power) it is now home to the International Center for the preservation of wild animals. Conservation is key at the Wilds where over 9000 acres of forest and grassland with 150 lakes is home to animals in a protected open range habitat (no pens, stables, and cages) designed to create an environment for reproduction. Check out the Mid-Sized Carnivore Conservation Center, where highly social animals such as cheetahs and African wild dogs wander. Take an open-air bus to view the other animals as they roam free in this preserve. You'll see many animals you don't see in zoos like African gazelles, reticulated giraffes, mountain zebras, tundra swans and red wolves in herds. With lots of "tender loving care" and adaptation exercises, injured animals may now roam free. You might also see real wild horses that look like a rhinoceros and a horse. They are very strong and tough (yet beautiful to watch). Other opportunities available to visitors include an education center where you can learn from interactive computer kiosks and various displays that focus on the relationship between humans and their environment.

Dellroy

ATWOOD LAKE RESORT

Dellroy - *2650 Lodge Road (off SR 212 to SR 542 or off SR 39 entrance) 44675.*
Phone: (330) 735-2211 or (800) 362-6406. www.atwoodlakeresort.com.

Family fishing memories...

Camping, hiking trails, boating & rentals, fishing, swimming, visitor center and winter sports. Beach with paddle boat rentals & food service. Dining and accommodations with indoor/outdoor pool at lodge. Comfortable, spacious 4 bedroom cabins with trails! Bring along the extended family and plan a mini-reunion. Because the cabins are spacious and have separate bedrooms, everyone can have their "space", yet convene in the center gathering area for games, conversation or television. Summertime kids activities, too.

Dennison

DENNISON RAILROAD DEPOT MUSEUM

Dennison - *400 Center Street (off SR 250 or SR 36, Dennison exit to Second St.-turn right along tracks) 44621. www.dennisondepot.org. Phone: (740) 922-6776 or (877) 278-8020. Hours: Tuesday-Friday 10:00am-5:00pm, Saturday 11:00am-4:00pm, Sunday 11:00am-3:00pm. Admission: $8.00 adult, $6.00 senior, $4.00 child (7-17). Miscellaneous: Special train rides depart each season. Check website for events.*

During WW II the Dennison Depot was located on the National Railway Defense Route. It was the main stopping point on the route because it was the exact mid-point between Columbus and Pittsburgh. One evening, a town's lady noticed the servicemen seemed sad, so she organized a few other friends to start a GI canteen. The community became so popular among the soldiers that it was called Dreamsville, USA. The canteen for WW II servicemen is now used as a museum of local history, a gift shop, an old fashioned candy counter and a theme restaurant. Lunch is served at the Canteen Restaurant, a unique 1940s family restaurant offering Victory Garden Salads and Dreamsville Desserts (groups: ask about the "hobo lunch" served in a souvenir bandana). Small admission to the museum includes kids being able to ring a steam locomotive bell, swing a lantern, climb a caboose and watch trains run on the model train layout.

RAILROAD FESTIVAL

Dennison - *Dennison Railroad Depot Museum. Enjoy the heritage and history of the famous World War II Dennison Depot with food, games, contests, rides and parade. Train rides. (week – mid. May)*

_____

POLAR EXPRESS

Dennison – *Dennison Railroad Depot Museum. Train trip in decorated coaches with Santa. Songs and treats. Dress warmly. Weekends only. Admission.*

_____

Dover

BROAD RUN CHEESEHOUSE

Dover - *6011 County Road 139 NW (4 miles west of I-77, old SR 39) 44622. Phone: (330) 343-4108 or (800) 332-3358. www.broadruncheese.com. Admission: $1.50 per person (age 5+). Tours: Monday – Saturday (Mornings), by reservation usually. 20 minutes long with samples. Miscellaneous: Gift Shop with novelties, cheese and sausage.*

Not just a window view but an actual tour of Swiss, Baby Swiss, Brick, and Muenster productions. They make 640,000 pounds of cheese from 8,000,000 pounds (yes, pounds!) of milk each year. After your factory tour you can sample cheese and as a souvenir, get an official cheesemaker paper cap (the one you wore during the tour). What happens to the cream that is separated off from the cheese? (hint: it's made into another tasty product). Ever seen thick, warm milk cut into cubes? (forms "curds" and "whey"). What makes the holes?

WARTHER CARVINGS

Dover - *331 Karl Avenue (I-77 to exit 83 to State Route 211 east) 44622. Phone: (330) 343-7513. www.warthers.com. Hours: Daily 9:00am-5:00pm (March-November). Monday-Saturday 10:00am – 4:00pm (December – February) Admission: $11.50 adult, $6.00 student (7-17). Tours: Last tour begins one hour before closing. Miscellaneous: Tree of Pliers – 500 interconnecting pairs of working pliers carved out of 1 piece of walnut wood! Mrs. Warther's Button Collection – Over 70,000 in museum! Gift Shop and garden trails. Short videos throughout the tour keep it interesting.*

For updates & travel games visit: **www.KidsLoveTravel.com**

A must see tour of the visions of a master craftsman! Mr. Warther started carving at age 5 with a pocketknife while milking cows and later during breaks working at a mill. Before your tour begins, take a peek into the original 1912 workshop or at the display of wood carved postcards. A favorite carving of ours was the steel mill (3 x 5 feet) with moving parts depicting the foreman raising a sandwich to eat, and another worker sleeping on the job. The Abraham Lincoln Funeral Train has thousands of mechanized movements powered by a sewing machine motor. See models of steam locomotives and trains using mostly walnut, ivory, and arguto (oily wood) for

> Ernest "Mooney" Warther turned his joy of carving wood and ivory into creations that the Smithsonian has called "priceless works of art".

moving parts which still run without repairs for over 60 years! The late Mr. Warther loved entertaining children with his carvings (George actually met him in 1970) and he would carve a pair of working pliers with just a few cuts in a piece of wood in only a few seconds! Now, one of

Hundreds of tiny moving parts... all carved by hand...amazing!

the family members still carves pliers for each child visiting (if you pay attention and sit in the front row). This is "Where enthusiasm is caught, not taught." Truly amazing!

VICTORIAN HOME OPEN HOUSE, J.E. REEVES

Dover - 325 East Iron Avenue. Buildings decorated for holidays, Santa visit, entertainment and light refreshments served. Great way to expose younger ones to historical homes that might be boring otherwise. Many other historic sites listed within the book have special holiday themes (see each separate listing for details). Admission. www.doverhistory.org. (begins thanksgiving weekend for one month of December)

East Liverpool

BEAVER CREEK STATE PARK

East Liverpool - *12021 Echo Dell Road (8 miles North of East Liverpool off State Route 7) 43920. Phone: (330) 385-3091. www.beavercreekwildlife.org.*

3,038 acres of camping, hiking trails, fishing and winter sports. Approximately sixteen miles of hiking trails take the visitor to historic canal locks and through a steep walled gorge. Hikers will find several beautiful waterfalls by exploring the many tributary streams. A short trail from the campground to Oak Tree Point gives an excellent panorama of the scenic valley. The park includes Little Beaver Creek, a state and national wild and scenic river, and acres of forest wilderness. The rich history of the area invites visitors to explore Gaston's Mill, pioneer village and abandoned canal locks. The Education Center has live turtles as well as several live native snakes for visitors to see. They also have over 300 mounted mammals including deer, bears, beaver, fox, coyote, badger, bobcat, mountain lion and a gray as well as both bald and golden eagles and many song birds that can be found in and around Columbiana County (Center only open weekends from May thru early October).

MUSEUM OF CERAMICS

East Liverpool - *400 East 5th Street (corner of Broadway) 43920. Phone: (330) 386-6001 or (800) 600-7880. www.ohiohistory.org/places/ceramics. Hours: Tuesday-Saturday and Holidays 9:30am-3:30pm. Closed most major holidays and November Election Day plus Max Gard Hike Day (second Wednesday in May). Admission: $4.00 adult, $2.00 student (all ages).*

The exhibits in the museum depict the growth and development of East Liverpool and its ceramic industry from 1840 to 1930, the period when the city's potteries produced over 50% of the ceramics manufactured in the United States. Displays cover good and bad times of the ceramic industry and the effects on its people. Life- sized dioramas of kiln, jigger and decorating shops with a collection of old and new ceramics make the museum easy to follow.

TRI-STATE POTTERY FESTIVAL

East Liverpool - www.tristatepotteryfestival.org. (330) 385-0845. Celebration of pottery heritage featuring pottery Olympics, industry displays, potters at work, ceramic museum, international doorknob tossing championships, factory tours (local companies like Hall China or Pioneer Pottery), art show, rose show, window displays, amusement rides and daily entertainment. (third weekend in June)

Frazeysburg

LONGABERGER MUSEUM & FACTORY TOUR

Frazeysburg - *5563 Raiders Rd (on State Route 16) 43822. www.longaberger.com.*
Phone: (740) 322-5588. Hours: Monday-Saturday 9:00am-5:00pm, Sunday Noon
- 5:00pm. Extended hours in the spring and summer and during special events.
Closed holidays. Admission: FREE. Tours: Arrive before 1:00pm, Monday –
Friday to see actual production. No production on Saturday or Sunday. Weaving
demonstrations daily in the Gallery with same setup as one of the factory
stations.

CORPORATE HEADQUARTERS: (State Route 16) Newark. A giant
7-story Market Basket design with towering heated handles (to melt the winter
ice) on top and painted / stenciled to look like wood. Incredible!

HOMESTEAD: Gift shops with tour baskets for sale, lots of home furnishings
and eateries. Tour a replica of the Longaberger Family Home where Dave

grew up with his 11 brothers and sisters.
JW's workshop may be toured also. The
Make a Basket Shop is where you can pay
a fee to actually create your own hardwood
maple Longaberger basket with the help of
a Master artisan (takes one hour). All
children (any age) can romp around at "The
Lookout Treehouse" (located within the
Homestead). Listen to the owl and the
sights and sounds of nature. Outdoor
Playground and special indoor Kid's
shopping areas. Eateries from ice cream to
sit down are offered.

FACTORY TOURS: Fascinating tours and lots to see in this tiny little town.
Longaberger manufacturers high quality, handmade hard maple baskets. The
one-quarter mile long factory is home to hundreds of weavers who make over
100,000 baskets per week (each initialed and dated). It's best to first watch a
13 minute video of the company's history and the manufacturing process that
takes sugar maple logs (poached and debarked) that are cut into long thin
strips. You'll be mesmerized when you go upstairs to the mezzanine to view
hundreds of crafters, each with their own station, weaving damp wood strips
around "forms", Each basket takes about 20-30 minutes to make. Can you
guess what a weaving horse is?

Gnadenhutten

GNADENHUTTEN

Gnadenhutten - 352 South Cherry Street (I-77 to SR 36 east) 44629. Phone: (740) 254-4143. http://gnaden.tusco.net/history/museum.htm. Hours: Tuesday-Saturday 10:00am-5:00pm, Sunday 1:00-5:00pm (June-August). Weekends only (September-October). Admission: $1.00 donation. Miscellaneous: A 'friendly' cemetery tour on the premises. Look at the graves tombstone hands- why are they turned in different directions-what does it mean?

Gnadenhutten (Huts of Grace) was settled five months after Schoenbrunn on October 9, 1772. Joshua, a Moravian Mohican Elder, brought a large group of Christian Mohican Indians from Pennsylvania to this location. This settlement grew rapidly and the group worked hard and prospered. Their standard of living was high for that era on the frontier, their cabins had glass windows, basements, they used pewter household utensils, they were adept in crafts and artwork, and loved music. It was here that the Roth child (first white baby in this territory) was born, July 4, 1773. All went well until the Revolutionary War began and the English at Detroit wanted all Indians to fight against the Americans. The local Indians refused. When they would not leave, in September 1781, troops and Indian warriors rounded up all the Indians living in New Schoenbrunn, Gnadenhutten, and Salem and took them to Captives town. During the winter in the captive town many died of diseases. Permission to go home was granted to 150. They arrived back home in February 1782 and were gathering food and belongings, when Pennsylvania Militiamen under Colonel Williamson surrounded them. After a night of prayer and hymn singing, ninety men, women and children were massacred, then all cabins were set afire on March 8, 1782. Two boys escaped to warn others and to tell the story. See the sites of the two buildings where the Indians spent the night before their death. Those buildings, the Mission House and Cooper Shop (the actual basement foundation where one boy hid - it will take your breath away!), have been restored and are located on their original sites. The story of the massacre is told in the outdoor drama "Trumpet in the Land".

PIONEER DAYS

Gnadenhutten - Historical Park & Museum. An 1840's pioneer encampment, entertainment, parade, arts and crafts. FREE. (first weekend in August)

Hartville

QUAIL HOLLOW STATE PARK

Hartville - *13480 Congress Lake Road (2 miles North of Hartville) 44632. Phone: (330) 877-6652. www.dnr.state.oh.us.*

Quail Hollow is a landscape of rolling meadows, marshes, pine and woodland trails surrounding a 40-room manor. Now called the Natural History Study Center, the former Stewart family home is primarily used for educational, nature-oriented and community activities. The home is open on weekends 1:00-5:00 pm. Quail Hollow has over 19 miles of trails ideal for hiking, jogging, nature study or cross-country skiing. Eight interpretive nature trails explore the unique natural habitats for which each is named. There is also a five-mile, day-use bridle trail and four-mile mountain bike trail. The Nature For All trail is a 2000 ft. paved interpretive trail for those visitors with a physical challenge. Interpretive audio tapes and brochures are available at the visitors center as well as along the trail.

PUMPKIN MAZE PLAYLAND

Hartville - Maize Valley Farm Market, 6193 Edison St. NE. Pumpkin Patches / Hayrides / Corn Mazes / Fall Playland - Admission (average $6.00). Plan on at least two hours playtime. Pumpkin cannon. Open weekends, some weekdays (by appointment) and weeknights. www.maizevalley.com. (Daily, late September-early November).

Kidron

LEHMAN'S HARDWARE

Kidron - *4779 Kidron Road (Rte. 30 east, exit Kidron Road, head south) 44636. Phone: (330) 857-5757. www.lehmans.com/index.jsp. Hours: Monday - Saturday 8:00am-5:30pm, Thursday until 8:00pm. Closed Sunday.*

Visit http://countrylife.lehmans.com/about/ online for free tips on how to live simply

Heading from Ohio Amish country west, you may be surprised to find some old-fashioned goodness in Wayne County. Try to plan a visit to Kidron on a Thursday - it's auction day. Next door, visit the famous Lehman's Hardware, where you'll find all the non-electrical appliances and equipment used by the

Amish. Lehman's was founded by Jay Lehman in 1955 to serve the Amish who believe in simple living without electricity or other modern innovations. From his Amish customers, Jay learned that non-electric products often give us the ability to complete a task faster and more efficiently than commonly accepted modern methods. In a twist of irony, the company's key customers (once the Amish) are now a key vendor. Don't forget to bring your toy and kitchen tools wish list. Look for the giant copper kettles and cast iron pots and plenty of toy wagons and farm games. Around every corner is a museum-quality artifact with a description.

You can browse here for hours for all kinds of unique items...

Lisbon

GUILFORD LAKE STATE PARK

Lisbon - *6835 East Lake Road (6 miles Northwest of Lisbon off State Route 172) 44432. Phone: (330) 222-1712.. www.dnr.state.oh.us.*

Guilford Lake State Park is a quiet fishing lake located in northeastern Ohio on the west fork of the Little Beaver Creek. The gentle rolling terrain of the area offers a serene escape for park visitors year round. A half-mile hiking trail skirts the scenic lakeshore and provides opportunities for exercise and wildlife observation. 488 acres of camping, boating, fishing, swimming and winter sports.

Magnolia

ELSON FLOURING MILL

Magnolia - *261 North Main Street (SR 183, southwest edge of town) 44643. Phone: (330) 866-3353. www.elsonmill.freeservers.com. Tours: Every Thursday at 10:00am and 2:00pm, April through November. Only by Appointment. Admission is $2.00 per person. The working mill conducts business 8:00am - 5:00pm weekdays and 8:00am - noon Saturdays.*

Visit this picturesque red mill in the center of a canal village. Founded in 1834 by the great-great grandfather of the present owners, it gives a glimpse of industry in the 1800's. Built of virgin timber cleared from the land on which the mill stands, it has been in continuous operation by the Elson Family. Corn meal has been made at the mill since 1834 and can be purchased still today.

Millersburg

GUGGISBERG CHEESE FACTORY

Millersburg - *5060 State Route 557 (Off State Route 39, I-77 exit 83) 44654. Phone: (330) 893-2500. www.guggisberg.com. Hours: Monday-Saturday 8:00am – 6:00pm, Sunday 11:00 am – 4:00pm) (April – December). Monday-Saturday 8:00am – 5:00pm (December – March)*

Home of the original Baby Swiss – you can watch through a window as cheese is being made (best time to view is 8:00 am – Noon weekdays). We learned milk is brought in the early mornings from neighboring Amish farms. Cultures and enzymes are added to form curd. Curd is pressed into molds and brine salted. Each cheese is aged at least a month for flavor. A short video is always playing that details this process if you can't view it personally.

ROLLING RIDGE RANCH

Millersburg - *3961 County Road 168 (Weaver Ridge Road) (I-77 exit Rte. 39 west to SR 62 north to CR 168) 44654. Phone: (330) 893-3777. www.visitrollingridge.com. Hours: Monday-Saturday 9:00am-One hour before sunset (April - mid-October). Admission: Drive thru in own car $5.00-$8.00 per person or $8.95-$13.95 per person (wagon ride tours).*

The ranch features 400-500 animals & birds from around the world. Take a 2-mile safari ride in your own vehicle or a horse drawn wagon to see animals from 6 continents. Feed the animals from a guided horse-drawn tour or from the safety of your own car. Experienced guides will identify different species and teach you about each animal's habitat, feeding habits and unique traits. You are welcome to bring along your camera, as you will be up close to the animals and birds. You may see zebras, water buffalo, African and Indian antelope, African Watusi cows, and Indian and Oriental deer. There is a petting zoo adjacent to the wildlife area and a gift shop. There are also picnic tables.

YODER'S AMISH HOME

Millersburg - *6050 State Route 515 (between Trail and Walnut Creek) 44654. Phone: (330) 893-2541. www.yodersamishhome.com. Hours: Monday-Saturday 10:00am-5:00pm (mid-April thru October). Admission: Tours $5.00 Adult, $3.00 Children (under 12). Buggy Rides $3.50 Adult, $2.00 Children (under 12). Add about $3.00 each for the tour of the school. Combo (all three tours) saves $1.50.*

Step back to a simple time and way of life. This home was built in 1866 and shows authentic furnishings from that period. Local, knowledgeable guides take you on a 30-40 minute tour through both homes on the property and the barn. Your guide will explain a great deal about the history and lifestyle of the Amish people. Learn what a "hoodle stup" is. Then step into an 1885 barn with animals to pet. Most popular tends to be the turkeys – (Yes, you can try to pet turkeys!). Buggy rides are given by retired real Amish farmers who are personable and tell stories during the ride.

OLD FASHIONED APPLE BUTTER STIRRING

Millersburg – *Yoder's Amish Home. Uncle Andy and Aunt Mattie, with some help from their boys, get the 30 gallon copper kettle on the fire in the morning and begin the process of apple butter. Do you know how many apples go in a 30-gallon batch? When you visit, you can take a turn stirring and try a sample too! They stir all day and fill up half pint jars to be sold. (first three Saturdays in October)*

HOLIDAYS AT THE MANSION

Millersburg - *484 Wooster Road. www.historicdowntownmillersburg.com. Holidays at the Mansion is a very special time to see the Victorian House in all its grandeur. Buildings decorated for holidays, Santa visit, entertainment and light refreshments served. Great way to expose younger ones to historical homes that might be boring otherwise. Admission. (mid-November thru December weekends)*

Minerva

MINERVA CHEESE FACTORY

Minerva - *430 Radloff Avenue 44657. www.cheesehere.com. Phone: (330) 868-4196. Hours: Monday-Friday Noon-6:00pm, Wednesday & Saturday 9:00am-3:00pm.*

Minerva Cheese & Butter plant has been family owned & operated since 1935. Producers of Amish-style, Ohio raw milk and goat cheeses, this factory strives to maintain a product free of hormones or antibiotics. Watch them at work through the viewing window. Free viewing and some samples. Say cheese, please.

Nashport

DILLON STATE PARK

Nashport - *5265 Dillon Hills Drive (8 miles west of Zanesville off State Route 146) 43830. Phone: (740) 453-4377. www.dnr.state.oh.us/parks/parks/dillon.htm.*

The wooded hills and valleys of the area offer outdoor adventure with 7690 acres of camping, hiking trails, boating and rentals, fishing, swimming (sandy beaches), and winter sports. The Ruffed Grouse Nature Trail is approximately 3/4-mile long and introduces the hiker to the varied habitats of the area. This trail is a branch of the 6-mile long Licking Bend Trail which skirts the lakeshore. Three other fascinating trails--Blackberry Ridge Trail (1 mile), King Ridge Loop (1.1 miles) and Hickory Grove Loop (1.5 miles) are located very near the camping and cottage area. Family deluxe cottages with A/C and cable. Nearby, in the Blackhand Gorge, carved by the Licking River, a sandstone cliff bore a soot blackened (Black Hand Sandstone) engraving of a human hand. This mysterious petroglyph is thought to have served as a guide marker for Indians searching for Flint Ridge.

New Concord

JOHN & ANNIE GLENN HISTORIC SITE

New Concord - *68 West Main Street (I-70 to New Concord exit, across from library) 43762. Phone: (740) 826-3305. www.johnglennhome.org. Hours: Wednesday-Saturday 10:00am-3:00pm, Sunday 1:00-4:00pm. (mid-April thru mid-October). Closed major holidays and winter months. Admission: $6.00 adult, $5.00 senior, $3.00 student. Educators: Bios of the Glenns are online.*

John Glenn, astronaut and politician, spent his boyhood in this home that has been moved and restored to its late 1930's appearance as a museum dedicated to telling 20th century American history through the lives of John and Annie Glenn. The backdrop are displays on the Cold War and the Space Race. Kids will like to view models of an F86 airplane, which John Glenn flew, and a Russian MIG, of which Glenn downed three in Korea. John Glenn's brand of heroism is steeped in small-town values. These values, along with patriotism, public service, and commitment to family are interpreted at the museum. "Grit is the theme of the museum," according to The New York Times.

New Philadelphia

MUSKINGUM WATERSHED CONSERVANCY DISTRICT LAKES

New Philadelphia -   *44663. www.mwcdlakes.com. Phone: (330) 343-6647 or (877) 363-8500.*

All of the MWCD parks feature camping all year long, so a getaway for a day or weekend is easy. Stays in family vacation cabins also are available for a few weeks at Pleasant Hill and Seneca parks, several months at Tappan Lake Park and all year at Atwood Lake Park. Contact the park of your choice for details. Hiking trails, boating and rentals, fishing, swimming, visitor center, lodge or cabins and food service. Nature programs.

SHOENBRUNN

New Philadelphia - *State Route 259, East High Avenue (4 miles East of I-77 exit 81) 44663. www.ohiohistory.org/places/shoenbr. Phone: (330) 339-3636 or (800) 752-2711. Hours: Wednesday-Saturday 9:00am-5:00pm; Sunday Noon-5:00pm (Summer). Weekends only (September-October). Admission: $7.00 adult, $3.00 student (all ages). Miscellaneous: Museum. Video orientation. Gift Shop. Picnic facilities. A special, interactive event is usually held one Saturday each month. Tape recorded tours available at no extra cost.*

CE Area

Take a self-guided tour of the reconstructed log building village founded by a Moravian missionary in 1772. The Moravian church founded Schoenbrunn

First settlement church

("beautiful spring") as a mission to the Delaware Indians. Being the first settlement in Ohio, Schoenbrunn claims the first civil code, the first church (learn about the love feast still occasionally held here, especially near Christmas), and the first school. Problems associated with the American Revolution prompted Schoenbrunn's closing in 1777. Today the reconstructed village includes seventeen log buildings and gardens...many occupied by costumed interpreters demonstrating period crafts and customs.

CE Area

TRUMPET IN THE LAND

New Philadelphia - *Shoenbrunn Amphitheatre (-77 to Exit 81) 44663. Phone: (330) 339-1132. www.trumpetintheland.com. Hours: Several performances per week (except Sunday) 8:30 pm (mid-June to late August) Admission: $15.00 adult, $13.00 senior, $7.00 child (under 12). Backstage tours a few dollars extra. Bargain days on Mondays and Tuesdays ($5.00-$10.00 per person). Miscellaneous: See listing for Gnanenhutten to review a more detailed history of this saga before you go. Other productions are either historical or contemporary.*

In an Ohio Frontier setting (the first settlement at Schoenbrunn), meet historical characters like David Zeisgerber (missionary converting Indians), Simon Girtz (renegade), Captain Pipe (young warrior who hated white men) and John Heikewelder (explorer)...all vital historical figures in the founding of Ohio. The Revolutionary War breaks out and Moravian Indian Christians would not take sides. Feel their stress and desires to try to remain neutral in a hostile environment. Sadly, in the end, American militia brutally massacre 90 Christian Indians at Gnadenhutten.

TUSCORA PARK

New Philadelphia - *South Broadway Street (I-77 to US 250 east) 44663. Phone: (800) 527-3387. www.tuscora.park.net.*

The central feature is the antique big carousel or the summer showcase concert series or swimming pool. What draws little ones and families is also the Ferris wheel, 6-8 kiddie rides (including a train ride and mini roller coaster), batting cages and putt-putt - all at low prices. Most rides are 50 cents and activities are around $1.00. Great alternative to higher priced amusement "vacations" during Summer Break (only open summertime).

Norwich

NATIONAL ROAD / ZANE GREY MUSEUM

Norwich - 8850 East Pike (U.S. 40 / I-70 Norwich Exit) 43767. Phone: (740) 872-3143 or (800) 752-2602. www.ohiohistory.org/places/natlroad. Hours: Wednesday-Saturday 9:30am-5:00pm, Sunday & Holidays Noon-5:00pm (Memorial Day weekend-Labor Day). Admission: $7.00 adult, $3.00 student (all ages).

"Head West Young Man" in a Conestoga wagon as you explore the history of US-40 National Road. Built based on a concept of George Washington, it stretches between western territories in Illinois to the eastern state of Maryland. It was vital to the development of the frontier heading west and later called "America's Main Street". Play a game where children locate all the different types of bridges on this route (examples: the "Y" and "S" Bridge). The facility also commemorates author Zane Grey and his western novels and the area's ceramic heritage.

Orrville

SMUCKERS COMPANY STORE AND CAFÉ

Orrville - 333 Wadsworth Road (Rt. 57, 1/4 mile north of Rt. 30) 44667. Phone: (330) 684-1500. www.smuckers.com/jm_smucker_company_store/default.asp. Hours: Monday-Saturday 9:00am-6:00pm. Closed Sunday.   Miscellaneous: Café offers delicious recipes made with ingredients from their family of brands. Enjoy a pizza made in their wood-fired oven.

You'll see the Simply Smuckers store brimming with your favorite jams and relishes - plus Pillsbury Dough Boys and Jif products. Walk through the on-site museum to learn about The Company's heritage and journey - spanning over 100 years. Follow the history "mailboxes" along one wall to learn fast facts about Smuckers like when they decided to go with the gingham-colored lids for brand identity. There are always delicious products to sample - usually something sweet and something savory - all in a beautiful timber frame barn.

JUMPIN PUMPKIN SPECIAL

Orrville - *145 South Depot Street. Orrville Railroad. www.orrvillerailroad.com. Phone: (330) 683-2426. The Jumpin' Pumpkin Jamboree features food, adult and children's games, pictures, parade, pumpkin decorating contest, and many other activities. They make available a one mile round trip train ride on the Orrville Railroad Heritage Society siding. Trains rides depart on the hour beginning at 12:00 Noon with the last ride at 5:00pm. The train will be leaving from and returning to the McGill St. Siding. Small Admission. (mid-October Saturday)*

Shreve

APPLE FESTIVAL

Shreve - *Whispering Hills RV Park. Apples & cider. Apple pie eating contests. Apple peeling contests. Apple butter. Candy apples. Wagon/hayrides. Apple Dumplings, Fritters, Donuts, etc. Parades. Pioneer crafts. Petting Zoo. www.whisperinghillsrvpark.com. (first weekend in October)*

Steubenville

JEFFERSON LAKE STATE PARK

Steubenville - *501 Twsp Rd 261A (16 miles Northwest of Steubenville on State Route 43) 43944. Phone: (740) 765-4459. www.dnr.state.oh.us.*

In the sandstone bedrock can be found layers of coal which were formed by decaying swamp vegetation. 933 acres of camping, rough hiking trails, boating, fishing, swimming and winter sports.

CREEGAN COMPANY ANIMATION FACTORY

Steubenville - *510 Washington Street (I-70 to State Route 7 North) 43952. Phone: (740) 283-3708. www.creegans.com. Tours: Reservations Preferred. (45 minute tour). Monday – Friday 10:00am-4:00pm. Saturdays only 10:00 am-2:00pm (during Christmas season). Walking on three levels with stairs. Miscellaneous: An area retail store (Treasure Island Flea Market, located nearby) sells Creegan's puppets and holiday items.*

Their theme is "We Make Things Move" and they're the nation's largest manufacturer of animated and costumed characters. (Some customers are Hershey Park and Disney

CE Area

World). A costumed mascot (Beary Bear) greets and guides your pre-arranged tour of Animation "Behind the Scenes". Start with the Craft Area where ribbon, yarn, and puppet props abound everywhere. Then, to the Art Department where workers paint faces on molded plastic heads and make costumes. (To make the plastic heads they use a machine press that uses molds to form faces out of sheets of plain white plastic.) In the sculpting area, shelves of hundreds of character head, feet, and hand molds line the walls and a woman sculpts new molds. Finally, peek inside some of the bodies of automated figures to

Plastic molded heads awaiting their bodies...A must see unique factory tour!

view the electronics that produce body movements (some are a little scary for young ones). An amazing place and tour…it's like Santa's workshop!

FORT STEUBEN, HISTORIC

Steubenville - *120 South Third Street 43952. www.oldfortsteuben.com. Phone: (740) 283-1787. Hours: Monday-Saturday 10:00am-4:00pm, Sunday Noon-4:00pm (May-October). Visitor Center open weekdays year-round.   Admission: $5.00 adult, $3.00 youth (6-12). Miscellaneous: Pick up a map at the CVB office here for the Steubenville City of Murals: During a self-guided tour (free) you can see 25 giant full color (almost 3D) murals with the theme "Preserving a Piece of America" on the sides of downtown buildings. Each has its own name with some of the most interesting being Stanton Park, Ohio River Oil Company and Steam Laundry*

– these all "jump" right off the wall and appear almost like a photograph.

Historic Fort Steuben is a reconstructed 18th century fort built on the original site overlooking the Ohio River that opened the Northwest Territory to expansion and settlement. The 150 soldiers garrisoned in the fort protected the surveyors from hostile tribes as they laid out the first Seven Ranges of the Northwest Territory. Exhibits depict military life in 1787. An active archaeological dig is part of the tour. Buildings housing exhibits include the hospital, the Officers'

Quarters, the Enlisted Men's Quarters, the Blacksmith, the Quartermaster's, and the newly opened Commissary. This is a nicely restored fort complex that kids can explore easily within parental view.

FORT STEUBEN FESTIVAL

Steubenville - This first American Regiment was built to protect government surveyors from hostile Indians. Next to the fort site is the first Federal Land Office built in the U.S. in 1801. Watch mountain men reenactment groups, storytellers and craftspeople. Admission. (third weekend in June)

Sugarcreek

ALPINE HILLS MUSEUM

Sugarcreek - 106 West Main Street 44681. www.oacountry.com. Phone: (888) 609-7592. Hours: Daily 9:00am-4:30pm, except Sundays (April - November). Extended summer hours.

Three floors of Swiss, German and Amish heritage. Many audio-visuals & push buttons "spotlight" parts of well-explained dioramas of an Amish kitchen, Swiss cheesehouse and a woodshop & printshop. Nearby, the best Swiss steak & mashed potatoes in town are at the Swiss Hat restaurant.

OHIO SWISS FESTIVAL

Sugarcreek - Downtown. (888) 609-7592. Experience the best of Switzerland from Polka bands, dancing, tons of Swiss cheese, Steinstossen (stone throwing) and Schwingfest (Swiss wrestling). FREE (last Friday & Saturday of September)

Walnut Creek

COBLENTZ CHOCOLATE COMPANY

Walnut Creek - 4917 State Route 515 and State Route 39 (I-77 exit 83 Dover to Rte. 39 west) 44687. www.coblentzchocolates.com. Phone: (330) 893-2995 or (800) 338-9341. Hours: Monday – Saturday 9:00am – 6:00pm (July – October). Close at 5:00pm (November-May). Best viewing is from 9:00am-3:00pm.

Watch through the kitchen windows as chocolate is stirred in large vats with automatic paddle stirs. They have a window going 65 feet along the side of the kitchen so you can see candy being made, from cooling to pouring onto tables to wrapping. Caramels, fruits, and nuts are hand dipped and layered on large trays to cool and dry. Also, see molds for chocolate forms used to create bars of barks and holiday shapes. Savor the sweet smell of fresh milk and dark chocolate as you decide which treats to buy. Our favorite was the chocolate covered Dutch pretzels with sprinkles or nuts on top. Can't make the trip in person, they have an online slide show tour that will make you salivate!

Wilmot

AMISH DOOR DINNER THEATRE

Wilmot - 1210 Winesburg Street, US 62 44689. www.amishdoor.com. Phone: (800) 891-6142. Hours: Doors open at 6:15pm. Shows generally begin around 7:00pm.

Come celebrate the joy of dinner and a show at the Amish Door. Through original plays, classic stories and festive songs, you'll experience light-hearted, fun biblical "twists" of classic themes and musicals. Tickets are $28.00-$35.00 per person and include a bountiful, all inclusive meal featuring all the Amish Door favorites.

GRANDMA'S ALPINE HOMESTEAD

Wilmot - 1504 US 62 44689. www.grandmashomestead.com. Phone: (330) 359-5454 or (800) 546-2572. Hours: Daily 9:00am-8:00pm (Spring-Thanksgiving). Serving lunch and dinner beginning at 11:00am.

This is home of the "World's Largest Cuckoo Clock". The Guinness Book of World Records has it listed as 23 ½ feet high, 24 feet long and 13 ½ feet wide. Trudy, a life-size mannequin with a German accent, opens shutters to greet you. The Swiss Village Market has viewing windows (to watch cheese-making), restaurants and shops.

Wooster

AMERIHOST INN WOOSTER EAST

Wooster - 2055 Lincoln Way East (SR 30A) 44691. www.amerihostinn.com. Phone: (330) 262-5008. Try this family-friendly hotel when in the area. Their best feature is right in front of the hotel - the indoor heated pool and whirlpool - a nice-sized area that was clean and inviting for kids and parents. Each morning, they offer free continental breakfast including fresh-made waffles and good coffee. Their rooms are nice and modestly priced.

AMISH DOOR RESTAURANT

Wooster - 6655 East LincolnWay (US 30 East. Exit at Applecreek Rd. South and Turn Right on Lincoln Way E.) 44691. Phone: (330) 263-0547. www.amishdoor.com. Hours: Monday -Saturday 7:00am-8:00pm Closed Sunday. Generous portions of homemade foods and real mashed potatoes in a country charm motif. Select your favorites from the menu or choose their bountiful all-you-can-eat family style. We liked their Express Lunch Buffet ($7.99) and a piece of homemade pie (our favs: black raspberry or pecan).

CE Area

🍽️

CAT'S MEOW VILLAGE

Wooster - 2163 Great Trails Drive (just off E LincolnWay, near Rte. 30) 44691. Phone: (330) 264-1377. www.catsmeow.com.

Just a few miles outside of downtown toward Wooster on SR 30, you'll find The Cat's Meow Village, maker of the two-dimensional wooden buildings found in gift shops around the country. Although homeworkers do the cutting and painting (no factory here), some kids may like the "Mewseum" where you can make your own piece or play some guessing games with Casper, the mascot. Did you know Casper is hidden on every Cat's Meow memory piece?

HARTZLER FAMILY DAIRY

Wooster - 5454 Cleveland Road 44691. www.hartzlerfamilydairy.com. Phone: (330) 345-8190. Tours: All tours are by appointment only. Mostly weekdays, some Saturdays. Small Tours (minimum 15 people) $3.00 per person. (includes single dip ice cream cone).

A true "family affair" with oodles of generations of kids working all about. Get the "scoops" from Mom Hartzler at the Ice Cream Shoppe. Tour the processing plant that is adjacent to

Cows drink 25-50 gallons of water each day--nearly a bathtub full!

the ice cream shoppe. Walk through the family farms and processing plant where you'll see milk bottling, butter churning and ice cream making - live and in person. Learn The History of Hartzler Farms, Their Family, and Their Dairy Business. Guided by a Hartzler Family Member, you'll determine the secrets about why their milk looks and tastes different than most.

MELVINS

Wooster - *359 West Liberty Street 44691. Phone: (330) 264-6263. Miscellaneous: Downtown Wooster: Looking for some new kitchen accessories or outdoor Little Tykes playstuff, stop in to the Everything Rubbermaid Store. Several little boutiques, The Wooster Book Company (nice kids section) and unique bakeries or cafes are in the square, too. After you've shopped and taken in some history, enjoy a delicious hot meal at Melvins on West Liberty. The brick oven smell will lure you in and their friendly wait staff and reasonable gourmet pricing (average dinner entree around $10.00) will please your appetite and they have a $2.99 Kids Menu, too. Dinner.*

OHIO AGRICULTURAL RESEARCH AND DEVELOPMENT CENTER

Wooster - *1680 Madison Avenue (off I-71 exit SR 83 or US 30 west to Madison Ave. exit) 44691. Phone: (330) 202-3507. www.oardc.ohio-state.edu/visitor/. Hours: Monday-Friday 7:30am-4:30pm (Summer). Monday-Friday 8:00am-5:00pm (September – June). Admission: FREE. Tours: Guided tours for groups of 10+ by appointment. Weekdays 9:00am-4:00pm. Self guided maps at visitor center. Miscellaneous: You can also visit the 88 acre Secrest Arboretum which has many walking trails and a children's play area. Enter off Madison at the main entrance to OARDC and drive through SECREST ARBORETUM. Get out and walk if it's spring and blooming.*

> Soybeans cover 14.7 million acres in Ohio - 32% of all of the state's farmland.

This center is the foremost, nationally known agricultural research Ohio State University facility with inventions to their credit such as crop dusting and adding vitamin D to milk. Many experiments on insects, greenhouses, honeybees and composting are going on. See how animals are raised, how the right wheat is important for successful bread making (maybe make some), how laser beams detect the size of water droplets in pesticide applications, and how a jellyfish gene can help soybean scientists. Stop in to the Visitors Center and take a picture with a cow or play with some food ideas. Also in the complex is the Bug Zoo (the

Center can give you a map of where to go). If you dare, hold a millipede or sample bug "treats" at special programs conducted every so often in Cafe

Insecta. Why are bugs like tools? Be sure to sign up for other popular programs for families or groups where you might be able to pull out DNA or plant

soybeans in plaster! Most importantly, they teach you how agriculture impacts everyone-everyday. If self-guided tours are your option, you can see the Center which contains some activities for children such as a microscope and computer display as well as the bug zoo. This might spark the future scientist within your child.

How can bugs be like tools?

WAYNE COUNTY HISTORICAL SOCIETY MUSEUM

Wooster - 546 East Bowman St. 44691. www.waynehistorical.org. Phone: (330) 264-8856. Hours: Wednesday-Sunday 2:00-4:30pm (February - October). Tours by appointment only November, December and January. Closed holidays. Admission: $5.00 adults; children under 14 and members of the Historical Society free.

A Historical complex complete with an 1873 schoolhouse, log cabin, mercantile shop and firehouse. From magnificent model ships to the weird seven-legged pig or the amusing squirrel Orchestra - taxidermied squirrels playing mini-instruments! The staff and volunteers here are so passionate about their artifacts and research stories. Here's some other sites to look at: Log Cabin (early settlers home life), Schoolhouse (McGuffy Readers, dunce cap and stool, and potbelly stove,

Large arrowhead collection...

it accurately recreates the atmosphere of a late 1800's learning center), Indians, Women's Vintage Dress Shop, and Outdoor Bake Oven (typical of the massive outdoor ovens which were once found on virtually all German farms in the area during the 19th century).

The famous Squirrel Orchestra

PUMPKIN MAZE PLAYLAND

Wooster - Ramseyer Farms. 3488 Akron Road. Pumpkin Patches / Hayrides / Corn Mazes / Fall Playland. Admission (average $6.00). Plan on at least two hours playtime. Open weekends, some weekdays (by appointment) and weeknights. www.ramseyerfarms.com. (late September - late October, closed Sunday and Monday).

Zanesville

LORENA STERNWHEELER

Zanesville - Moored at Zane's Landing Park (West End of Market Street – I-70 to Downtown Zanesville Exit – Follow signs) 43701. Phone: (740) 455-8883 or (800) 246-6303. www.visitzanesville.com/lorena_sternwheeler. Hours: Wednesday and Saturdays (June – August). Weekends Only (September to mid-October). Admission: Public Rides: $8.00 adult, $7.00 senior, $4.00 child (average 4x/ month). $15.00-$30.00 lunch and dinner cruises.

There was a mythical sweetheart of the Civil War named Lorena who inspired a song written by the famous Zanesvillian, Rev. Henry Webster. The 104' long, 59-ton boat was christened "Lorena" after that popular song. A one-hour cruise on the Muskingum River at a very reasonable rates (afternoon and some twilight cruises).

STARS & STRIPES ON THE RIVER

Zanesville - Zanes Landing Park, Downtown Riverfront. (740) 453-7889. A full day of parades, rides, entertainment and fireworks. (July 4th).

APPLE FESTIVAL

Zanesville - McDonald's Greenhouse, www.mcdonaldsgreenhouse.com. 3100 Adamsville Road. Apples & cider. Apple pie eating contests. Apple peeling contests. Apple butter. Candy apples. Wagon/hayrides. Apple Dumplings, Fritters, Donuts, etc. Parades. Pioneer crafts. Petting Zoo. Giant sand box, pumpkin painting. (daily, September)

Zoar

ZOAR VILLAGE

Zoar - *198 Main Street (State Route 212 – I-77 to Exit 93) 44697. Phone: (800) 262-6195 or (330) 874-3011. www.zca.org. Hours: Wednesday-Saturday 9:30am-5:00pm, Sunday, Holidays Noon-5:00 pm (Summer). Weekends Only (April, May, September, October). Restricted hours for FREE Museum. Admission: $8.00 adult, $4.00 child (6-12). Miscellaneous: Video presentation first explains Zoar history. Probably best to tour with an emphasis on early Ohio home and community life (w/German-American heritage) theme vs. a focus on their political and religious practices (cult-like aspects).*

Zoar means "a sanctuary from evil". They, as a society of Separatists (separation between church and state), were known for their bountiful gardening designs based on the bible. The 12 block district of 1800's homes and shops include a dairy, bakery, museum, gardens, storehouse, tin shops, wagon shops, and blacksmith. They are actual original buildings in a real town of 75 families. Some buildings are staffed, others open by guided tour. Volunteers give craft demonstrations during the many yearly special events. Walk along streets dispersed with restored residences and shops for modern clients.

HARVEST FESTIVAL

Zoar – *Zoar Village. Horse drawn wagon rides, craft show, food, entertainment, kids activities in the garden. Admission for adults. (first weekend in August)*

CHRISTMAS IN ZOAR

Zoar – *Zoar Village. Carolers, crafters and cooks bring back memories of Christmases of the 1850s village decorated for the holidays. This event is a good place to start Christmas shopping and enjoy the culinary treats of the season. Admission. (first weekend in December)*

CE Area

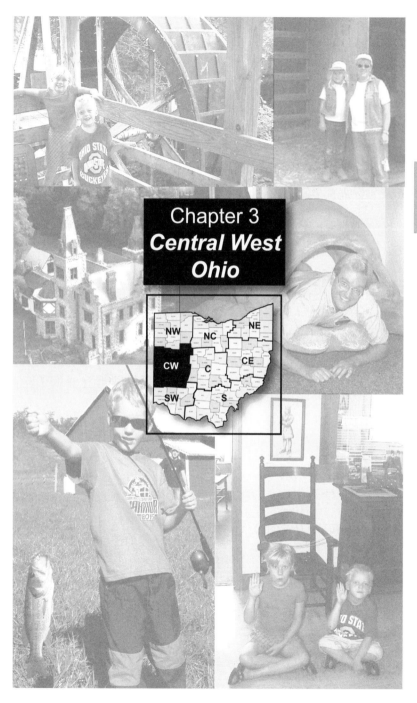

Chapter 3
Central West Ohio

CW Area

Arcanum
- Kinda Kooky Korn Maze

Bellefontaine
- Zane Shawnee Caverns

Clifton
- Clifton Mill

Dayton
- Aullwood Audubon Center And Farm
- Boonshoft Museum Of Discovery
- Carillon Historical Park, Dayton History
- Citizens Motorcar Packard Museum
- Cox Arboretum
- Dayton Art Institute
- Dayton Philharmonic Orchestra
- Dayton Sports
- Dunbar House
- Family New Year's Eve Celebration
- Learning Tree Farm
- Riverscape
- Sunwatch
- Wright Cycle Company Complex

Dayton (Fairborn)
- National Museum Of The USAF

Dayton (Huber Heights)
- Carriage Hill Farm And Museum

Dayton (Miamisburg)
- Miamisburg Mound
- Wright B. Flyer

Dayton (Vandalia)
- Dayton Air Show

Fort Recovery
- Fort Recovery

Greenville
- Annie Oakley Days
- Bear's Mill
- Garst Museum, Annie Oakley Center
- Kitchenaid Experience & Factory Tours

Jackson Center
- Airstream Factory Tour

Lakeview
- Indian Lake State Park

Lockington
- Lockington Locks

Ludlow Falls
- Lights At Ludlow Falls

Minster
- Lake Loramie State Park

New Bremen
- Bicycle Museum Of America

New Carlisle
- Pumpkin Maze Playland

Piqua
- Piqua Historical Area Tour

Springfield
- Buck Creek State Park
- Fair At New Boston

St. Mary's
- Grand Lake St. Mary's State Park

St. Paris
- Kiser Lake State Park

Trotwood
- Sycamore State Park

Troy
- Brukner Nature Center
- Idle Hour Ranch
- Troy Strawberry Festival

Urbana
- Cedar Bog
- Freshwater Farms Of Ohio

Wapakoneta
- Armstrong Air And Space Museum

West Liberty
- Mad River Theater Works
- Ohio Caverns
- Piatt Castles (Mac-O-Chee And Mac-A-Cheek)

Wilberforce
- National Afro-American Museum And Cultural Center

Xenia
- Blue Jacket
- Greene County Historical Society Museum

Yellow Springs
- John Bryan State Park
- Young's Jersey Dairy Farm

Zanesfield
- Marmon Valley Farm

CW Area

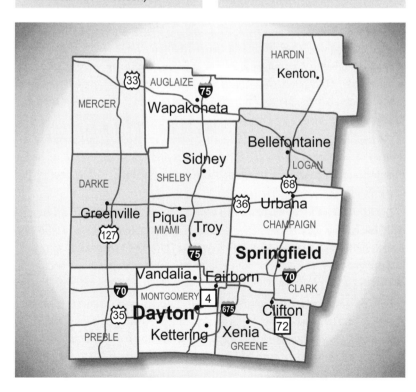

A Quick Tour of our Hand-Picked Favorites Around...

Central West Ohio

CW Area

Meet the inventors of flight and the pilots of space in this area. The dream of flight was imagined by many, but achieved by Orville and Wilbur Wright, two brothers from Dayton who built and flew the first mechanically powered airplane. Their **Wright Cycle Company** and **Carillon Park** are probably the most kid-friendly sites to catch a glimpse of their genius. Walk on the same workshop floors of these famous folks who wouldn't stop at a "no" until they had a "yes". The **National Museum of the U.S. Air Force**, located just east of Dayton, also tells the story of the 100-plus years of flight, from its beginning to today's stealth age. ..and it's a FREE attraction. The world's only B-2 stealth bomber on public display is here, too. North of Dayton in Wapakoneta is the **Armstrong Air & Space Museum** where you'll see another form of aviation. Astronaut Neil Armstrong has permitted display of many space artifacts and a wonderful interactive area that immerses kids into "space."

Canals, not planes, are the hot topic at **Piqua Historical Area**. Ever tried to churn butter by hand? What about trying some ice cream or butter freshly made by costumed 1800s-period folks? Later, take a "slow ride" on the canal with mules leading the way.

Dayton is host to some other great sites like the **Boonshoft Museum of Discovery** where interactive techno exhibits combined with a zoo and planetarium make for more than a day's worth of fun. Their sister location nearby is **Sunwatch** – an ancient Indian village recreated from actual archeological digs in the area. What did they find and where did the Indians go?

Ever pow-wowed with famous Indians like **Tecumseh**? Xenia is the place. Pioneers and Indians, oh my! At the local county museum you'll find a log cabin tucked away in a complex of buildings. This is the home of Rebecca Galloway – a white girl who was adored by Shawnee chief, Tecumseh. Actually view the chair he sat in while waiting for his date.

Finally, head out into the quaint countryside for a "meet-n-greet" with some farm animals of very different sorts. Visit Ohio's largest indoor fish hatchery and retail fish farm market – **Freshwater Farms**, in Urbana. Start your tour by petting a sturgeon fish. Why can you touch them, but not catfish? Next, stop for yummy ice cream and visit with the cows that made it famous at **Young's Jersey Dairy** in the picturesque town of Yellow Springs, near Springfield. The cutest cows in the world make the sweetest milk for creamy ice cream. Plan an entire day here as there's petting areas, pre-arranged group tours, putt-putt, eateries, and some of the best seasonal festivals anywhere.

CW Area

Sites and attractions are listed in order by City, Zip Code, and Name. Symbols indicated represent:

 Festivals   Restaurants   Lodging

Arcanum

KINDA KOOKY KORN MAZE

Arcanum - Brumbaugh Fruit Farm, 6420 Hollansburg-Arcanum Road. Pumpkin Patches/ Hayrides/ Corn Mazes/ Fall Playland - Admission (average $6.00). Plan on at least two hours playtime. Open weekends, some weekdays (by appointment) and weeknights. www.brumbaughfruitfarm.com. (early September - late October).

Bellefontaine

ZANE SHAWNEE CAVERNS

Bellefontaine - 7092 State Route 540 (5 miles east of town) 43311. Phone: (937) 592-9592. www.zaneshawneecaverns.net. Hours: Daily 10:00am-5:00pm. Admission: Caverns $11.00 adult, $5.00 child (under age 12). Museum $7.00 adult, $4.00 child. Pioneer Village $3.00-$6.00. Cavern & Museum pkg. Rate. Miscellaneous: There are a lot of extras like hayrides, gift shop, snack bar, and camping. Remember to dress appropriately because the temperature in the caverns is a constant 48-50 degrees F.

See crystals in objects formed like straws, draperies, and popcorn. They boast the only "cave pearls" found in Ohio. This property is now owned and operated by the Shawnee People. The Museum has artifacts from actual tribe members and some from prehistoric Indian digs (Hopewell, Ancient). Separate display cases give a special look to other Native American cultural areas including: Great Lakes Tribes, Northern Iroquois, Southwestern Tribes, Great plains, Southeastern Tribes and the Eskimo People. Also on display is the evolution of corn - Zea Maize to modern corn and Native American weapons along with several dioramas. Probably the best time to visit are Pow Wow weekends.

Clifton

CLIFTON MILL

Clifton - 75 Water Street (I-70 West to SR 72 South) 45316. Phone: (937) 767-5501. www.cliftonmill.com. Hours: Monday-Friday 9:00am-4:00pm, Saturday-Sunday 8:00am-5:00pm. Admission: Restaurant serves kids meals around $3-5.00. Adult meals are double. Miscellaneous: Restaurant and store. Walk off your meal by parking down the road at Clifton Gorge Nature Preserve and "hiking" the small sand/gravel walkway past bridges and on platforms that give you a "crows nest" view of the gorge - beautiful.

A surprise treat tucked away in a small town where Woody Hayes grew up. Built in 1802 on the Little Miami River, it is the largest operating water powered gristmill in the nation. Before or after a yummy breakfast or lunch overlooking the river, take a self-guided tour for a small fee. There are 5 floors to view. The 3rd floor (main operations) is where you see how everything on the other floors above and below

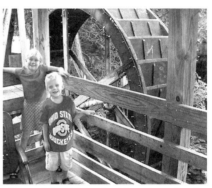
Jenny & Daniel by the big water wheel...

come together. The turbine takes the flowing water's energy to move a system of belts to the grindstones. As the stones rotate, raw grain is poured into the

Christmas is magical here...

hopper, through a chute and into a space between the stones which grind it. The most interesting part of the tour is the belt to bucket elevators that are the "life of the mill" transporting grain and flour up and down 5 levels. Restaurant seating with a view of a waterwheel, river and covered bridge. Pancakes, mush, grits and bread are made from product produced at the mill. Best pork barbecue sandwich ever! Breakfast and lunch only. Be sure to buy some pancake mix to take home!

CLIFTON MILL LEGENDARY LIGHT DISPLAY

Clifton - *Clifton Mill. Miniature village, Santa's workshop and 1802 log cabin. 3.2 million lights. Promptly lit at 6:00pm. (month of December)*

Dayton

DAYTON SPORTS

DAYTON BOMBERS HOCKEY - Erwin J. Nutter Center, Fairborn. (937) 775-4747 or www.daytonbombers.com. East Coast Hockey League.

DAYTON DRAGONS BASEBALL - Fifth Third Field. I-75 to First Street Exit 53. (937) 228-BATS or www.daytondragons.com. Class A team. Check out the new FunZone. Located behind the batters eye, the Dragons FunZone consists of : Pop-a-Shot (challenge a friend and winners can take home bragging rights); Speed pitch (unleash your fastball) and Inflatable Bounce house (features a slide). Tickets are $1 each.

DUNBAR HOUSE

Dayton - *219 North Paul Lawrence Dunbar Street (2 blocks north of 3rd Street, east of US35) 45401. www.ohiohistory.org/places/dunbar. Phone: (937) 224-7061 or (800) 860-0148. Hours: Wednesday-Saturday 9:30am-5:00pm, Sunday & Holidays Noon-5:00pm (Memorial Day-Labor Day). Weekends Only (April, May, September, October). Admission: $6.00 adult, $3.00 student (all ages). Educators: Excellent Curriculum Resources/Lessons with word games, vocabulary and discussion questions are online - click on Site Education Programs.*

The restored home of the first African American to achieve acclaim in American literature. From a young poet at age 6 to a nationally known figure (until his death at age 33 of tuberculosis), the guide helps you understand his inspiration especially from his mother and her stories of slavery. Personal belongings, like his bicycle built by the Wright Brothers and a sword presented to him by President Roosevelt, are noted as the guide leads you to his bedroom where he wrote 100 novels, poems and short stories.

Dunbar House *(cont.)*

> *"We smile, but, O great Christ, our cries*
>
> *To thee from tortured souls arise.*
>
> *We sing, but oh the clay is vile*
>
> *Beneath our feet, and long the mile;*
>
> *But let the world dream otherwise,*
>
> *We wear the mask!"*

-Paul Laurence Dunbar, from the poem, "We Wear the Mask"

CITIZENS MOTORCAR PACKARD MUSEUM

Dayton - 420 South Ludlow Street - Downtown (I-75 to US 35 exit, head east a few blocks) 45402. Phone: (937) 226-1917. www.americaspackardmuseum.org. Hours: Monday-Friday Noon-5:00pm, Saturday and Sunday 1:00-5:00pm. Open Every Day except Easter, Thanksgiving, Christmas, and New Years Day. Admission: $6.00 adult, $5.00 senior, $4.00 student.

See the world's largest collection of Packard automobiles in an authentic showroom. The art deco Packard dealership interior exhibits are spread through 6 settings, including the service area and period decorated salesman's office.

DAYTON PHILHARMONIC ORCHESTRA

Dayton - 125 East First Street (many performances at the Schuster Center for the Performing Arts) 45402. Phone: (937) 224-9000. www.daytonphilharmonic.com.

Plays classical, pops, and Summer outdoor concerts. Young People's Concerts and Magic Carpet Concerts. The Family Concert Series often features Side-by-Side appearances with the Youth Orchestra with themes like Clowns, Bach to the Future or Mozart for the Mind.

RIVERSCAPE

Dayton - 111 E. Monument Avenue (MetroPark's RiverScape, I-75 exit 53B) 45402. Phone: (937) 278-2607. www.riverscape.org.

Enjoy the RiverScape landscaped gardens, a free summer concert, major community festivals and family walks and bike rides along the river corridor recreation trails. A focal point of RiverScape is the Five Rivers Fountain of Lights, a series of five fountains that shoot water upwards of 200 feet and 400 feet across at the confluence of the Great Miami and Mad Rivers (May through October). And, don't forget your bathing suit. A popular spot for visitors looking to cool off on hot summer days is the Interactive Fountain where multiple fountain jets shoot water as high as 15 feet into the air choreographed to the sounds of family friendly music. And, the fun isn't over when it gets cold -MetroParks' invites you to come "Skate the Scape" as RiverScape becomes home to the regions only outdoor ice skating rink, festive light displays and other family winter activities. Concessions available.

CITYFOLK FESTIVAL

Dayton – Riverscape. www.cityfolk.org/festival/festival.html. Hundreds of the country's best folk performers and artists entertain you with shows, activities, games, crafts and food. (first weekend in July)

CW Area

DAYTON ART INSTITUTE

Dayton - *456 Belmonte Park North (I-75 exit 53B or 54B) 45405. Phone: (937) 223-5277 or (800) 296-4426. www.daytonartinstitute.org. Hours: Daily 10:00am-4:00pm (except Mondays - closed). Thursday nights until 8:00pm. Admission: FREE.*

Overlooking the Great Miami River and downtown Dayton, The Dayton Art Institute's Italian Renaissance-style building houses an extensive permanent collection of American, European, Asian and African art. Experiencenter (features 20 hands-on activities) encourages interaction with art and experimentation with artistic elements of line, pattern, color, texture and shape. A gallery bag and an alphabet book are also available at the Entrance Rotunda desk allowing families to further explore featured special exhibits through the use of games and learning activities.

WRIGHT CYCLE COMPANY COMPLEX

Dayton - *22 South Williams Street (I-75 exit 53A, off West 3rd Street) 45407. Phone: (937) 225-7705. www.nps.gov/daav/. Hours: Daily 8:30am-5:00pm except major winter holidays. Admission: Donation. Tours: Join a ranger for a walking tour of the historic Wright-Dunbar Village, the neighborhood of the Wright brothers and Paul Laurence Dunbar. Visitors are advised to carry water on hot days. (offered daily during summer)*

This is the neighborhood in which the Wright brothers lived and worked. This is the neighborhood in which they started their printing business, entered into the bicycle business and became involved with the mystery of flight. The Wright Cycle Company complex consists of the Wright Cycle Company building and the Wright–Dunbar

Interpretive Center (the restored Hoover Block building) and the Aviation Trail Visitor Center and Museum. The brothers operated their second print shop here as Wright & Wright, Job Printers. In this location, the Wrights edited and published newspapers for West Side patrons, including the Dayton Tattler, written by Paul Laurence Dunbar. The bicycle craze in America began in 1887 with the introduction from England of the safety bicycle (two wheels of equal size). It made the freedom of cycling accessible to a much wider market. The Wright brothers' best known pre-aeronautical occupation was bicycle repair and manufacture. This building

Learn the bicycle history of the Wright Brothers

is the actual site where the Wright Brothers had a bicycle business from 1895-1897 and developed their own brand of bicycles. On this site, they also developed ideas that led to the invention of flight almost 7 years later. The dream of flight was imagined by many, but achieved by Orville and Wilbur Wright - just two brothers from Dayton who happened to fly the first mechanically powered airplane. You'll walk on the same floorboards that the brothers did and see actual plans for a flying bicycle!

Did You Know?

On September 7, 1904, the Wright brothers use a catapult launching device for the first time at Huffman Prairie Flying Field, Dayton, Ohio.

CARILLON HISTORICAL PARK, DAYTON HISTORY

Dayton - *1000 Carillon Blvd. (I-75 to Exit 51) 45409. www.carillonpark.org. Phone: (937) 293-2841. Hours: Monday-Saturday 9:30am-5:00pm. Sunday and Holidays Noon - 5:00pm, closed on Thanksgiving, Christmas Eve, Christmas Day, New Year's Eve and New Year's Day. Admission: $8.00 adult, $7.00 senior, $5.00 child (3-17). Miscellaneous: Museum Store sells period toys, snacks and candy. Wooded park with Ohio's largest bell tower, the Carillon Bell Tower (57 bells), also has many shaded picnic areas. CULP'S CAFE, reminiscent of Culp's Cafeteria located in downtown Dayton in the 1930s and 1940s, serves soup, salads, and sandwiches, ice cream and sodas. (937) 299-2277.*

A must see - very comfortable and educational - over 65 acres of historical buildings and outdoor exhibits of history, invention and transportation. Called the "Little Greenfield Village" in Miami Valley and we definitely agree! Inventions like the cash register, innovations like flood control, and industries like Huffy Corporation are represented throughout the Park. Many of the oldest buildings from the early 1800's are represented too (tavern, home, school). As

you enter most buildings, a costumed guide will orient you to colorful stories of the famous people who once occupied them. The highlight of the collections is the 1905 Wright Flyer III, the world's first practical airplane. Our favorites are the Deed's Barn (learn about the Barn Gang

and the big companies they started) and the rail cars that you can actually board-the Barney & Smith is ritzy!

AULLWOOD AUDUBON CENTER AND FARM

Dayton - *1000 Aullwood Road 45414. http://aullwood.center.audubon.org. Phone: (937) 890-7360. Hours: Monday-Saturday 9:00am-5:00pm, Sunday 1:00-5:00pm. Closed holidays. Admission: $4.00 adult, $2.00 child (2-18).*

The Discovery Room has more than 50 hands-on exhibits. Visitors can begin walks on five miles of hiking trails here. Around the building are special plantings of prairie and woodland wildflowers and a butterfly - hummingbird garden. The nearby Farm (9101 Frederick Pike) is the site of many special events. Cows, pigs, horses, chickens, turkeys, sheep, goats and barn swallows can all be found here if you come at the right time. The sugar bush, organic garden, herb garden and access to the trails are here. The glacial erratics are the start of the Geology trail. On it, you can explore the recent erosion of the land and the water cycle, the leavings of the continental glacier, and the old bedrock with its load of Ordovician fossils.

MAPLE SYRUP FESTIVAL

Dayton *– Aullwood Audubon Center and Farm. Syrup making demos. Pancake breakfasts. Sugarbush tours by foot or wagon. (weekends late February and/or March)*

APPLE FEST

Dayton – *Aullwood Audubon Center and Farm. The whistle of Ken Ullery's antique steam engine and the delicious aroma of simmering apple butter beckon one and all to the festivities. Sample pie and everything apple flavored, enjoy live entertainment, visit farm-friendly animals, and hop on a horse drawn wagon. Meet Johnny Appleseed or watch the herding of sheep. (last weekend in September. Enchanted Forest hike is last weekend in October)*

BOONSHOFT MUSEUM OF DISCOVERY

Dayton - 2600 DeWeese Parkway (North of downtown I-75 to exit 57B, follow signs) 45414. Phone: (937) 275-7431. www.boonshoftmuseum.org. Hours: Monday-Friday 9:00am-5:00pm, Saturday 11:00am-5:00pm, Sunday Noon-5:00pm. Closed major winter holidays. Admission: $8.50 adult, $7.50 senior, $7.50 child (2-12). $1.00-$3.00 additional for Space Theater. Miscellaneous: With memberships here, you also can get free or discounted admissions to many museums in Ohio and surrounding states. Vending area. Discovery Shop.

A Children's Museum, a Science Center, Nature Center and Planetarium all in one place! Interactive technology exhibits combined with a zoo and planetarium make for more than a day's worth of fun. Here's highlights of each space:

DISCOVERY CENTER - mastodon bones, desert animals (daytime vs. nighttime creatures using flashlights!), touch tide pool (ever seen a red sea cucumber? Touch one!), rainforest and a treehouse with binoculars for outdoor window views.

A treehouse of discovery...

WILD OHIO – An indoor tree house & zoo with small animals in natural surroundings. Visit the den of bobcat Van Cleve or a coyote, river otter, groundhog, fox or turtle. A Falcon nest Web Cam is a popular area - something new is always happening with that family. Both parents will tend to the chicks so keep an eye out for both Mercury and Snowball at the nest.

Dad feeling very "turtley?"...

For updates & travel games visit: **www.KidsLoveTravel.com**

ANCIENT WORLD – Egyptian artifacts with 3000 year old mummy, a replica of the Rosetta Stone and some African jewelry.

SCIENCE CENTRAL – Inventions stations (water table w/ sticky water, airfort and force (tubes & funny windbag blower machines), chemistry lab, and a climbing discovery tower (nets, tubes & slide) provide hands-on adventures.

KIDS' PLAYCE - baby garden, pioneer cabin, dig, slide & little creatures. Dress up spot.

LEARNING TREE FARM

Dayton - 3376 South Union Road   45418. www.learningtreefarm.org. Phone: (937) 866-8650. Hours: Dawn to Dusk. Best weekdays when most facilities are open or during special programs. Admission: Hands on the Farm: $6.00 general self-guided. Special Programs: guided $7.00 general. $1.00 discount per person for groups (12+).

The history of the family which originally owned the farm, from their initial voyage to Ohio to the present day, has been researched and displayed. Visitors may tour the house, visit the farm animals, hike on the farm's land, and participate in hands-on activities like caring for animals, crafts, and sheep shearing. Special programs like "Finding Freedom on the Farm" highlights storytelling, quilts used by escaping slaves, and a clue game played thru nearby land and daily activities of the safe house station.

SUNWATCH

Dayton - 2301 West River Road (I-75 to Exit 51, west on Edwin C. Moses Blvd., cross South Broadway, turn left) 45418. www.sunwatch.org. Phone: (937) 268-8199. Hours: Tuesday-Saturday 9:00am-5:00pm. Sunday and Holidays Noon – 5:00pm. Closed major winter holidays. Admission: $5.00 adult, $3.00 child (6-17) & senior (60+). Tours: Guided tours daily at 1:30pm. (Summer) Miscellaneous: Occasional Flute Circle weekends offer music, storytelling and food like Bison burgers, Indian tacos and summer Indian corn. Visitor's are welcome to carry-in their own food. A beverage vending machine is available.

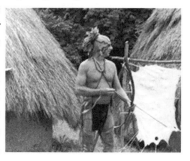

SunWatch Indian Village/Archaeological Park is a partially reconstructed Fort Ancient period Native American village along the Great Miami River. Here visitors can explore Dayton's first neighborhood, walk in reconstructed houses, hear the intriguing history of the Fort Ancient people, and discover the role the sun played in daily life. Archaeological excavations at a site near the Great Miami River uncovered evidence of an 800-year-old village built by the Fort Ancient Indians. The reconstructed 12th Century Indian Village has self-guided tours of the thatched huts, gardens, and artifacts of the lifestyle of a unique culture. When touring the museum exhibits be sure to study the trash pits - you can learn a lot from people's trash. Study their ancient calendars - can you tell the season? Some activities include story telling, archery, toys and games, harvesting, a multi-media presentation, and best of all, learn to tell time by charting the sun. See how the Indians used flint and bone to create jewelry and tools - then buy some as souvenirs. This is a nice family-friendly introduction to ancient Indian lifestyles - be sure to view the orientation film first.

KEEPING THE TRADITIONS POW WOW

Dayton – Sunwatch. www.tmvcna.org/4powwow.htm. Native American dancing, singing, foods. The event features both men's and women's dances, including the men's grass dance and the women's shawl and jingle dance, performed wearing full regalia. In addition, traditional American Indian food and arts and crafts will be available from vendors. One of the largest Pow Wows in Ohio. Admission (age 13+). (last weekend in June)

17TH CENTURY REENACTMENT

Dayton – Sunwatch. The event features both men's and women's dances, including the men's grass dance and the women's shawl and jingle dance, performed wearing full regalia. In addition, traditional American Indian food and arts and crafts will be available from vendors. Included with regular admission. (Mid-October weekend)

COX ARBORETUM

Dayton - 6733 Springboro Pike (I-75 exit 50B to OH 74 south) 45449. Phone: (937) 434-9005. www.metroparks.org. Hours: Daily 8:00am to dusk. Visitor Center weekdays 8:30am-4:30pm and weekends 1:00-4:00pm.

Cox Arboretum MetroPark is a hands-on landscaping arboretum. Best family features are: Water Garden & Rock Garden; the Bell Children's Maze; and the Butterfly House and Garden (Butterfly House is a seasonal display). 170 acres total including the nationally recognized Edible Landscape Garden. Every season has something special to offer, from spring's splashes of bright color to winter's textures. In addition to exploring gardens, hike trails through mature forests and colorful meadows. FREE admission.

FAMILY NEW YEAR'S EVE CELEBRATION

Dayton - *Riverscape MetroPark. A family oriented non-alcoholic event with indoor and outdoor activities such as kid's/parent's food, entertainment and crafts, and a countdown to midnight. Admission. www.metroparks.org. (New Years Eve)*

CW Area

NATIONAL MUSEUM OF THE USAF

Dayton (Fairborn) - *Wright Patterson Air Force Base (I-75 to State Route 4 East to Harshman Road Exit) 45433. www.nationalmuseum.af.mil/. Phone: (937) 255-3286. Hours: Daily 9:00am-5:00pm. Closed Thanksgiving, Christmas and New Years. Admission: FREE. Tours: The free USAF Heritage Tour begins at 1:30pm Monday through Friday. Saturdays 10:30am & 1:30pm. No reservation required. Educators: Online lesson plans and Scavenger Hunt - click on Education, then*

Educators for printable links. Miscellaneous: Largest Gift Shop imaginable. Concessions.

IMAX THEATER - 6 story with hourly 40 minute space/ aviation films - feel like you're flying with the pilots. Fee. (937-253-IMAX. Morphis MovieRide Theater - actually move, tilt and shout. extra fee).

HUFFMAN PRAIRIE FIELD - Rte. 44 (937-257-5535). See where The Wright Brothers first attempted flight.

This museum tells the story of the 100-plus years of flight, from its beginning to today's stealth age. For the best in family entertainment / educational value, this museum is definitely a must see! You'll have a real adventure exploring the world's oldest and largest military aviation museum that features over 50 vintage WWII aircraft (even the huge 6-engine B-36) and 300 other aircraft and rockets. See everything from presidential planes, to Persian Gulf advanced missiles and bombs, the original Wright Brothers wind tunnel, to the original Apollo 15 command module. Look for the observation balloon (easy to find—just look up ever so slightly), Rosie the Rivetor and "Little Vittles" parachuted goodies. Discovery Hangar Five follows a common museum trend and focuses on the interactive learning of why things fly and different parts of airplanes. Continuous films played at stations throughout the complex (with chairs-take a break from all the walking). This attraction houses more than 400 total aircraft and missiles, including the world's only B-2 stealth bomber on public display. National Aviation Hall of Fame is next door.

JULY 4TH CELEBRATIONS

Dayton (Fairborn) – *National Museum of the USAF. The day includes parades, rides, entertainment and fireworks. Balloon Festival.*

CARRIAGE HILL FARM AND MUSEUM

Dayton (Huber Heights) - *7860 East Shull Road (I-70 to Exit 38 - State Route 201 north) 45424. Phone: (937) 278-2609. www.metroparks.org/parks/carriagehill/. Hours: Monday-Friday   10:00am-5:00pm,   Saturday-Sunday   1:00-5:00pm. Admission: Donation   Miscellaneous: Picnic area, fishing, horseback riding, cross country skiing, hayrides and bobsled rides. No bikes on trails, though.*

Farm life in the 1880s comes alive at Carriage Hill Farm. Stop at the Visitor Center for exhibits highlighting lifestyles of a century ago, a children's interactive center and the Country Store gift shop. The self-guided tour of an 1880's working farm is a great benefit to the community. The farm includes a summer kitchen, workshop, blacksmith and barns. Household chores and farming are performed as they were 100 years ago and a variety of farm animals fill the barn. They are best to visit when workers are planting or harvesting gardens.

MIAMISBURG MOUND

Dayton (Miamisburg) - *(I-75 to State Route 725 exit 44, follow signs) 45342. Phone: (937) 866-5632. www.ohiohistory.org/places/miamisbur. Hours: Daily Dawn to Dusk. Admission: FREE. Miscellaneous: Park, Picnic tables and playground.*

Take the 116 stairs up a 68-foot high and 1.5 acre wide mound built by American Indians. This is the largest conical burial mound in Ohio. Archaeological investigations of the surrounding area suggest that it was constructed by the prehistoric Adena Indians (800BC - AD100). The mound measures 877 feet in circumference.

WRIGHT B. FLYER

Dayton (Miamisburg) - *10550 Springboro Pike (I-75 exit 44, State Route 741 – Dayton Wright Airport) 45342. www.destinationdayton.com/wrightb/hanger.html. Phone: (937) 885-2327. Hours: Tuesday, Thursday, and Saturday 9:00am-2:00pm. Admission: There is no charge for the museum or to look at the aircraft. Aircraft ride certificates may be purchased for $150.00. This entitles the certificate bearer to an orientation ride replicating the Wright Brothers' original flight patterns over Huffman Prairie! Otherwise, only donations.*

A group decided to build a flying replica of the first production aircraft ever built - the Wright Brothers B Model Airplane. The result is a fully operational flying aircraft that closely resembles the original Wright B Model that flew over Huffman Prairie in 1911. This hangar houses a flyable replica of the 1911 plane built by Wilbur and Orville Wright. They also have a half scale model of the plane and other aviation exhibits and souvenirs.

CW Area

DAYTON AIR SHOW

Dayton (Vandalia) - Dayton Int'l Airport. (I-75 exit 64). www.daytonairshow.com. This is the leading event of its kind highlighted by the outstanding civilian and military air show performances. The event includes ground flight simulators, aerobatics, barnstormers, air races, pyrotechnics and sky divers. Parade, entertainment and Kids Hanger. Admission ($16-19.00, age 6+) - Discount tickets at area Krogers). (third weekend in July)

Fort Recovery

FORT RECOVERY

Fort Recovery - *One Fort Site Street (State Route 49 and State Route 119) 45846. Phone: (419) 375-4649. www.ohiohistory.org/places/ftrecovr. Hours: Daily Noon-5:00pm (Summer). Weekends Only (May and September). Admission: $1.00-$3.00 (student and adult). Educators: a link to www.ohiohistorycentral.org online leads you to many related articles that would be useful for research papers.*

The remaining blockhouses with connecting stockade wall are where General Arthur St. Clair was defeated by Indians in 1791. Later, in 1794, General "Mad" Anthony Wayne defended the fort successfully. A museum with Indian War artifacts and dressed mannequins is also displayed on the property.

Greenville

BEAR'S MILL

Greenville - *Bear's Mill Road (5 miles East on US 36 then South) 45331. Phone: (937) 548-5112. www.bearsmill.com. Tours (self-guided): Tuesday-Sunday 11:00am – 5:00pm (March-December), extended morning hours on Saturdays. Weekends only (January-February). Guided tours by appointment. Miscellaneous: Store-sells flours ground at the mill, gift baskets, handmade pottery.*

Bear's Mill, built in 1849, is an authentic example of a stone grinding flour mill of its time. It is still in use today grinding cornmeal, whole-wheat flour, and rye flour. Tour the mill built in 1849 by Gabriel Bear where grinding stones (powered by water flowing beneath the building) grind flour and meal. The process is slow and kept cool to retard deteriorating wholesome nutrients. Everyone who comes to Bear's Mill during business hours is welcome to take a self guided tour of the 4-story structure and take a walk in the scenic woods surrounding the mill. Best times to take the family: Candlelight Open House (first Friday night in December) and Fall Open House (first weekend in October) with entertainment and great seasonal foods.

GARST MUSEUM, ANNIE OAKLEY CENTER

Greenville - *205 North Broadway 45331. www.garstmuseum.org. Phone: (937) 548-5250. Hours: Tuesday-Saturday 11:00am-4:00pm, Sunday 1:00-4:00pm. (February-December). Closed month of January. Admission: $2.00-$5.00 (age 6+).*

The main feature of the museum is Darke County's most-famous daughter sharp-shooter and entertainer Annie Oakley (artifacts from her professional and private life -newly renovated Center). View displays about: world-traveler, broadcaster, author and adventurer Lowell Thomas; pioneering aviator Zachary Lansdowne; The Treaty of Greeneville and a lot of other history of the county including 30 individual room settings. Even something on Lewis and Clark, Anthony Wayne, Native American artifacts and Village of shops, too. Crossroads of Destiny, their new permanent exhibit, is a chronological walking tour that includes 28 displays. Each display has authentic artifacts that relate a story that begins with prehistoric Native Americans and climaxes as America's Crossroads of Destiny in 1795 with the signing of the Treaty of Greeneville that included 12 Indian nations and the United States.

KITCHENAID EXPERIENCE & FACTORY TOURS

Greenville - *423 South Broadway/ 1701 KitchenAid Way (I-70 exit US 127 north to town) 45331. Phone: (888) 886-8318. www.KitchenAid.com/experience. Hours: Experience store Monday-Saturday 10:00am-6:00pm, Sunday Noon-5:00pm. Admission: Tours are $5.00 per person. Tours: Weekdays at 10:00am and 1:00pm (subject to manufacturing schedules) or groups over 8 with appointment. Enclosed footwear required. Safety glasses provided, must be at least 12 YEARS OLD.*

The site that houses the KitchenAid Experience was the Turpin House Hotel and later a five and dime store. The Greenville connection started way back in 1908 with a mixer produced for commercial bakers. Visit the heritage exhibits, take a kids cooking class, or tour. The work force produces hundreds of mixers every day. Walk through the whole process, peeking over workers shoulders.

ANNIE OAKLEY DAYS

Greenville - *Darke County Fairgrounds, SR 49. www.annieoakleyfestival.org. Annie Oakley's hometown celebrates with a parade, live entertainment, a sharpshooter's contest and a contest to name Miss Annie Oakley. (last weekend in July)*

Jackson Center

AIRSTREAM FACTORY TOUR

Jackson Center - *419 West Pike Street (I-75 exit 102, SR 274 east) 45334. Phone: (937) 596-6111. www.airstream.com. Tours are: Monday - Tuesday - Wednesday-Thursday - Friday at 2:00 pm. Friday Tours are after normal production hour. This is a walking tour approximately ¾ mile in length. The tour begins in the Service Lobby and travels outside to the production facility. Eye protection and hearing protection are required. No sandals or open toe shoes.*

Airstream's founder Wally Byam said, "Let's not make any changes – let's only make improvements!" Wally began Airstream as a single man with a most singular dream: to build the perfect travel trailer. Airstream, the world's leader in travel trailers and motor coaches, are completely manufactured and assembled in Jackson Center, Ohio. This is your chance to come see how it's done. From chassis assembly through final quality assurance, you'll be able to witness it all, first hand. The Airstream way is no automotive assembly line process mind you. These travel trailers and motor homes are custom assembled, by hand, in stages throughout the manufacturing process. You won't believe your eyes as you watch them come together in this 90-minute tour.

Lakeview

INDIAN LAKE STATE PARK

Lakeview - *12774 State Route 235 N (US 33, 20 miles east of I-75) 43331. Phone: (937) 843-2717. www.dnr.state.oh.us.*

Indian Lake is an important resting stop for birds such as Canada geese, ducks, grebes, swans, egrets and herons. Many stay over the summer to nest. The present and much larger lake lies along one of the country's major avian migration routes. The Cherokee Trail, a 3-mile easy walk through brushy habitat, is located west of the camp. The Pew Island Trail, a 1-mile path, encircles Pew Island. Access is available to Pew Island from a causeway. This trail affords a spectacular view of Indian Lake. A paved bikeway is located on the West Bank between Old Field Beach and Lakeview Harbor. The bikeway is 3 miles long. Walkers and joggers are welcome to use the bikeway. Two public beaches, Old Field Beach and Fox Island Beach, invite swimmers to relax in the cool waters of Indian Lake. 6448 acres of camping, hiking trails, boating, fishing, swimming and winter sports.

Lockington

LOCKINGTON LOCKS

Lockington - *5 miles North of Piqua-Lockington Road (I-75 to exit 83 West on State Route 25A) 45356. www.ohiohistory.org/places/lockingt/index.html. Phone: (800) 686-1535. Hours: Daily Dawn to Dusk. Admission: FREE.*

These stair step locks, among the best preserved in Ohio, were part of the Miami and Erie Canal System, which opened for navigation in 1845 and connected Cincinnati and the Ohio River to Toledo and Lake Erie. For several decades, the canal provided Ohio with valuable transportation and waterpower. View portions of five original locks (elevation adjusters for canal boats) and the aqueduct that lowered boats 67 feet into the Miami-Erie Canal.

Ludlow Falls

LIGHTS AT LUDLOW FALLS

Ludlow Falls - SR 48. (937) 698-3318. Hundreds of thousands of lights & holiday / storybook characters. Daily, evenings. FREE, donations accepted. (during Winter Break)

CW Area

Minster

LAKE LORAMIE STATE PARK

Minster - 4401 Ft. Loramie Swanders Road (3 miles Southeast of Minster off State Route 66) 45865. Phone: (937) 295-2011. www.dnr.state.oh.us.

One of the original canal feeder lakes, Lake Loramie State Park offers visitors a quiet retreat in rural Ohio. Swim from the sandy beach, hike along the old canal towpath, stay a night in a shaded campsite or boat the lazy waters of Lake Loramie. The hiking opportunities at Lake Loramie include more than eight miles of trail. A portion of the trail system follows the Miami-Erie Canal from the park to Delphos. This route is also a part of the Buckeye Trail and the North Country National Scenic Trail.

New Bremen

BICYCLE MUSEUM OF AMERICA

New Bremen - 7 West Monroe Street (I-75 exit 102, west on SR 274) 45869. Phone: (419) 629-9249. www.bicyclemuseum.com. Hours: Monday – Friday 11:00am - 5:00pm (til 7:00pm in the summer). Saturday 11:00am – 2:00pm. Admission: $3.00 adult, $2.00 senior, $1.00 student   Educators: click on the For Students link and download pdfs to help with research papers.

A department store has been converted into a showcase of the world's oldest bike (w/out pedals) to the Schwinn family collection (including the 1,000,000th bicycle made). High-wheelers to side-by-side doubles and quads. Celebrity bikes and bikes from balloon tire to banana seat bikes will amuse you. Learn about bicycle history in the theatre.

New Carlisle

PUMPKIN MAZE PLAYLAND

New Carlisle - *Meadow View Farm, 755 N. Dayton-Lakeview Rd.(I-70 & SR 235) Pumpkin Patches / Hayrides / Corn Mazes / Fall Playland - Admission (average $6.00). Plan on at least two hours playtime. Open weekends, some weekdays (by appointment) and weeknights.www.meadowview.com. (late September - late October).*

Piqua

PIQUA HISTORICAL AREA TOUR

Piqua - North Hardin Road (I-75 to exit 83 County Road 25A West to State Route 66 North) 45356. www.ohiohistory.org/places/piqua. Phone: (937) 773-2522 or (800) 752-2619. Hours: Wednesday-Saturday 9:30am-5:00pm, Sunday and Holidays Noon-5:00pm (April-October). Admission: $8.00 adult, $4.00 student (all ages). Includes canal boat ride. Miscellaneous: Canal rides a few times during the afternoon in the summer. Educators: click on the Site Education Programs link for vocabulary, discussion questions and a complete Teachers Guide (printable) that covers 1800 years of history that occurred on site (including quizzes and projects)!

The Piqua Historical Area State Memorial celebrates two thousand years of Ohio's rich history from prehistoric Indians to Ohio's canal era. The focal point of the peaceful 200-acre park is John Johnston--farmer, public official, and United States Indian Agent for western Ohio from 1812 to 1829. Tour the

Johnston Farm which includes an 1808 massive log barn which is probably the oldest such barn in Ohio. In the farmhouse, the kids will probably be most interested in the beds made of rope and hay filled sacks. Eight girls slept in one room (ages 2-20) and three boys in another. Many youth games of that time period are displayed.

Ride the General Harrison canal boat...

The Winter Kitchen is also very interesting – especially the size of the walk-in fireplace. The Farm buildings have costumed guides describing and interacting with youth as they demonstrate chores on the farm. Before you visit the canal, stop in the museum where excellent exhibits, inside and out, explain the treacherous job of building a canal and why. The General Harrison canal boat is powered by two mules which pull the boat down and back on a section of the Old Miami-Erie Canal (Cincinnati to Toledo). The cargo boat was once used to transport produce and meat at a speed limit of 4 MPH. The boats were fined $10.00 for speeding although many paid the fine and continued going 10 MPH. Once the railroads came, canals became obsolete.

CW Area

Springfield

BUCK CREEK STATE PARK

Springfield - *1901 Buck Creek Lane (4 miles East of Springfield on State Route 4) 45502. Phone: (937) 322-5284. www.dnr.state.oh.us/parks/parks/buckck.htm.*

Buck Creek State Park lies in a fertile agricultural area, rich in Ohio's history. The park's recreational facilities center around the 2,120-acre lake, offering endless water-related opportunities. The spotted turtle, a state endangered animal, is found in the area. The northernmost region of the park is an excellent area to observe waterfowl. The shallow waters provide a stopover for thousands of migrating ducks. More than 7.5 miles of hiking trails offer opportunities for nature study, bird watching and other wildlife observation. A scenic 7.5-mile bridle trail is also open to snowmobiling, weather permitting. The U.S. Army Corps of Engineers manages a visitor center and recreational site near the dam. The center provides displays, programs and dam operation tours. 4030 acres of camping, hiking trails, boating and rentals, fishing, swimming and winter sports. 26 family cabins with A/C.

FAIR AT NEW BOSTON

Springfield - *George Rogers Clark Park. (937) 882-9216 or www.grcha.org. Area where General Clark defeated Shawnee to open NW Territory. Early 1800's frontier life & Indian village. Re-enactors, craft demonstrations, authentic open fire, wood cooked food and folk entertainment. Admission. (Labor Day Weekend)*

St. Mary's

GRAND LAKE ST. MARY'S STATE PARK

St. Mary's - *834 Edgewater Drive (2 miles West of St. Mary's on State Route 703) 45885. Phone: (419) 394-3611. www.dnr.state.oh.us.*

Originally constructed as a feeder reservoir for the Miami-Erie Canal, Grand Lake St. Mary's was for many years recognized as the largest man-made reservoir in the world. Nature programs. 14,000 acres of camping, boating and rentals, fishing, swimming, sport courts, putt-putt and winter sports. Ohio's largest inland lake. A new Fur-Ever Friends Dog Park opened in 2009.

ST. MARY'S FISH FARM: After boating or swimming on Grand Lake, wander through 52 acres of ponds where pike, catfish, etc. are raised. The farm is one of only three in Ohio and is the only farm with a large mouth bass and yellow perch hatchery. (East Side of Grand Lake, Phone: (419) 394-5170, Hours: Daily 7:00am-3:30pm)

St. Paris

KISER LAKE STATE PARK

St. Paris - *4889 N. St. Rt. 235 (17 miles Northwest of Urbana on State Route 235) 43072. Phone: (937) 362-3822. www.dnr.state.oh.us.*

The rolling wooded hills and diverse wetlands add to the beauty of this scenic lake known for its clean, clear waters. Five hiking trails are located within the park and provide 5.1 scenic miles of walking pleasure. Red Oak and the Nature Preserve Boardwalk trails are located near the family camp area at the east end of the lake. The North Bay Trail follows the lake shoreline for 1.5 miles. Seven miles of horse trails are located near State Route 235. 870 acres of camping, hiking trails, boating and rentals, fishing, swimming and winter sports.

Trotwood

SYCAMORE STATE PARK

Trotwood - *4675 N. Diamond Mill Road (1 mile North of Trotwood on State Route 49) 45426. Phone: (937) 854-4452. www.dnr.state.oh.us.*

The meadows, woodlots and still waters of Sycamore State Park provide the perfect setting for picnicking, hiking, fishing, camping, snowmobiling and horseback riding. The 3-mile Ghost Hedge Nature Trail offers the hiker an opportunity to explore the Wolf Creek Valley. Giant sycamore trees form a picturesque canopy over the trail. The 1.5-mile Beech Ridge Trail explores the surrounding woodlots and meadows. Horsemen can enjoy 15 miles of bridle trail, including the snowmobile routes when not snow covered.

Troy

BRUKNER NATURE CENTER

Troy - *5995 Horseshoe Bend Rd. (Exit # 73 off of I-75, west on SR 55 3 miles) 45373. Phone: (937) 698-6493. www.bruk!nernaturecenter.org. Hours: Monday-Saturday 9:00am-5:00pm, Sunday 12:30 - 5:00pm. Admission: Small admission charged on Sundays.*

This 164 acre nature preserve's attractions include 6 miles of hiking trails, a wildlife rehabilitation center and the interpretive center. The 1804 Iddings log house was built by the first settlers in Miami County. The Center's animal rehabilitation has over 65 permanent residents on display. The top floor contains a glass-enclosed vista room for watching and listening to birds as they feed. A ground-level viewing station for mammals also is available. They are best known for their Night Hikes, Star Gazes, Wild Journeys and Seasonal events.

IDLE HOUR RANCH

Troy - 4845 Fenner Road (I-75 exit 73 west) 45373. www.idle-hourranch.com. Phone: (937) 339-9731. Hours: Saturday & Sunday Noon-6:00pm (June - October). Admission: $8.00 adult, $5.00 child.

CW Area

Ever want to hitch a ride with a kangaroo? See the world from a giraffe's point of view? Well, Idle Hour Ranch is just the place for you. If you love animals, Idle Hour Ranch is definitely the perfect experience for you and your family, or for groups of all ages. Unlike a zoo, IHR allows you to get up close & personal with the animals. Interact with & see over 200 animals including: Camels, Kangaroo, Wallabies, Cougar, Zebu, Llamas, Alpaca, Reindeer, Nilgai, Yak, Wolves, Cavies, Horses, farm animals and many, many more! Special areas included: the North American River Otter Exhibit, the Giraffe Observation Deck & the Farm Market. Otter feeding at 3:00pm. Look for "babies" every now and then.

TROY STRAWBERRY FESTIVAL

Troy - Public Square, I-75 exit 73 or 74. The Strawberry Capital of the Midwest. www.troyohiostrawberryfestival.com. Public Square. The first full weekend in June the fountain on Town Square runs pink water! Loads of fresh-picked berries and strawberry foods (donuts, pizza, fudge) are sold. Bed races, waterball, Kids' Crawl and Pie eating contests. Parade, entertainment and hot-air balloons. Free. (first weekend in June)

Urbana

CEDAR BOG

Urbana - 980 Woodburn Road (off Route 68 North / I-70 to Springfield / off State Route 36) 43078. Phone: (937) 484-3744. www.ohiohistory.org/places/cedarbog. Hours: Wednesday-Sunday 9:00am-4:30pm (April-October). Volunteer staffing so call ahead to be sure open. Admission: $3.00-$4.00 per student or adult. Educators: Nine different tours are offered to school groups for study during themed guided tours.

An almost mile long boardwalk guides the visitor through this preserve. Ohio's only fen - a wetland with water that rises to the surface - that is still surrounded with white cedar, just as it was thousands of years ago after the last great glacier disappeared. Mastodons probably fed here, and all of the Indian cultures of Ohio lived around here. A bog is a remnant of the Ice Age and public tours take you to the boardwalk over this bog. Below, you'll see the black, wet, slimy muck and chilly dampness created by a constant water table and cool springs. In contrast, see excellent orchid, prairie and woodland wildflowers. The Education Center is new in 2009 and sure to highlight features of the bog not seen every day naturally.

FRESHWATER FARMS OF OHIO

Urbana - *2624 US 68 (north of downtown circle) 43078. Phone: (937) 652-3701 or (800) 634-7434. www.fwfarms.com. Hours: Store - Monday-Saturday 10:00am-6:00pm. Closed major holidays. Tours: FREE. Self-guided tour include trout feeding and a sturgeon petting zoo. Guided tours of the fish farm require advanced registration and a small fee, and can include a gourmet sampling of Freshwater Farms smoked trout appetizers and all-natural smoked trout spreads.*

You even get to "pet" a fish...

Miscellaneous: Bring a cooler if you plan to purchase any fish. Supplies for ponds at home - compatible fish, frogs. Produces several hundred thousand trout sold to premium restaurants. The Douglas Inn (111 Miami St., 937-653-5585) downtown Urbana serves this wonderful fresh trout in a historic early 1800s bldg.

Visit Ohio's largest indoor fish hatchery and retail fish farm market. Start your tour by petting a sturgeon fish. Why can you touch them, but not catfish? They raise rainbow trout that are bred in large water tanks. Farmer Smith, a marine biologist with a doctorate in nutrition, and his father (an engineer), developed a system of tracks and tanks using re-circulated pure cleaned water. The fish are really pampered with a special diet and solar-heated hatchery. View the spring water "ponds" with gravel bottoms (outside) and put a quarter in the machine to get fish food to feed the fish. Other newer exhibits of live fish are the jumbo freshwater shrimp and their "loopy" eyes! These fish are really spoiled, aren't they?

Wapakoneta

ARMSTRONG AIR AND SPACE MUSEUM

Wapakoneta - *500 South Apollo Drive (I-75 to Exit 111) 45895. Phone: (419) 738-8811 or (800) 860-0142. www.ohiohistory.org. Hours: Tuesday-Saturday 9:30am-*

5:00pm. Sunday Noon – 5:00pm. Closed Winter Holidays. Admission: $8.00 adult, $4.00 student (6-12).

The museum honors Neil Armstrong (a Wapakoneta native) and other area aeronauts (like the Wright Brothers) and their flying machines. After greeted by a NASA Skylaneer flown by Armstrong in the early 1960's, trace

the history of flight from balloons to space travel. Look at the Apollo crew spacesuits, a real moon rock, or watch a video of lunar space walks. In the Astro Theater, pretend you're on a trip to the moon. Try a lunar or shuttle landing interactive. Look at Space Food, even dessert! Another favorite is the Infinity Cube – 18 square feet covered with mirrors that make you feel like you've been projected into space. Interactives and videos are abundant. Blast OFF! …

West Liberty

MAD RIVER THEATER WORKS

West Liberty - *319 North Detroit 43357. www.madrivertheater.org. Phone: (937) 465-6751.*

Their purpose is to create and produce plays that explore the concerns of rural people and to perform these works for multi-generational, primarily rural audiences. They interview local residents and research historical issues with contemporary relevance (i.e. John Henry, slavery, Casey Jones). This material is used to craft plays with music that are drawn from and produced for the people of the rural Midwest. This is a touring company that is booked for events and special showings each year.

OHIO CAVERNS

West Liberty - *2210 East State Route 245 (I-70 to US 68 north to SR 507 east) 43357. Phone: (937) 465-4017. www.ohiocaverns.com. Hours: Daily 9:00am-5:00pm (April-October). 9:00am – 4:00pm (November – March). Admission: $12.50 Adult, $7.00 Children (5-12). Historic tour costs more. Miscellaneous: On the premises is a park and gift shop with gemstone mining.*

This tour is a 45 minute guided regular or historic tour of the largest cave in Ohio. The cave formations are still actively in the process of development. Still photography is welcome to capture you memories. The temperature here is 54 degrees F. constantly so dress appropriately. Look for the Palace of the Gods and stalagmites that look like cacti or a pump.

PIATT CASTLES
(MAC-O-CHEE & MAC-A-CHEEK)

West Liberty - *State Route 245 (Route 33 West to State Route 245 East) 43357. Phone: (937) 465-2821. www.piattcastles.org. Hours: Daily Noon–4:00pm (April-October), 11:00am-5:00pm (Summer). Weekends only, 11:00am-4:00pm (mid-*

March thru late May & early September thru early November). Admission: $9.00 adult, $8.00 senior (60+), $6.00 student (5-15). Prices listed are for each castle. Discount combo prices for both castles. Miscellaneous: Hands-on activities for families (summer).

Castles in Ohio? Catch the eerie, yet magnificent old castles furnished with collections ranging from 150-800 years old. Both castles were built in the mid-1800's and give a good sense of what the lifestyle of the upper-class Piatt brothers family was like. This self-guided tour is

Castle Mac-O-Chee

somewhat manageable for school-aged (pre-schoolers not suggested) children and includes lots of land to explore outside. Telling friends they were in a castle is fun too. Because the furniture is original, the homes have an old smell and the rooms look frozen in time. Ceiling paintings and the kitchen/dining area were most interesting.

TRADITIONS OVER TIME HOLIDAY TOUR

West Liberty – *Piatt Castles. Buildings decorated for holidays, Santa visit, entertainment and light refreshments served. This program traces the origins and evolution of decorating trees at Christmas, caroling, gift giving, holiday games, and family gatherings. Visitors of all ages are invited to enjoy a game from the past, make a holiday card, share a favorite memory, and leave a letter in Santa's mail box at Mac-A-Cheek Castle. Great way to expose younger ones to historical homes that might be boring otherwise. Admission. (first few weekends of December)*

Wilberforce

NATIONAL AFRO-AMERICAN MUSEUM AND CULTURAL CENTER

Wilberforce - 1350 Brush Row Road (off US 42 - Next to Central State College) 45384. Phone: (800) BLK-HIST. www.ohiohistory.org/places/afroam. Hours: Tuesday -Saturday 9:00am-5:00pm. Closed holidays except MLK holiday. Admission: $4.00 adult, $1.50 children.

Wilberforce was a famous stop on the Underground Railroad and became the center (Wilberforce University) for black education and achievements. The University was the first owned and operated by Afro-Americans. Best feature is the "From Victory to Freedom - the Afro-American Experience of 1950 - 1960's". This exhibition chronicles the trends, struggles and social changes that occurred within this crucial period in American history through a variety of photographs and artifacts, but also through life-sized scenes of a typical fifties lifestyles. These include a barber shop, a beauty salon, and a church interior complete with pews, pulpit and choir stand. These exhibits are made real to the visitor through the accompaniment of recorded speaking voices and gospel music.

Xenia

GREENE COUNTY HISTORICAL SOCIETY MUSEUM

Xenia - 74 Church Street (near center of town) 45385. Phone: (937) 372-4606. Hours: Tuesday-Friday 9:00am-Noon, Saturday and Sunday, 1:00-3:00pm (Summer). Weekends Only (Rest of Year). Admission: Donations suggested.

Restored Victorian home and 1799 James Galloway log house where Tecumseh tried to "woo" Rebecca Galloway (actually view the chair Tecumseh sat in near the fireplace!). First, pick herbs from a 1700's garden, smell them and then try to enter the front door of the log house. No door knob or latch? How did they open the door? The Carriage House has a wonderful display of farm equipment, general store (candy), china, books, furniture, toys, railroad exhibit, and school. In the Big House, easily explore the many rooms looking for old-fashioned toys, the kiddie potty, or, the old hair crimpers and curling irons - try one - how does it work? On your way here, stop by Clifton Mill for a hotcake breakfast with freshly milled flour. History and hotcakes is a nice way to make it fun for the kids.

Tecumseh's famous "courting chair"...

Yellow Springs

JOHN BRYAN STATE PARK

Yellow Springs - *3790 State Route 370 (2 miles Southeast of Yellow Springs on State Route 370) 45387. Phone: (937) 767-1274. www.johnbryan.org.*

750 acres of camping, hiking trails, fishing and winter sports. The park contains a remarkable limestone gorge cut by the Little Miami River which is designated as a state and national scenic river. Clifton Gorge State Nature Preserve is located adjacent to the park. The Clifton Gorge is a limestone gorge cut by the river (a national natural landmark). Nature lovers can enjoy any of the nine different trails found in the park. Trails follow the scenic river gorge and meander through majestic woodlands.

YOUNG'S JERSEY DAIRY FARM

Yellow Springs - *6880 Springfield-Xenia Road (On Route 68, off I-70) 45387. Phone: (937) 325-0629. www.youngsdairy.com. Hours: Daily 6:00am–10:00pm (April-October). Open later in the summer and closes earlier in the winter. Admission: Grounds are FREE. Each activity averages $5.00 per person. Tours: Scheduled groups Monday – Friday (April – October). $4.00 Children – FREE for Teachers and Chaperones. Minimum of 10 paying participants for tours. The one hour tour starts with a short video in the barn full of small animals such as ducks, rabbits and chicks. The video shows the farming process: from feeding the cows*

CW Area

(amazing how much food they need - 25 gallons of water, over 100 lbs of hay/ grain), milking the cows, bottling the milk (quick chilled) and making the ice

cream (what's their secret?), watching the operations through the processing window, to selling the milk and ice cream in the store and restaurant. The children then visit the animals in the big barn. They see what a cow eats, feed the goats (why can't they bite?), and visit with the other farm animals. The next step is a wagon ride. Finish the tour with some homemade ice cream.

The Dairy store began in 1960 and is still operated by members of the Young family. Choose from the following activities: Udders and Putters Miniature Golf, Driving Range, Batting Cage, Corny Maze (a 3 acre corn field maze open weekends, August

thru October), Wagon Rides & Moo-ver & Shaker Barrel Cart rides on weekends, Petting Area – Baby Jersey (pretty-faced calves) cows, pigs and sheep; or Water Balloon Toss (summertime). Go to the petting area and then the wagon ride with a treat at the end in one of the restaurants. They make and sell 110 flavors a year - try something fun like Cake Batter Rainbow Chip, Green Apple Sorbetto, Cow Chip? or Wooly Wonka. Young's attracts mostly families. Parents and grandparents love to bring children and friends to the farm and visit. Our family has fallen in love with this farm amusement park!

EASTER EGG HUNTS

Yellow Springs – Young's Jersey Dairy Farm. Easter Bunny appearance, treat stations, egg hunts, and kids' entertainment and crafts. Usually held the Saturday before Easter. Over 4000 colored Easter eggs. Free.

FALL FARM FESTIVAL

Yellow Springs – *Young's Jersey Dairy Farm. Pumpkin Patches / Hayrides / Corn Mazes / Fall Playlands. All sites charge admission (average $6.00). Plan on at least two hours playtime. Open weekends & weekdays (by appointment) and weeknights (late September - late October).*

Zanesfield

MARMON VALLEY FARM

Zanesfield - *7754 SR 292 (off US 33 northwest, exit Mad River Mtn. Area) 43360. Phone: (937) 593-8051. www.marmonvalley.com. Hours: Call for details. Educators: Farm (younger ones) or Ohio Homesteading (upper elementary) field trips offered with instruction.*

Winter and summer activities are available at Marmon Valley Farm. They have live farm animals and a fun barn with rope bridges, rope swings and barn games. Hiking and horseback riding (year-round trail rides, on ponies, or in the indoor arena) are available. If it's very cold, try ice-skating. When there's snow, you may want to take your sled along for some great sled riding hills. Overnights combine activities with just enough time left to wander and make new friends. Activities like archery, fishing, a challenge course, indoor arena sports, and the new indoor barn rock climbing wall fill a sport gal or guy's day.

Life-long memories are made here...

This one didn't get away!

An evening hayride followed by silly barn line dancing and s'mores by the fire pit are a great way to end the day. Overnighters ride the wagon each morning over to the cowboy chuck wagon camp for yummy, open-air cooked, big breakfasts followed by a nature hike with Wrangler Matt. Look to attend their seasonal events if you can't arrange a group visit.

FALL FARM FESTIVAL

Zanesfield – *Marmon Valley Farm. Enjoy Farm favorites like horse drawn wagon rides and pony rides. Activities like indoor rock climbing, archery, hay tunnels, a kids fishing derby, leather crafts and pumpkin painting are just a few of the opportunities for fun that day. Experience old west gun fights, stick horse rodeo games, live musical entertainment and contests for kids, too! (Trail rides and some Make-it and Take-it crafts are not included in the admission cost.) Riding reservations are recommended. Food Concessions and snacks will be available throughout the day. Stick around for a barn dance that evening, too. Admission. (first Saturday in October)*

A COUNTRY CHRISTMAS

Zanesfield – *Marmon Valley Farm. Costumed characters, carolers, live animals in a presentation of the Nativity story. Hayride wagons take guests to different scenes around the barns and fields. Hot chocolate, goodies, singing, Christmas crafts. By reservation. (First two weekends in December).*

CW Area

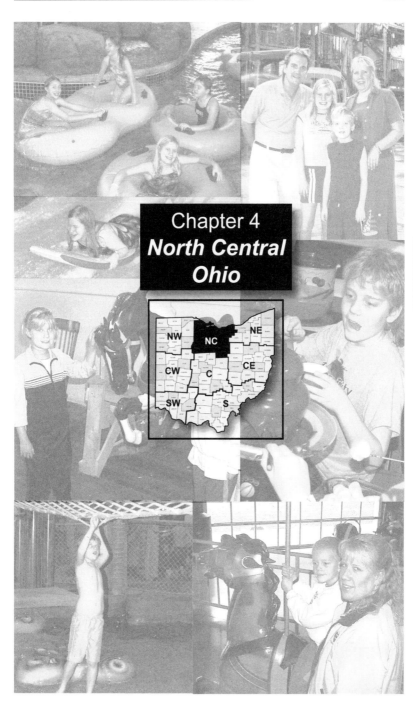

Chapter 4
North Central Ohio

NW   NC   NE
CW   C   CE
SW   S

Ashland
- Ashland Balloonfest
- Bookmasters

Bellevue
- Historic Lyme Village
- Mad River & Nkp Railroad Museum

Berlin Heights
- Berlin Fruit Box Company

Bucyrus
- Cooper's Cider Mill Apple Butter & Jelly Factory
- Pfeifer Dairy Farms

Butler
- Prairie Peddler

Castalia
- Castalia State Fish Hatchery

Catawba
- Miller Boat Line Ferries

Elyria
- Apple Festival

Flat Rock
- Seneca Caverns

Fremont
- Hayes Presidential Center

Lakeside
- Lakeside

Lexington
- Mid Ohio Sports Car Course

Loudonville
- Great Mohican Indian Pow-Wow
- Landoll's Mohican CasTle Resort
- Mohican State Park Resort

Lucas
- Malabar Farm State Park

Mansfield
- Biblewalk
- Carousel Magic! Factory & Richland Carousel Park
- Christmas Wunderland
- Freedom Festival
- Kingwood Center
- Ohio Bird Sanctuary
- Ohio State Reformatory
- Pumpkin Maze Playland
- Spruce Hill Inn & Cottages

Marblehead
- East Harbor State Park
- Kelleys Island Ferry Boat Lines
- Marblehead Lighthouse State Park
- Prehistoric Forest & Mystery Hill
- Train – O – Rama

Milan
- Edison Birthplace Museum
- Melon Festival
- Milan Historical Museum

New Washington
- Pumpkin Maze Playland

Oberlin
- Oberlin Heritage Center

Perrysville
- Mohican-Memorial State Forest

Port Clinton
- African Safari Wildlife Park
- Crane Creek State Park & Magee Marsh Wildlife Area
- Great Lakes Popcorn Company
- Jet Express
- Lake Erie Islands Regional Welcome Center
- Lake Erie Islands State Park
- Monsoon Lagoon
- Walleye Madness At Midnight

Put-In-Bay
- Aquatic Visitors Center
- Butterfly House
- Chocolate Café & Museum
- Crystal Cave & Heineman's Grape Juice Winery

Put-In-Bay (cont.)

- Lake Erie Islands Museum
- Perry's Cave & Family Fun Center
- Perry's Victory And International Peace Memorial
- Put-In-Bay Tour Train
- Stone Laboratory

Rittman

- Apple Festival

Sandusky

- Castaway Bay
- Cedar Point & Soak City
- Goodtime I
- Great Wolf Lodge Indoor Waterpark
- Kalahari Indoor Waterpark Resort
- Lagoon Deer Park
- Maui Sands Indoor Waterpark Resort
- Merry-Go-Round Museum

Tiffin

- Tiffin-Seneca Heritage Festival

Upper Sandusky

- Indian Mill

Vermilion

- Festival Of The Fish
- Woollybear Festival
- Inland Seas Maritime Museum & Lighthouse

Wellington

- Findley State Park

Willard

- Celeryville, Buurma Vegetable Farms

NC Area

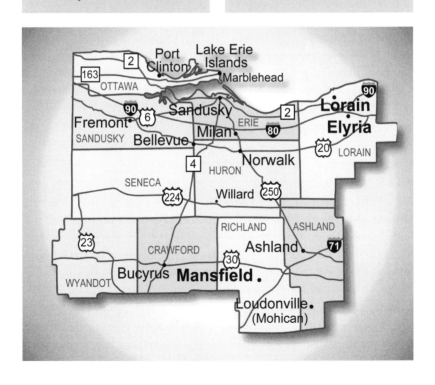

A Quick Tour of our Hand-Picked Favorites Around...

North Central Ohio

Be sure to stop in the **Lake Erie Islands** Regional Welcome Center to view the dioramas of the area and meet the friendly staff. The kids can gaze at the 600 gallon aquarium or do nature rubbings while the parents work out a plan. They can also tell you about eateries in the area that specialize in perch and walleye…any way you like it.

Did you know you could escape to an island, just off the shores of Sandusky? The Islands are a Midwest vacation hot spot. Just a short ferry ride from the mainland, and you'll forget you are in Ohio! Whatever your pleasure, coastal relaxation or on-the-go excitement, the islands have got it covered!

A favorite paradise oasis in any season – Sandusky and its numerous **Indoor Waterparks**, may just be the "Orlando of the Midwest!" Tweens and teens thrive at Kalahari, while the younger set (ages 1-10) are more content at any of the other parks as they're smaller and more manageable with "softer" rides and activities.

Down the road towards **Marblehead** are quaint shops, train or dinosaur attractions, eateries, plus the Marblehead Lighthouse. Their stories of old lighthouse keepers lugging 40 pound buckets of whale oil up those 77 stairs are so interesting.

If history or nature are more your thing, we recommend **Perry's Monument**. The DVD presentation of the War of 1812 and the Battle of Lake Erie are so worth seeing. While island hopping, make sure you don't miss walking into a giant geode (**Crystal Cave**) or walking across **Glacial Grooves** (Kelleys Island). Remember, try to leave Put-in-Bay island by 4:00pm to avoid the "party scene".

Thomas Edison developed the incandescent light bulb, phonograph and early motion picture camera. **Edison's Birthplace**, in Milan (around the corner from the Sandusky area), is where you can count how many tries it took to make the light bulb work; what was first recorded on the phonograph; and what silly thing the first movie was about.

Closer to Central Ohio is **Mohican Country**, near Mansfield...the land of skiing, canoeing, hiking and other outdoor sports. But, several unusual attractions are hidden here too. Ride the Richland Carousel downtown, grab a bite at the Diner and then make an appointment to visit the **Carousel Magic! Factory** just down the street. See them start with a hollow box and create a magical colorful animal. After lunch, plan to spend a couple hours at **BibleWalk** – the only wax museum in Ohio and full of several choices of themed walkways to explore. It's very emotional, too. You can overnight in the area from your choice of lodge, cabins, tents, or even a castle!

Sites and attractions are listed in order by City, Zip Code, and Name. Symbols indicated represent:

 Festivals   Restaurants   Lodging

Ashland

BOOKMASTERS

Ashland - *30 Amberwood Parkway (I-71 exit 186, SR 250 west) 44805. Phone: (800) 537-6727 ask for Plant Manager. www.bookmasters.com. Tours: Monday –*

Friday 10:00am – 2:00pm. Appointment necessary. Group size (6 – 40).

While visiting, kids will learn step-by-step how books (like the "Kids Love" books) are produced. Start by seeing what materials are needed, then see the pre-press division, the printing area (with huge, monster-like printers), and the final book binding area. See all phases of books being made through production and view finished books at the end of the tour.

ASHLAND BALLOONFEST

Ashland - *Main Street, downtown. www.ashlandballoonfest.org. Hot air balloon races and twilight balloon glow. Ashland is a top balloon manufacturer – factory tours available. (long weekend near 4th of July)*

Bellevue

HISTORIC LYME VILLAGE

Bellevue - 5001 State Route 4 (south of SR 113) 44811. Phone: (419) 483-4949. www.lymevillage.com. Hours: Tuesday-Saturday 11:00am-4:00pm, Sunday Noon-4:00pm (Summer months). Sunday only (September & October). Admission: $8.00 adult, $7.00 senior (65+), $4.00 child (6-12). Miscellaneous: Gift Shop and concessions. Best to visit during special events. No pets allowed on grounds.

This 19th Century Ohio Village includes the Wright Mansion, Annie Brown's log home that she owned for 82 years (early Ohio settler exhibits inside), a blacksmith shop, schoolhouse, barns, a church, and the Cooper-Fries general store. All original buildings were moved to this location. Of special interest is the National Museum of Postmark Collector's Club (with the world's largest single collection of postmarks) in a restored post office.

PIONEER DAYS

Bellevue – Historic Lyme Village. Early 1800's frontier life & Indian village. Re-enactors, craft demonstrations, authentic open fire, wood cooked food and folk entertainment. (weekend after Labor Day)

CHRISTMAS CANDLELIGHT TOURS

Bellevue – Historic Lyme Village. Take a self-guided tour of the village by candlelight, where you'll discover buildings decorated for Christmas and interpreters located inside with delicious food samples. (second or third Saturday in December)

MAD RIVER & NKP RAILROAD MUSEUM

Bellevue - 233 York Street (Just South of US 20) 44811. Phone: (419) 483-2222. www.madrivermuseum.org. Hours: Daily Noon-4:00pm (Memorial Day-Labor Day). Weekends Only (May, September, October). Admission: $7.00 adult, $6.00 senior (60+),$4.00 child (3-12).

Look for steam engines, diesel engines, or the huge snow plow. Once you find them, browse through their collections of full-scale locomotives, cabooses, and mail cars – many that you can climb aboard. The hands-on museum stands on the former Henry Flagler family estate, near the first chartered railroad in the State and the largest railroad museum in Ohio. Tour guide volunteers are usually retired railway personnel who are knowledgeable and excited to tell you stories about the old railway days.

Berlin Heights

BERLIN FRUIT BOX COMPANY

Berlin Heights - *51 Mechanic Street (off SR 61) 44814. Tours: Workshop open for tours weekdays from 9:00am-3:00pm. $5.00 per adult. About one hour long. Must schedule appointment. www.samuelpattersonbaskets.com.*

The sixth generation family-run company makes beautiful hardwood Maple and American Black Cherry decorative baskets for the home, plus farm baskets. Complete production on site, including log veneering and clipping demos. If you can't organize a tour, you may be interested in attending a special event: Spring Open House (two middle weekends in March) and Christmas Open House (Thanksgiving weekend and first weekend in December). The Open Houses are held at the workshop and include log veneering and clipping demonstrations, basket weaving, activities for kids and refreshments. You can even weave your own basket! (Appointment highly recommended.)

Bucyrus

COOPER'S CIDER MILL APPLE BUTTER & JELLY FACTORY

Bucyrus - *1414 North Sandusky Avenue (US Route 30 bypass & State Route 4) 44820. Phone: (419) 562-4215. www.coopersmill.net. Hours: Open Monday-Saturday 8:30am-6:00pm. Admission: FREE. Tours: Monday-Friday 9:00am-11:30am and 1:00-3:30pm, by reservation usually. Miscellaneous: Farm Market - taste test jellies and homemade fudge.*

Jelly Factory tour lets you watch fruit spreads being made the old fashioned way. With "Grandma" recipes, watch the cooking of fine jams and apple butter. Take time to go into the screened-in porch to watch the apple butter bubbling in open 50 gallon copper kettles over a wood fire. Or, observe the delicious ripe fruits cooking into jelly. They cook in small batches and use home-canning jars.

PFEIFER DAIRY FARMS

Bucyrus - *301 S. Sandusky Ave. 44820. www.bucyrus.org. Phone: (866) 562-0720.*

A modern dairy farm milking around 300 cows twice a day. Here their story and see the actual milking of cows the modern way. Plus you may bottle feed a calf if you want. This is an excellent tour to actually experience where milk comes from. Times for this tour are limited to milking times each day. Many people have never seen the actual milking of a cow...here is the opportunity.

NC Area

Butler

PRAIRIE PEDDLER

Butler - Bunker Hill Woods, State Route 97. (419) 663-1818. www.prairietown.com. Almost 200 costumed craftspeople offer their items made with frontier style tools, foods cooked over open fires and bluegrass music. Horse drawn wagon rides. Stop by the Medicine Show and buy a bottle of elixir. Admission. (last 2 weekends of June & first two weekends in October)

Castalia

CASTALIA STATE FISH HATCHERY

Castalia - 7018 Homegardner Road (SR 6 to SR 269 south for 2 miles) 44824. Phone: (419) 684-7499. www.dnr.state.oh.us. Hours: Monday-Friday 8:00am-3:00pm.

The hatchery raises steelhead and rainbow trout and offers self-guided tours of 90-acres of serene grounds including outdoor raceways, a half-mile section of the Cold Creek and a "blue hole" aquifer. Because the water from the blue hole has no oxygen and high levels of nitrogen, it is treated before being used by the hatchery. The remaining two raceways are supplied with water diverted from Cold Creek. This cold water supply allows the hatchery to raise steelhead and rainbow trout. All of the state's steelhead production occurs at this hatchery. Rainbow trout are raised to catchable size before being stocked in Ohio lakes in both the spring and fall. The facility offers great wildlife viewing opportunities and also offers a limited lottery-style fishing program on the portion of Cold Creek that runs through the hatchery grounds. The area also provides excellent bird watching opportunities. FREE admission.

Catawba

MILLER BOAT LINE FERRIES

Catawba - Catawba Point (SR 2 to Route 53 north) 43456. Phone: (800) 500-2421 or (419) 285-2421. www.millerferry.com.

Trips run spring, summer & fall, "family friendly" fares, free mainland parking, Put-in-Bay summer trips every half hour as late as 9:00pm service to Put-in-Bay and Middle Bass Island (late March-October). Low rates $6.50-$8.00 adult, $1.50-$3.00 child, (one way), most frequent trips. It is the only scheduled service to Middle Bass Island. The ferry trip to Put-in-Bay takes 18 minutes, and 40 minutes to Middle Bass. Cars, motorcycles, RVs, boats, trailers and

NC Area

bicycles are welcome aboard - and Miller Ferry is the only service that takes both passengers and vehicles to these islands. Rental transportation, including bikes and golf carts, available near the dock.

Elyria

APPLE FESTIVAL

Elyria - *Ely Square, downtown. www.elyriaapplefestival.com. Apples & cider. Apple pie eating contests. Apple peeling contests. Apple butter. Candy apples. Wagon/hayrides. Apple Dumplings, Fritters, Donuts, etc. Parades. Pioneer crafts. Petting Zoo. (third weekend in September)*

Flat Rock

SENECA CAVERNS

Flat Rock - *15248 Twp. Road 178 (SR 4 off turnpike, south of SR 269) 44811. Phone: (419) 483-6711. www.senecacavernsohio.com. Hours: Daily 9:00am-7:00pm (Summer). Weekends 10:00am - 5:00pm (May, September, October). Admission: $13.00 adult, $10.00 senior (62+), $6.50 child (5-12). Miscellaneous: Light jacket is suggested as the cave is a constant 54 degrees F.*

"The Caviest Cave in the U.S.A." is one of the most unique underground natural wonders in Ohio and the United States. The one hour guided tour includes walking and climbing natural stone steps and pathways. The 110 foot deep limestone cave has many small rooms, seven levels and the "Ole Mist'ry River". The cave is actually an earth crack discovered by two boys out hunting in 1872. To make the tour really fun, stop by Sandy Creek Gem Mining and let your little explorers pan for gems.

Fremont

HAYES PRESIDENTIAL CENTER

Fremont - *1337 Hayes Avenue (Rt. 6), Spiegel Grove (turnpike exit 91, SR 53 south to SR 6 west) 43420. www.rbhayes.org/hayes/. Phone: (419) 332-2081 or (800) 998-7737. Hours: Monday-Saturday 9:00am-5:00pm. Sunday and Holidays Noon - 5:00pm. Closed Easter, Thanksgiving, Christmas & New Year's Day. Admission: $6.00 adult, $5.00 senior, $2.00 child (6-12) Home or Museum. Combo prices offered to tour both. Miscellaneous: Museum Store. Educators: wonderful biography online.*

Disputed Election? Contested Florida votes? Popular vote vs. Electoral College vote? It all happened in 1876 with the campaign of Rutherford B.

Hayes. The iron gates that greet you at the entrance were the same gates that once stood at the White House during the Hayes administration. The 33-room mansion estate was the home of President and Mrs. Rutherford B. Hayes and is full of family mementos, private papers and books. They give you the sense he dedicated himself to his country. The museum displays the President's daughter's ornate dollhouses and the White House carriage that the family used. As 19th President, Hayes contended with the aftermath of Reconstruction in the South, the problems of our black citizens, and the plight of the American Indian.

CIVIL WAR ENCAMPMENT & REENACTMENT

Fremont – *Hayes Presidential Center. Puts you in the middle of the action as Union and Confederate forces prepare to meet in battle. You can walk amid the tent camps of both armies as soldiers prepare meals on open fires, sleep on mattresses of straw, and speak in hushed tones lest the nearby enemy hear them. Costumed reenactors immerse themselves in the lifestyles of the 19th century to help visitors better understand the war, the hardships it caused, and the heavy toll it exacted in American lives lost. An exciting highlight of their efforts is the re-creation of the Battle of Opequon Creek - a conflict in which Rutherford B. Hayes played a decisive role. Three battle re-creations take place (two Saturday, one Sunday). Small admission. (first weekend in October)*

HAYES TRAIN SPECIAL

Fremont – *Hayes Presidential Center. A 12 x 24-foot operating model train display featuring six 19th-century-style trains used during the life of the 19th President. Interactive buttons let visitors control signals, gates, whistles, and more. Victorian Teas. Sleigh/ Carriage Rides through Spiegel Grove (end of month). Take a tour through the 25-acre estate of 19th U.S. President Rutherford B. Hayes using the mode of transportation he used. Weather determines if sleighs or carriages will be used. Admission. (month-long in December thru weekend after New Years)*

Lakeside

LAKESIDE

Lakeside - *236 Walnut Avenue 43440. Phone: (419) 798-4461 or (866) 9-LAKESIDE. www.lakesideohio.com.*

Chautauqua – like resort with programs in a historic enclave on Lake Erie. (June – September). The entire area is a Christian family retreat of shops, eaties, entertainment, lectures, worship services and family-rated movies. Daily, weekly and season pass admission prices are charged (average $10.00 per person per day-ages 10+). This gated community is safe for families and offers a huge dock, lake swimming, a sailing area (learn to sail), mini-golf, a town movie theatre, and seasonal festivals. It is like stepping back in time!

Lexington

MID OHIO SPORTS CAR COURSE

Lexington - *Steam Corners Road (I-71 exit SR 97 or SR 95, follow signs) 44904. Phone: (419) 884-4000 or (800) MID-OHIO. www.midohio.com.*

Indy Car, Sport Car, AMA Motorcycles, Vintage Car Races. General, Weekend, Paddock (walk through garages & see drivers) passes available. Weekends (June – mid September)

Loudonville

LANDOLL'S MOHICAN CASTLE RESORT

Loudonville - *561 Twp. Rd 3352 44842. www.landollsmohicancastle.com. Phone: (800) 291-5001.*

If you really want an upscale, enchanted getaway in the Mohican Area... Landoll's Mohican Castle complex is the place! Stay overnight in a castle with

royal family suites or cottages! Castle suites have fireplaces, jacuzzis, mini-kitchens, heated tile floors, and complimentary euro-style continental breakfast. Euro-gardens and cobblestone paths lead into the 30 miles of hiking/golf cart trails (golf cart rentals available). The royal suites are great for small families, but the newly remodeled royal cottages are the best for large families or extended family and friends. The patio, two-floor, two-bedroom cottages connect in the middle and each unit sleeps 6+. We loved visiting with friends in the connecting great rooms and were up until late playing board games and watching DVD's (one player in most every room, by the way). Both floors have a large deck to sit and watch the leaves change or the flowers bloom. In colder weather (mid-November thru March), the Landoll's have nearly one million lights outside the castle and all the "kingdom structures". Basically, every season has its own natural enchantment set around the intriguing castle. Enjoy the indoor pool/fitness/gameroom complex - then after a great workout - try the wonderful blueberry piefin (made with fresh organic blueberries grown on the property) if available for purchase. Overnight stays begin around $200 up to around $400 per night.

MOHICAN STATE PARK RESORT

Loudonville - *3116 State Route 3 44842. Phone: (419) 994-4290 or (419) 938-5411 Resort. www.mohicancamp.com or www.mohicanresort.com.*

The striking Clearfork Gorge, hemlock forest and scenic Mohican River offer a wilderness experience while the resort lodge and cottages provide comfortable accommodations. Most people come to stay at riverfront family cabins (with A/C, fireplaces and cable) or the Lodge rooms (with indoor/outdoor pools, sauna, tennis, basketball and shuffleboard facilities). Family playground activity center. Over 13 miles of trails take the visitor to the more interesting areas of the park and forest. Lyons Falls trail follows Clear Fork Gorge and features two waterfalls. The Hemlock trail leads to the scenic wooden bridge, and Pleasant Hill trail follows the lake shoreline and offers beautiful views of the lake (a favorite trail as it leaves from the lodge and is super scenic). Among the resort's most popular attractions are birds of prey presentations conducted by experts from the Ohio Bird Sanctuary. Nearby activities include visiting four canoe liveries, Mohican Water Slide, five golf courses, two horse stables, and downhill ski resorts. 1,294 acres of camping, bridle trails, boating and rentals, marina, bike rentals, fishing and winter sports.

GREAT MOHICAN INDIAN POW-WOW

Loudonville - *Mohican Reservation Campgrounds & Canoeing. 23270 Wally Road (CR 3175). (800) 766-CAMP. www.mohicanpowwow.com. Nine different tribes gather to a pow-wow featuring foods, music, crafts, hoop dancers and storytellers. Learn the proper throwing of a tomahawk or a new Native American custom. Admission. (second weekend in July and third weekend in September)*

Lucas

MALABAR FARM STATE PARK

Lucas - 4050 Bromfield Road (I-71 to Exit 169, follow signs) 44843. Phone: (419) 892-2784. www.malabarfarm.org. Hours: Tuesday-Saturday 10:00am-5:00pm, Sunday Noon-5:00pm. Weekends only each winter. Admission: Big House Tour, $4.00 adult,$2.00 child (6-18). Tractor Drawn Wagon Tour, $2.00 (6+). Tours: Begin at 10:00am, last tour at 4:00pm. Wagon tours are generally only on weekends (May-October). Miscellaneous: Malabar Inn. 1820's stagecoach stop restaurant.

A writer and lover of nature, Louis Bromfield, dreamed of this scenic land and home. Today, visitors can see the house and farm existing just as they did in Bromfield's time. The outbuildings and pastures still house chickens, goats and beef cattle. It is still a working farm and the place where Bromfield discovered new farming techniques. The guides at the Big House tell captivating stories. During seasonal events, kids can watch harvesting or planting, ride an authentic wagon, or help with daily chores @ 3:30pm. The new Visitors Center has easy to understand farm exhibits (even milk a mechanical cow!) and nature study. Over 30 interactive exhibits let visitors explore and experience agriculture, the environment, energy, and Bromfield's legacy as author AND farmer. There are twelve miles of trails for the hiker or horseperson to enjoy. Trails traverse scenic fields and forests. Bridle trails, fishing, hiking trails, camping and winter sports are also available park-wide.

> **Special note to grandparents...**
> Humphrey Bogart & Lauren Bacall were married on these beautiful grounds.

MAPLE SYRUP FESTIVAL

Lucas – Malabar Farm State Park. Take a horse-drawn wagon ride and see demonstrations of sugar making through history and pioneer life. Enjoy live music and food. Maple syrup, fudge and other maple products are for sale. (first and second weekend in March)

OHIO HERITAGE DAYS / HARVEST TOURS

Lucus – *Malabar Farm State Park. Enjoy demos by 70 traditional crafters, along with vintage farm machinery, draft horse competitions, pressing cider, butter churning, hayride tours, open-fire cooking and eating. (last weekend in September & every weekend in October)*

CANDLELIGHT CHRISTMAS TOURS

Lucas – *Malabar Farm State Park. Tour the decorated home of Louis Bromfield and enjoy yuletide crafts, refreshments, caroling and holiday stories. Admission. (second week of December)*

NC Area

Mansfield

CAROUSEL MAGIC! FACTORY & RICHLAND CAROUSEL PARK

Mansfield - 44 West 4th Street (behind the Gift Horse) (I-71 Exit State Route 13 North to downtown) 44901. Phone: (419) 526-4009 factory or (419) 522-4223 carousel. www.carouselmagic.com.   Admission: Factory Tour $5.00 adult, $1.50 child (5-12). Carousel $1.00 – (2) ride tokens. Tours: Factory tours start at the back of the Gift Shop Tuesday-Saturday 10:00 pm – 4:00pm. 30-45 minutes long. (late April thru mid-December, except Thanksgiving). Reservations necessary for

parties of 10 or more. Miscellaneous: For lunch, stop at the Coney Island Diner on Main Street with its genuine old-time tables, stools and "Blue Plate" specials.

Step back in time as you watch skilled craftsmen use time honored techniques of carving, finishing and painting to transform hardwood blocks into prancing ponies and magical menagerie figures. Watch the wood carousel horses being

It's fascinating to watch how the carousel figures are carved...

made starting from a "coffin box" with a hollow center, then the carving with special tools, and finally the painting. The artisans casually show off their skill. Your tour guide will explain carousel history and construction as they guide you through displays showing the history of American carousels, and the process of creating magical animals from a pile of boards. Why do some

carousels run backwards? Why were they built in medieval times? Now that you know how they're made, walk over to the wonderful carousel in the center of town (Main & Fourth Street-indoor/ outdoor style - open daily). There really is Carousel Magic!

Jenny & Daniel's new friend...

OHIO BIRD SANCTUARY

Mansfield - *3773 Orweiler Road (west of Lexington off SR 97, turn north on Bowers Rd, then east) 44903. www.ohiobirdsanctuary.com. Phone: (419) 884-HAWK. Hours: Visitors Center open Tuesday- Saturday 10:00am-4:00pm, Sunday 1:00-5:00pm. Trails open daily during daylight hours, restricted winter hours, and group tours by reservation (small fee). Educators: online Teachers guides, Vocabulary guide and Education Boxes under Teacher Resources.*

The Ohio Bird Sanctuary is located on the headwater of the Clearfork River. The marsh and old growth forest offers great birding and hiking. Enjoy seeing birds up close at the Birds Of Prey. The Sanctuary is also a wildlife rehabilitation for native bird species. Nine species of birds of prey including our national emblem, the Bald Eagle, reside in large display areas. If you are a fan of songbirds you will enjoy the walk through Songbird Aviary where birds fly around you and nibble at your hand in search of food. Groups can schedule "Falcon & Friends", a live bird presentation. Picnic tables, gift shop. FREE.

SPRUCE HILL INN & COTTAGES

Mansfield - *3230 O'Possum Run Road (I-71 exit 169, Rte. 13 turn up the hill beside Cracker Barrel) 44903. Phone: (419) 756-2200. www.sprucehillinn.com.*

Right next to Snow Trails Ski Resort are sets of cottages (rent for $125 peak) and a lodge or house (for groups or extended families) to rent overnight while in the area. Nestled on the hill overlooking the ski trails, you'll have easy access to the slopes. The cottages include a jacuzzi tub in the bathroom, a queen bed and some have a tower room w/ futon bed or an outside deck. Walking around the sloped property and pond is a fun activity. They serve a light continental breakfast at the carriage house each morning. Just minutes from attractions or nearby Mohican Country - canoeing, hiking and other outdoor sports.

BIBLEWALK

Mansfield - *500 Tingley Avenue (I-71 to US 30 West to State Route 545 North) 44905. Phone: (419) 524-0139 or (800) 222-0139. www.livingbiblemuseum.org. Hours: Monday-Saturday 9:00am-6:00pm, Sunday 3:00-7:00pm. Admission: $3.75-$4.50 adult, $3.50-4.25 senior (50+), $2.75-$3.50 youth (6-18), $10.00-$20.00 family. This is the price per adjoining museum. There are 4 museums: Life of Christ, Miracles of The Old Testament, Christian Martyrs, or Heart of Reformation (church history). Discount for families and for combo of all 4 museums. Miscellaneous: Solomon's Snack Bar (Saturday only) serves aptly named sandwiches and snacks (ex. Samson Burger, Goliath Dog or Eve's Fruit Salad). Dinner Theater productions different every season (Saturdays only). Gift Shop. Collection of rare bibles and religious woodcarvings.*

The only life-size wax museum in Ohio – it features figures from the Old and New Testaments (non-denominational). Featured stories include the Life of Christ, Daniel in the Lions Den, Jonah and the whale, and Adam and Eve. You can choose to study more recent martyrs and figures in Christian history, too. The tour guide takes you through dimly lit hallways that add a theatrical, dramatic effect. Your personal tour guide will assist you through dioramas from the Bible, each with its own audio text, music, and some with special effects. At the end of the tour you will be left emotional (a small chapel is available to reflect). What an excellent way to dramatically, unforgettably, walk through the bible and church history.

KINGWOOD CENTER

Mansfield - *900 Park Avenue West (I-71 exit State Route 30) 44906. Phone: (419) 522-0211. www.kingwoodcenter.org. Hours: 8:00am - 30 minutes before dusk.*

Forty-seven acres of gardens, woods and ponds surrounding the King French Provincial mansion. Greenhouses with a specialty of tulips and perennials and short hiking trails are family friendly. Maybe the best time to visit is for the KINGWOOD CHRISTMAS DISPLAY (thanksgiving thru December)

OHIO STATE REFORMATORY

Mansfield - *100 Reformatory Road (I-71 to SR 30 west & SR 545 North) 44906. Phone: (419) 522-2644. www.mrps.org. Hours: Sunday 1:00-4:00pm (Mid-May to September). Admission: $8.00 adult, $6.00 student (7-17). Add on a tour is $5.00 extra. Tours: Phone Reservations Preferred. Children under 9 and pregnant* *women should use caution because of stairs and lead-based paint. Best as a "tough love" educational visit for tweens and teens. 45 minutes. Daily (Tuesday-Friday only) group tours (10+) by appointment.*

A castle prison? This 1886 structure was built as a boy's reformatory. The original cellblocks and offices remain intact and were used to film 4 major motion pictures including "The Shawshank Redemption" and "Air Force One". The East Cell Block houses the world's largest free-standing steel cell block - 6 tiers. Ask about the story of the seven-foot Jesus. Tours to choose from:

- EAST CELL BLOCK TOUR - Travel the length of the East Cell Block, the world's largest freestanding steel cell block. Strenuous because of stair-climbing. Includes Central Guard Room and Catholic Chapel.

- WEST TOWER TOUR - wind up the spiral staircase of the Guard Tower for a view of the cemetery in which inmates were buried with only a number on their grave. Stop at the Big Dig underground tunnel system. Lots of stair-climbing.

- HOLLYWOOD TOUR - See the Shawshank Warden's Office and Andy Dufresne's escape tunnels. Take a trip into the sinister "Hole". View the 1886 West Cell Block used as a Russian prison in Air Force One.

NC Area

FREEDOM FESTIVAL

Mansfield *- Downtown. A full day of parades, rides, entertainment and fireworks. Airport air show. (July 4th)*

PUMPKIN MAZE PLAYLAND

Mansfield *- Apple Hill Orchards, 1175 Lex-Ontario Rd. Pumpkin Patches / Hayrides / Corn Mazes / Fall Playland - Admission (average $6.00). Plan on at least two hours playtime. Scavenger Hunt Kids Day. Open weekends, some weekdays (by appointment) and weeknights. www.applehill.biz. (late September - late October).*

CHRISTMAS WUNDERLAND

Mansfield *- Richland County Fairgrounds, 750 North Home Rd. Hundreds of thousands of lights & holiday / storybook characters. Daily, evenings. www.richlandcountyfair.com. Admission. (December - January 1)*

Marblehead

EAST HARBOR STATE PARK

Marblehead - *(8 miles East of Port Clinton on State Route 269) 43440. Phone: (419) 734-4424. www.dnr.state.oh.us.*

Located on the shores of Lake Erie, East Harbor State Park has unlimited opportunities for outdoor recreation. Boating, fishing, swimming (large sandy beaches), picnicking and camping (large campground) are popular while nature enthusiasts will enjoy the abundance of waterfowl, shorebirds and other species of wildlife found in the park's scenic wetlands. Nature programs. 1,152 acres of hiking trails and winter sports. Disc golf is now available.

KELLEYS ISLAND FERRY BOAT LINES

Marblehead - *510 W. Main St. (Take 163 E into Marblehead - across from the Police Department, and Fire Station.) 43440. Phone: (419) 798-9763 or (888) 225-4325. www.kelleysislandferry.com.*

They offer the only daily service (passenger & auto) to Kelleys Island with a short enjoyable 20 minute boat ride, departing every half-hour during peak times. Available year-round, weather permitting. Admission fees.

MARBLEHEAD LIGHTHOUSE STATE PARK

Marblehead - *110 Lighthouse Drive (SR 2 to SR 269 to SR 163 at the tip of the peninsula) 43440. Phone: (419) 798-4530 or (800) 441-1271. www.ohiodnr.com/parks/. Hours: Monday-Friday 1:00-5:00pm, and on the second Saturday of the month*

(June-Labor Day). Some Saturdays there are pioneer demos at the lightkeeper's house. Admission: FREE.

The oldest working lighthouse on the Great Lakes. Marblehead Point has been known for having the roughest weather along Lake Erie. To warn ships of the danger of being dashed against the rocks by winds from the north, the federal government constructed the Marblehead Lighthouse in 1821. Built of native limestone, it is the oldest light in continuous operation on the Great Lakes. The reflector lamp originally burned whale oil, lard oil, coal oil, and now it's electric.

Their stories of old lighthouse keepers lugging 40 lb. buckets of whale oil up those 77 stairs are so interesting. From the top, you can see Cedar Point rides, Kelley's Island and Put-in-Bay. The cute little museum and gift shop (in the lightkeepers house) have many inexpensive coloring books and puzzles to buy and artifacts to explore.

PREHISTORIC FOREST & MYSTERY HILL

Marblehead - 8232 East Harbor Road - State Route 163 (8 miles East of Port Clinton off State Route 2) 43440. Phone: (419) 798-5230. www.prehistoricforest.com. Hours: Daily 10:00am-Dark (Memorial Day-Labor Day). Weekends Only (May and September). Admission: $6.95-$8.95 (4 and over) - Mystery Hill and Prehistoric Forest. Coupons on website. Miscellaneous: "Sleep with the Dinos" sleeping cabins (w/AC) sleep up to 5 available to rent. Mini golf course and Water Wars extra.

PREHISTORIC FOREST: Learn the eating habits and lifestyles of dinosaurs in a forest full of them. Start your walk in the forest by going through

the volcano with a 35 foot waterfall. The volcano rumbles and smokes. Look out for the creatures that live in this place. There are Dino bones, serpent, Pterodactyl a dino egg nest and a little guy that likes to hide, he will show himself at just the right time, can you find him? Dig for dinosaur footprints and bones or get your picture taken with dinos. The T-Rex now "follows" you, the Stenonychosaurus is the brainiest, and the dinosaurs are pretty much life-size!

MYSTERY HILL: The "Illusion of Nature" House where water runs uphill and chairs stick to the walls. Is it Magnetic or Magic? In one place you feel OK and only a few inches away you feel strange. They will answer any question that have an answer. Be sure to volunteer for the fun demonstrations at Mystery Hill.

TRAIN – O – RAMA

Marblehead - 6732 East Harbor Road (Route 161 East) 43440. Phone: (419) 734-5856. www.trainorama.net. Hours: Monday-Saturday 11:00am-5:00pm, Sunday 1:00 – 5:00pm. Admission: $7.00 adult, $6.00 senior, $5.00 child (4-11). Online coupon. Miscellaneous: Train Gift Shop.

See the life-long collection and passion of Max Timmons that has become Ohio's largest operating multi-gauge model train display open to the public.

Milan

EDISON BIRTHPLACE MUSEUM

Milan - 9 Edison Drive (off State Route 250, Downtown, near exit 118 off Turnpike) 44846. Phone: (419) 499-2135. www.tomedison.org. Hours: Tuesday-Saturday 10:00am-5:00pm, Sunday 1:00-5:00pm (Summer). Tuesday-Sunday 1:00-5:00pm (April-May and September-October). Wednesday-Sunday 1:00-4:00pm (February-March and November-December). Closed Easter and January. Admission: $6.00 adult, $5.00 senior (59+), $3.00 child (6-12). Miscellaneous: The Milan Historical Museum Complex is across the street. Educators: look on their History page for Related Resources link and then Edison Related Links for bios, timelines, inventions and video.

Thomas Edison enjoying one of our favorite inventions...the Power Nap!

Edison was born here in 1847 and raised in this home until age 7. Your tour guides may be one or two of Edison's great-great-great-grandnieces. The original family mementos give you a feeling of being taken back in time. The room full of his inventions (he had 1,093 American patents) gives you a sense of his brilliance! Most famous for his invention of the light bulb and phonograph (first words recorded were "Mary had a little lamb"), you may not know he was kicked out of school for being a non-attentive/slow learner! So, his mother home-schooled him. Part of the Edison family belongings include slippers, Derby hat, cane, Mother Edison's disciplinary switch (still hanging in the original spot in the kitchen), butter molds and "Pop Goes the Weasel" yarner. Two practical inventions of the time you'll want to see are the pole ladder (a long pole that pulls out to a full size ladder) and the slipper seat (a cushioned little seat, low to the ground, so it is easier to put your slippers or shoes on).

MILAN HISTORICAL MUSEUM

Milan - 10 Edison Drive (off SR 113, Turnpike exit 118) 44846. Phone: (419) 499-2968. www.milanhistory.org. Hours: Tuesday-Saturday 10:00am-5:00pm, Sunday 1:00-5:00pm (Summer). Tuesday-Sunday 1:00-5:00pm (May, September) Admission: $6.00 adult, $5.00 senior, $3.00 child (6-12). Miscellaneous: Gift Shop with video and slide presentations. Educators: Provide excellent school tour packets of study. Some of the materials (Canals, coloring, word search) are printable online on the Teachers Resources page or the Children's Area page.

Tour includes several buildings in a complex featuring different themes like the Galpin Home of local history, dolls, toys and a collection of mechanical banks. There are several other homes along with a blacksmith and carriage shop and everything you might want to buy from the 1800's is sold in the general store. The pharmacist behind his counter would fill your prescription. On a chilly day the warmth of the pot-bellied stove drew menfolk to linger for a game of checkers. Be sure to add this to your visit to Edison's Home, one block away.

MELON FESTIVAL

Milan - Downtown, SR 113. (419) 499-4909. www.accnorwalk.com. Melons in baskets, by the slice, muskmelon ice cream and watermelon sherbet. Melon eating contests. Parade, rides, crafts and a kiddie pedal tractor pull. Free. (Labor Day Weekend)

New Washington

PUMPKIN MAZE PLAYLAND

New Washington - Iron Spring Farm, 5930 SR 103E. Pumpkin Patches / Hayrides / Corn Mazes / Fall Playland - Admission (average $6.00). Plan on at least two hours playtime. Open weekends, some weekdays (by appointment) & weeknights. www.bucyrus.org. (late September - late October).

Oberlin

OBERLIN HERITAGE CENTER

Oberlin - 73 South Professor Street, James Monroe House (State Route 38 and State Route 511) 44074. www.oberlinheritage.org/visit.html. Phone: (440) 774-1700. Hours: Tuesday, Thursday, Saturday 10:30am and 1:30pm. The tour is of most interest to adults and children above the age of 10 years. Tours last 1.25 hours and walking is involved. Summer Saturdays have more family-oriented programming suitable for children (most are FREE). Admission: $6.00 per person. Educators: Oberlin History for Kids link online with suggested games, crafts and books.

Oberlin is a town with strong ties to the Underground Railroad. The First Church in Oberlin served as headquarters for the Oberlin Anti-Slavery Society, and Oberlin's public school system was an early proponent of integration. Learn about abolition and the Underground Railroad, student life around campus through the years, and a little red school house with a collection of lunch pails and McGuffey Readers. Start the tour in James Monroe's home. He was an important abolitionist, advocate of voting rights for African Americans, and friend of Frederick Douglass. Monroe taught at Oberlin College. On display in the Jewett House is an exhibit on "Aluminum: The Oberlin Connection" that includes a recreation of Charles Martin Hall's 1886 wood shed experiment station. Maybe you'll also want to catch a movie at the Apollo, the local one-screen movie theatre that's been operating in Oberlin since the 1910s, and which introduced the "talkies" to Oberlin in 1928. (Showings cost a whopping $3.00 every day except Tuesday and Thursday, when admission is $2.00. That's hard to beat!)

HOLIDAY OPEN HOUSE

Oberlin – *Oberlin Heritage Center. Jewett House, (440) 774-1700. Gingerbread house contest display.*

Perrysville

MOHICAN-MEMORIAL STATE FOREST

Perrysville - *3060 County Road 939 44864. www.dnr.state.oh.us. Phone: (419) 938-6222.*

4,498 acres in Ashland County. Hiking trails (24 miles), bridle trails (22 miles), "Park & Pack" camping sites (10), snowmobile trails (7 miles - weather permitting), state nature preserve. Also War Memorial Shrine and Mohican State Park is adjacent.

Port Clinton

AFRICAN SAFARI WILDLIFE PARK

Port Clinton - *267 Lightner Road (Off State Route 2 exit SR 53, follow signs) 43452. Phone: (419) 732-3606 or (800) 521-2660. www.africansafariwildlifepark.com. Hours: Daily 10:00am-5:00pm (April, May, September, October). Daily 9:00am-7:00pm (Memorial Day-Labor Day).   Admission: $~11.00-$17.00 per person (summer). $3.00 discount (spring & fall). Admission ages 3+.   Miscellaneous: Safari Grill and gift shop. Jungle Junction Playland and petting zoo.*

Don't miss this unique drive-thru Safari. Get up close and personal with Nature's friends. See the "horse of a different color" - the rare white zebra! See more than 400 animals (including llamas, alpacas, and zebras) as they wander freely around your vehicle as you drive through a 100-acre park. This is the only drive through safari park in the Midwest. The giraffe lean their long necks over to check you out through your car windows. The friendliest animals

are the camels and ponies and you can ride them, too (at no additional charge). The ugliest are probably the warthogs. Another favorite is the "Porkchop Downs" pig races. Boy, do they snort loud when they're trying to win!

CRANE CREEK STATE PARK & MAGEE MARSH WILDLIFE AREA

Port Clinton - *(Rte. 2, west of Port Clinton) 43452. Phone: (419) 898-0960. Hours: Open dawn to dusk, year-round. www.stateparks.com/crane_creek.html.*

Located on the scenic shore of Lake Erie, Crane Creek State Park offers a vast freshwater marsh and spacious sandy beach for enjoyment. This coastal environment is home to more than 300 species of birds. Herons, waterfowl, warblers, gulls and the magnificent bald eagle make this park one of the best birdwatching areas in the country. We loved the boardwalk viewing, the beach and especially, the Eagle's Nests and spring migration. It's amazing how many birds come thru this area! The park was named for the abundance of blue herons - misidentified as cranes years ago. Park also has boating and swimming access to Lake Erie shores.

The boardwalk sure makes exploring easy...

GREAT LAKES POPCORN COMPANY

Port Clinton - *60 N. Madison Street (downtown) 43452. Phone: (419) 732-3080 or (866) 732-3080. www.GreatLakesPopcorn.com. Hours: Daily 10:00am-5:30pm (Sunday 11:00am-4:00pm). Extended Seasonal hours. Tours: Available for school-age children.*

Look for the bright red & white awning and listen for the "island music" as you and your children find this fun adventure! All of their equipment is located within view of customers standing at the counter. They turn the coaters at an angle so you can see inside of them and see the popcorn churning in the machines. Sample many varieties of popcorn including "Bubble Gum", "Root Beer", "Jelly Bean" and "Wild Walleye". The "Popcorn Tasting Station" is where kids and families alike can sample any, or all, of the 30 plus flavors.

JET EXPRESS

Port Clinton - *5 North Jefferson Street (docks at foot of Perry Street Bridge, SR 163) 43452. Phone: (800) 245-1JET. www.jet-express.com. Admission: Children 5 and under ride FREE! Each way is $12.00 for adults, $2.00 child (6-12) and $3.00 more for bikes. (April-October)*

Indoor and outdoor seating on the fastest catamaran to Islands. 22 minute trip with some boat facts weaved in. Nice ride and the docks are located right in the hub of activity. Free parking nearby or parking fee at terminal.

LAKE ERIE ISLANDS REGIONAL WELCOME CENTER

Port Clinton - *770 S.E. Catawba Road (just off Rte. 2 & Rte. 53 N) 43452. Phone: (800) 441-1271. www.lake-erie.com.*

The clever silhouette building design and replica dioramas inside really orient you to all the area has to offer. The staff is very friendly. The kids can gaze at the 600 gallon aquarium or do nature rubbings while the parents work out a visitors plan. Their movie theater highlights the Lake Erie region. A Kids play area resides within a replica of Oliver Hazard Perry's flagship, THE LAWRENCE, from the Battle of Lake Erie during the War of 1812. Gander at replicas of the Tin Goose, the first airplane to service the Lake Erie Islands. The Birdwatching display has an interactive telescope. Look for the replica of the Marblehead Lighthouse or listen for a Talking walleye, plus more surprises. They can also tell you about eateries in the area that specialize in perch and walleye…any way you like it. The Crow's Nest has their famous, warm Hot Apple Walnut Pie and Nate's has the tangy Sunburst Salad…both great add-ons to your fresh fish meal.

LAKE ERIE ISLANDS STATE PARK

Port Clinton - *4049 E. Moores Dock Road 43452. Phone: (866) 644-6727 for camping. www.dnr.state.oh.us. Hours: Daylight hours.*

Limestone cliffs, historic wineries, crystal caverns and a shimmering Great Lake greet visitors to the Lake Erie Islands state parks. These five state parks offer unique island retreats with an atmosphere both festive and casual. Fishing, boating and swimming can be enjoyed at each park.

CATAWBA ISLAND STATE PARK: (419) 797-4530, off SR 53.

SOUTH BASS ISLAND: (419) 285-2112 seasonally. Some overnight camping is available. See separate attraction descriptions under Put-n-Bay city listings.

KELLEY'S ISLAND STATE PARK: (reached only by ferry or boat) Six miles of hiking trails lead to scenic vistas, historic sites and two nature preserves. The islands were formed during the glacial period when massive ice sheets entered Ohio. **GLACIAL GROOVES STATE MEMORIAL** is a must see and a great way to study Ohio geology. Located on the north side of the island, the largest easily accessible grooves were formed when ice once covered solid limestone bedrock. Looking safely over fence, you see a giant groove passage that seems unbelievable. Placards along the trail detail the

history of glaciers moving through the area. Prior to the War of 1812, the Lake Erie Island region had been occupied by Ottawa and Huron (Wyandot) Indian tribes. A testimony to their existence on the islands is carved in **INSCRIPTION ROCK STATE MEMORIAL**. The flat-topped limestone slab displays carvings of animals and human figures. Discovered partly buried in the shoreline in 1833, the 32 feet by 21 feet rock is now entirely exposed (protected by a roof and viewing platform). Archaeologists believe the inscriptions date from sometime between AD 1200 and 1600. (419) 746-2546 or (419) 797-4530 (Rock) or (419) 797-4025 (Grooves).

See actual groves made by huge glaciers "creeping along"...

MONSOON LAGOON

Port Clinton - *1530 S. Danbury Rd. N (Danbury N Road exit off Rte. 2) 43452. Phone: (419) 732-6671. www.monsoonlagoonwaterpark.com. Hours: Generally 11:00am-dusk (Memorial Day weekend-Labor Day)   Admission: Rates range $10.00-$16.00 per day. Golf, boats and go-carts $5.00 extra. Coupons online. Miscellaneous: Picnics and coolers are not allowed as well as any outside food. Monsoon Lagoon offers a concession stand with very reasonable prices.*

If your kids like water and the outdoors, head over to the Monsoon Lagoon. They have Adventure Island with 150 water toys, a lazy river, two giant water slides plus eatery, mini-golf, bumper boats, go-karts and a game room. Take a ride on the six great waterslides, including the three stories tall Typhoon Rush Slide Tower or.... Splash around on the Adventure Island Tree House with one-hundred and five water play stations on seventeen different levels. Little ones can splash and play in the Little Squirts Play Pool. And Mom and Dad can relax in the adult pool.

WALLEYE MADNESS AT MIDNIGHT

Port Clinton *- downtown. A family oriented non-alcoholic event with indoor and outdoor activities such as kid's/parent's food, entertainment and crafts, and a countdown to midnight. Watch a 20 foot fiberglass walleye descend during the countdown to the New Year. www.walleyemadness.com. Admission. (New Years Eve)*

Put-in-Bay

A Ship House?

As your ferry approaches Put-in-Bay, be sure to look for a famous private residence that is actually the front part of a retired freighter, the "Benson Ford" (no tours available - just fun to see!)

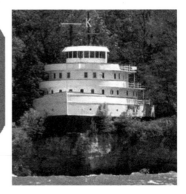

AQUATIC VISITORS CENTER

Put-in-Bay - *Peach Point   43456. Phone: (419) 285-3701 or (419) 625-0062. Hours: Tuesday-Saturday 11:00am - 6:00pm. (May - August). Admission: FREE.*

The Ohio Division of Wildlife invites kids to learn about fish and fishing. Displays highlight the story of this historic fish hatchery, live fish exhibits, Ohio's fishery resources, the wealth of recreational fishing activity offered on Lake Erie, and hands-on children's activities. A children's playroom includes a touch tank, coloring activities, wooden puzzles, wildlife videos and a hands-on fishing game. Kids can fish off the docks with rod and bait provided.

BUTTERFLY HOUSE

Put-in-Bay - *979 Catawba Avenue (on grounds of Perry's Cave Family Fun Center) 43456. Phone: (419) 285-2446. www.perryscave.com. Hours: Daily 9:00am-6:00pm (summer - May thru September). Weekends only April and October. Admission: $7.50 adult, $4.50 child (6-12).*

Walk among hundreds of exotic butterflies in their fully-enclosed garden. Enjoy the tranquil environment with soothing fountain, Koi fish pond & lush flowers and soothing music. The kids will enjoy the secret walkways throughout the garden to get up close with the butterflies in their natural environment. Teach the kids about how butterflies are created by asking staff questions. A 15-minute educational presentation is also included at no extra charge. Stay as long as your heart desires. Unique educational gift shop including framed butterfly specimens, nature gifts, candles & ceramics, butterfly & Put-in-Bay souvenirs.

CHOCOLATE CAFÉ & MUSEUM

Put-in-Bay - *820 Catawba Avenue 43456. www.chocolateohio.com. Phone: (419) 734-7114. Hours: Daily 7:00am-10:30pm (May-September). Miscellaneous: Golf Cart Rentals available. Receive one free pound of chocolate with a daily cart rental.*

Visit a fun Chocolate Museum and learn the history and making of chocolate! Featuring South Bend Chocolate Company handmade chocolates (our favorite Indiana chocolate factory tour!) Learn the history and making of chocolate while viewing a fine collection of antique chocolate collectibles. Learn even more about chocolate - watch a film, or have your picture taken with Lucy at the Chocolate Factory. The unique bistro celebrates fine chocolate & coffee. Decadent cheesecakes and ice cream treats guarantee something for everyone.

NC Area

CRYSTAL CAVE & HEINEMAN'S GRAPE JUICE WINERY

Put-in-Bay - *Catawba Ave. 43456. www.heinemanswinery.com/crystal_cave.cfm. Phone: (419) 285-3412. Hours: Daily (early May-Late September). Call for schedule (basically 10:00am-5:00pm except Noon on Sundays) Admission: $6.00 adult, $3.00 child (6-11).*

The Crystal Cave (located below the factory) is well worth the visit! Discovered by workers in 1897 while digging a well for the winery 40 feet above them. The walls of this cave are covered in strontium sulfate, a bluish mineral called celestite. These crystals range from 8 to 18 inches long. The original cave was much smaller than what appears today, as

Inside the "Crystal Cave"...Very Unique!

crystals were harvested and sold for the manufacturing of fireworks. You'll walk right into the world's largest geode! Every crystal (mostly bluish green) has 14 sides. We promise a WOW on this one! Another tour option is the juice/ wine factory. Although you may be hesitant to have children tour a winery, they really put emphasis on the grapes (varieties, flavor, color, etc.) and the chemistry of making juice. Did you know they use air bags to press the juice out of grapes?

LAKE ERIE ISLANDS MUSEUM

Put-in-Bay - *441 Catawba Avenue (adjacent to the Put-in-Bay Town Hall parking lot) 43456. Phone: (419) 285-2804. www.leihs.org. Hours: Daily 11:00am-5:00pm (May, June and September). Daily 10:00am-6:00pm (July and August). Weekends only in October. Admission is $2.00 (age 12+). Miscellaneous: Island Bike Rental, 419-285-2016. Bicycles can be rented near both boat docks. Children's seats and helmets are available. Golf carts are also available. Rates range from $10 to $16 per hour, depending on the number of seats.*

Boating, sailors, and shipping industry artifacts. Video shown is an excellent trip to the past. Why did so many Grand Hotels burn? What are the major industries on the island...a hint...one is a fruit! Usually live displays of Box Turtles, Painted Turtles, and island snakes can be seen at the wildlife building. Look for ship models scattered throughout.

PERRY'S CAVE & FAMILY FUN CENTER

Put-in-Bay - *979 Catawba Avenue (South Bass Island, 1/2 mile from town) 43456. Phone: (419) 285-2405. www.perryscave.com. Admission: $7.50 adult, $4.50 child (6-12). Lantern Tours $20.00 per person (includes t-shirt) - must have at least 4 in group. Other amusements are an additional $4.50-$7.50. Tours: Daily 10:30am - 6:00pm. Tours leave every 20 minutes in the summer. Fewer times rest of year.*

Inside the cave you'll see walls covered with calcium carbonate (the same ingredient in antacids) that has settled from years of dripping water. Rumor says Perry kept prisoners and stored supplies in the cave during the Battle of Lake Erie. At the Gem Mining Company, mine for real gems and minerals. After-hours lantern tours available by reservation. Chart your course around the War of 18 Holes, the brand new 18-hole miniature golf course with a War of 1812 theme. In the Antique Car Museum, stroll through the past as you view Ford Model A's & T's as well as the island's oldest automobile. Find your way in Fort Amazen. The Butterfly House has a separate listing.

PERRY'S VICTORY AND INTERNATIONAL PEACE MEMORIAL

Put-In-Bay - *93 Delaware Avenue (Ohio Turnpike to SR 53 and SR 2. There are several ferry lines that service the island, the Jet Express, The Miller Boat Line, and the Rocket) 43456. Phone: (419) 285-2184. www.nps.gov/pevi. Hours: Daily 10:00am-7:00pm (Mid-June - Labor Day). Daily 10:00am-5:00pm (Late April - Mid-June & September and mid-October). Daily 10:00am-6:00pm (mid-May to mid-June). Admission: $3.00 per person (age 17 and up). Must climb two flights of stairs first for elevator to top of monument.*

Built of pink granite, 352 feet high and 45 feet in diameter, this memorial commemorates the Battle of Lake Erie and then the years of peace. Commodore Perry commanded the American fleet in the War of 1812. In September of 1813 he defeated the British and Perry then sent his famous message to General William Henry Harrison "We have met the enemy and they are ours". Interpretive actors outside chat with you on busy days and weekends. The new Visitors Center facility has extensive exhibits, an auditorium featuring a film with surround sound,

"We have met the enemy and they are ours"

and an expanded bookstore. The exhibits tell the story of the Battle of Lake Erie, the War of 1812, construction of the monument and the international peace that it represents. A live feed camera system provides views from the top of the monument enabling those who are unable or decide not to make the trip to the observation deck to witness the view. The DVD presentation of the War of 1812 and the Battle of Lake Erie are so worth seeing.

JULY 4TH CELEBRATION

Put-in-Bay – *Perry's Victory Memorial. 3 days full of parades, rides, entertainment, reenactments and fireworks.*

_____

HISTORICAL WEEKEND

Put-In-Bay - *Perry's Victory Memorial. www.lake-erie.com or (800) 441-1271. Military living history camps with displays of Indian wars to the present. Boy Scout camporee. Parade, live entertainment. (second long weekend in September).*

_____

PUT-IN-BAY TOUR TRAIN

Put-In-Bay - *(South Bass Island) 43456. www.put-in-bay-trans.com. Phone: (419) 285-4855. Hours: Daily 10:00am-5:00pm (Memorial Day-Labor Day). Weekends Only (May and September). Admission: $10.00 adult, $3.50 child (6-12)   Miscellaneous: South Bass Island State Park, 419-797-4530, 419-285-2112, Reservations: (866) OHIOPARKS. Stone beach, ice skating, flush restrooms with showers (summer*

only), ice fishing, campsites, cabins (a combination of cabins & tents, picnic shelter, launch ramp, and fishing pier.

A tram departs frequently from the village depot for an one hour tour of the island. Stops include Perry's Cave, Heineman's Winery, Crystal Cave, War of 18 Holes Miniature Golf Course, Alaskan Wildlife Museum, and Perry's Victory and International Peace Memorial. Departing every 30 minutes, the train trolley allows passengers to depart and re-board (without additional cost) at any time. The tour is especially interesting and gives a clear understanding of all that occupied the island thru the years.

STONE LABORATORY

Put-in-Bay - *Field Station, Box 119 43456. Phone: (614) 247-6504 or (419) 285-2341. http://ohioseagrant.osu.edu/stonelab/. Hours: Workshops (open mid-April thru October). Wednesdays in the summer, they co-host Put-in-Bay Eco-History (a.k.a. Passport) tours open to everyone. Admission: Workshops: $20.00-$40.00 per student (4th grade and up). Meals and lodging extra. Field Station Tours: $10.00 per person. All workshops and tours are prearranged and require transport to the Island from Put-in-Bay or privately. Tours: Four-Site Passport Package (includes only South Bass Island Lighthouse, ODNR. Aquatic Visitors Center, Lake Erie Islands Historical Society, and Perry's Victory & International Peace Monument) Five-Site Passport Package (includes admission to the all of the sites above, including Stone Laboratory on Gibraltar Island).*

Stone Lab's science workshop program offers a variety of activities ranging from water sampling on a research vessel in the lake, to identifying microscopic aquatic organisms you've collected, or dissecting fish in a lab. You can specialize island activities by adding an invertebrate walk, bird walk, edible plant walk, exotic species slide show, or seining. Groups may arrange a one-hour historical/scientific tour of the Gibraltar Island facilities. Cooke Castle, Perry's Lookout, glacial grooves, and brief classroom activities will provide participants with a well-rounded program overview.

Rittman

APPLE FESTIVAL

Rittman - *Bauman Orchards, 161 Rittman Avenue. ww.baumanorchards.com. Apples & cider. Apple pie eating contests. Apple peeling contests. Apple butter. Candy apples. Wagon/hayrides. Apple Dumplings, Fritters, Donuts, etc. Parades. Pioneer crafts. Petting Zoo. (last two Saturdays in September, first Saturday in October)*

Sandusky

CASTAWAY BAY

Sandusky - *2001 Cleveland Road (at the entrance to Cedar Point Causeway) 44870. Phone: (419) 627-2106. www.castawaybay.com. Hours: Generally 9:00am-9:00pm. Closed some Tuesdays and Wednesdays (visit website for calender).*

In the elaborate enclosed natural setting of palm trees, huts, inland lagoons and plenty of water lies numerous water attractions. Highlights include a tall water roller coaster that propels riders uphill, then downhill; a dozen water slides; a large wave pool w/ 3 foot waves; an action pool with water basketball and floating logs; concessions and the center attraction: a gigantic multi-story interactive play area including a 1,000 gallon tipping bucket that downpours every few minutes. The waterpark is open to overnight guests at the resort featuring rooms starting at $200 per night. Day Passes run $29.00 per person (without overnight stay). Each overnight stay includes park admission for three to six, depending on the size of room. All rooms feature extras such as microwave and mini-frig. The resort has two mid-priced restaurants, an indoor pool, whirlpool, exercise room, arcade and adjacent marina within the property.

CEDAR POINT & SOAK CITY

Sandusky - *State Route 4 (I-80 to Exit 118 or 110. Follow Signs) 44870. Phone: (419) 627-2350. www.cedarpoint.com. Hours: Vary by season. (May-October). Generally open at 10:00 or 11:00am until dark. Admission: $20.00-45.00, Small children (under 48") – General (ages 4-59). Children age 2 and under are FREE. Separate admission for Soak City ($17.00-$30.00). Combo, 2 day & Starlight rates. Parking $10.00. Miscellaneous: Stroller rental. Picnic area. Food Service. Miniature golf. CHALLENGE PARK (additional admission)– Rip cord Sky coaster (fall 150 feet and then swing in a 300-foot arc. Grand Prix Raceway.*

More rides than any other parks in the world! The amusement extravaganza on the shores of Lake Erie includes 17 Roller Coasters and a total of 70 rides. Most new rides are super thrillers, not for kids, but maybe the parents. Here are some of the themed areas or rides: SOAK CITY – wave pool, water slides, Adventure Cove, Eerie Falls (get wet in the dark). LIVE SHOWS – 50's, Motown, Country, Ice Shows. CHAOS – turn sideways & upside down at the same time. MILLENNIUM & MAGNUM XL - tallest and best coasters. MAVERICK in Frontiertown. CAMP SNOOPY, PLANET SNOOPY & KIDDY KINGDOM - with piped-in kids music and child sized play like Red Baron airplanes, Woodstock's express family coaster, Peanuts 500 Speedway. Also Sing-along Show with Peanuts characters. And, of course, the traditional carousels and classic spinning/ circular rides. Cedar Point continues to hold the title of "Best Amusement Park in the World."

GOODTIME I

Sandusky - *(docked at Jackson Street Pier) 44870. Phone: (419) 625-9692 or (800) 446-3140. www.goodtimeboat.com. Admission: $15.00 - $25.00 (ages 4 and up) Tours: Depart 9:30am, Arrive back 6:30pm (Memorial Day-Labor Day). Tuesday night cruises available.*

The M/V Goodtime I is a sleek all-steel vessel built for ocean-going cruises. She is 117 feet long and Coast Guard approved to carry 355 Passengers. The Goodtime I Departs from Sandusky, Ohio daily on a Daytime Island Hopping Cruise. Stop for awhile at each island.

GREAT WOLF LODGE INDOOR WATERPARK

Sandusky - *4600 Milan Road (SR250) (Ohio Turnpike, exit 118, north on SR250) 44870. Phone: (419) 609-6000 or (888) 779-BEAR. www.greatwolflodge.com. Hours: Waterpark daily 9:00am-10:00pm. Wristbands are good day of arrival until closing the next day. Checkout is 10:30am. Admission: Lodge room suites include 4-6 waterpark passes. Rooms vary from $149-$300+ per night. Additional*

waterpark passes $20.00 each. Check out local supermarket discounts online. Miscellaneous: All suites: Family, KidCabin (log cabin in room with bunk beds), microwave, refrigerator. Arcade and outdoor pools, gift shops. Bring Coast Guard approved swim vests for non-swimmers (limited number of vests available at park, too). This park is excellent for kids 11 and under. Check out the wonderful holiday theme packages they offer for Easter, Fall Harvest, Thanksgiving and Christmastime.

Well, we've gone to explore this family-friendly resort several times....and the verdict...we are always VERY impressed! Even though it's a resort...it still was comfy for the both kids and parents. Bring you own food to prepare or eat in one of two on site restaurants - GITCHIE GOOMIE GRILL and LUMBER JACK'S COOK SHANTY (pass it around family style). All the kid's menu prices for both restaurants are around $5.00 and includes beverage & dessert. BEAR TRACK LANDING Indoor Waterpark is the highlight! The minute you step into the Outdoor/Northwoods ambiance (and gently heated, no musty or chlorine smell-they ozonate the water) you have

The best place for fun with friends and family...

hours of fun. Your favorite treehouse, Fort Mackenzie, is now home to two new Otter Run body slides. Play as you may in the 4-story interactive fun center featuring 12 levels of water based antics or get "dunked" by the giant bucket. If you don't scream from excitement in the Fort, you're sure to on the giant inner tube slides (best for elementary ages and up). In 5 pools (all age levels), 7 waterslides, and the water fort you'll find watchful and helpful lifeguards - there for safety and are excellent for crowd control. Smaller guests will delight in the redesigned Soak'n Oak Springs, a water play fort, just for toddlers, complete with slides and water spouting bear cubs. Teens and Tweeners can take on the challenge of climbing an Aqua Rock Wall (additional fee required). Take breaks. Two areas for the 10 and under crowd are the nightly Story time by the lobby fireplace (come in your pajamas) or the craft room, Cubs Cabin. Each month they change the seasonal theme of the crafts offered and most are free. The staff and quality of craft received high ratings from our crew! With a little planning of resources, you will get your money's worth in memories and fun for sure!

KALAHARI INDOOR WATERPARK RESORT

Sandusky - *7000 Kalahari Drive (located on State Route 250, just 10 minutes south of Cedar Point) 44870. www.kalahariresort.com. Phone: (419) 433-7200 or (877) KALAHARI. Admission: Overnight packages (lodging, waterpark, dry play area included) run $129.00-$349.00 per night. Waterpark only: $39.00-$42.00 for all day pass. Miscellaneous: Check-in is 4:00pm, Checkout is 11:00am. You may stay to play after checkout until 3:00pm that day. Other dry spaces include an indoor playground, small indoor mini-golf course, Pottery Pizzazz create station and they have daily crafts (especially loved the cookie decorating).*

Welcome to the largest indoor waterpark in the U.S.!!! Guests enter an authentic African-themed environment with safari bellmen, giant elephant

and rhino sculptures, and there's even a live baby lion cub habitat. Now, with the latest expansion, many may be curious how much better bigger could be? With a tween and teen in tow (our fav ages to recommend for this park as it is mostly "high adventure on safari"), we ventured north to find out.

WATERPARK: You can choose from a water treehouse, lazy river or water sport pools, but the kids over 10 spend more time in the rides area. Kids Favs: the Zip Coaster (extreme exhilaration, especially at the beginning-keep your head low) and the Victoria Falls family raft slide. Parents Favorites: the indoor/outdoor hot tub (in the winter, snowflakes melt on your nose). The new area is bright and inviting – and, actually makes the whole park appear more well-lit. Brighter lighting comes from the Texlon Transparent Roof over much of the new area. The "intelligent" roof system creates a comfortable vacation "feel" allowing natural light in while softening the acoustics. Now, what do you do first? We mistakenly went down the extreme Tanzanian Twister ("toilet bowl ride") as our first ride of the weekend. Once we caught our breath at the bottom – I think we actually liked it! The new Rippling Rhino family raft ride was next and not as extreme (but it was almost totally in the dark). I told you, high adventure! And the Wave Pool – so nice and wide and warm (other indoor wave pools tend to be smaller and cold). The "action" waves ride longer than most making this our family's favorite indoor waterpark wave pool! Now, with two indoor Flow Riders – your tweens and teens don't have any excuse to not try the ride. Give them some encouragement and you'll be amazed at what they can do. Outside (open

The Flowrider was soooo coool!

seasonally) are volleyball courts and attractions for the little ones and lively ones from slides to fountains. (Preschool Note: under 42" youngster set in tow? The new indoor Kids Safari is a much needed area for them – its two tall giraffes welcome kids to a "safe" play area just for them – set off to the side away from the "buzz" of action).

DINING: Kahunaville was our top priority. Plan to bring the kids around 5:00-7:00pm dinnertime when they have a DJ playing all the hip tunes. About 3 times per hour, the DJ begins a new activity such as a coloring contest, limbo, chicken dance, or line dancing. Multi-colored exotic lighting excites the kids to activity while the grown-ups watch or catch a game on the big screens. It's a party environment, for sure. Most entrees have an Asian bent and "pineapple" and "firecracker" are examples of two words used in descriptions. Try one of those festively decorated kids beverages or some fun exotic appetizer with sticks and color shooting everywhere. The Great Karoo Marketplace Restaurant features a lavish buffet with some African/Asian inspired items (you can order from the menu also). Unusual breakfast casseroles and the cinnamon buns were the hit in our family. We noticed many of the tables were set up for, and occupied by, parties of 6-8 to 10. Karoo was definitely a haven for multi-family vacationers. Other "snack stops" were the Café Mirage (the 20" Big Kahuna is the biggest pizza we've ever had) and Zulu Grille. The Café is across from the arcade – so, with a twenty minute wait – we HAD to use the time wisely playing games. Our old favorite is Skeeball, our new favorite is Deal/No Deal. Daniel won 200 tickets one game! We also liked having the Zulu Grille right smack in the middle of the rides – with plenty of tables to sit

down and eat at. Once you're in the park and wet – a quick bite "fits in" to the "happy family plan" at times. Because they make fresh product most every day, the Candy Hut's (located in main lobby) dipped pretzels and cheese/caramel corn were crunchy and perfectly seasoned. (dining budget note: every room has a minimum of a mini micro/frig unit. We noticed in-house Pizza Pub room service deliveries were abundant. Use discount coupons and order extra for reheats later. Plus, almost every guest checking in brought a large cooler – full of snacks, sodas and frozen entrees maybe?)

ROOMS: All rooms and suites include waterpark wristbands, at least one TV, micro/frig and coffee makers. Add bunk beds, Murphy beds or sofa beds for

four or more guests. The Village Suite is just perfect for large parties as each family has their own "space" for privacy yet a large communal full kitchen, dining and family room for fellowship. Once you're inside the resort complex, plan on staying cozy inside your entire stay. With so much to do and eat, it would take you a week to play, relax and taste everything you wanted to. (Budget note: check out their online specials – if you're somewhat flexible with your dates, you can get a room for $119.00 per

Back at the suite...it was a chocolate fountain...life is good!

night/family. And their packages/add-ons are a nice value treat. Get a wonderful mother/daughter pedicure or try a cabana rental).

LAGOON DEER PARK

Sandusky - *1502 Martins Point Road, State Route 269 (between State Route 2 and US 6) 44870. Phone: (419) 684-5701. www.lagoondeerpark.com. Hours: Daily 10:00am-6:00pm (May - mid-October). Admission: $8.00 adult, $4.00 child (3-12). Pay Fishing available in stocked lake.*

Hand feed and pet hundreds of deer, llamas, miniature donkeys and other tame species. Altogether, they have 250 exotic animals from Europe, Japan, Asia, South and North America. Approximately 75 baby animals are born here each year.

MAUI SANDS INDOOR WATERPARK RESORT

Sandusky - *5513 Milan Road (intersection of SR 250 & SR 2 44870. Phone: (888) STAY MSR. www.mauisandsresort.com. Hours: Daily Noon-11:00pm. Admission: Day Passes run $39.00 per day (age 3+). Day Passes are provided based on resort occupancy. Lodging rates vary from $109 to $269 base (waterpark admission is included). Miscellaneous: 70 cabanas for rental. Overnight Rooms (connected to waterpark): Guests can choose from five price tiers that include a mix of unique suite and room types. 1. Royalty Suites - Three-room suites with a living room and two separate bedrooms; 2. Island Paradise Suites - Family suites with kids-only bunk bed tiki huts, in-room whirlpools or SurfRider-side lanais; 3. Sweet Escape Suites - Family suites with kids-only bunk bed tiki huts; 4. Ocean Breeze-Hawaiian tropical rooms with two queen beds; 5. Coastline Comfort - Holiday Inn Express rooms go Hawaiian, with complimentary breakfast.*

Maui Sands Indoor Waterpark Resort is the second-largest indoor waterpark in Sandusky..second only to Kalahari…and introduces a few water rides that are new to the area. Riders will get to experience a bowl ride, which shoots people down a slide into a bowl that will eventually pull them through the bottom. Also inside the park is the SurfRider attraction. The SurfRider is a stationary wave that creates a never-ending two-foot high Waikiki breaker. The attraction pushes out 150,000 gallons of water per minute with a 16-inch high water flow and riders can either bodyboard or stand up. It is the only deep-water standing wave generator in existence in North America and riders use a real finned surfboard. The kiddie areas feature milder waterslides and an aquatic play structure. Then there's a teen activity center equipped with basketball hoops, two 40-person heated whirlpool spas (one inside and one outside), and a lazy river. On the dry side is a huge video game arcade and a full-service salon and spa. Several dining options all feature either seafood or American fare with an Hawaiian flare. This 55,000-square-foot water playground features more than 10 state-of-the-art water attractions including daredevil slides, adventurous activity pools, and attractions for kids ages two to 92.

NC Area

MERRY-GO-ROUND MUSEUM

Sandusky - *West Washington and Jackson Streets (State Route 6, downtown) 44870. Phone: (419) 626-6111. www.merrygoroundmuseum.org. Hours: Monday-Saturday 11:00am-5:00pm. Sunday Noon - 5:00pm (Summer). Weekends Only (January & February). Wednesday - Sunday (Rest of the Year). Admission: $5.00 adult, $4.00 senior (60+), $3.00 child (4-14). Includes carousel ride. Tours: Guided tours of the current exhibition are scheduled. Miscellaneous: Gift Shop.*

This colorful, bright, big museum was the former Post Office. Once inside, you'll see all sorts of carousel memorabilia and history. Each year, a new exhibit space is highlighted with colorful displays of carousel designers or companies. Next, tour the workshop to watch craftsman make carousel horses with authentic "old world" tools. Finally, ride the Herschel 1930's indoor merry-go-round.

Tiffin

TIFFIN-SENECA HERITAGE FESTIVAL

Tiffin - Hedges Boyer Park. (888) SENECA1. Living history village and entertainment, food, fireworks. Tours of area glass factory (888-298-7236). (third weekend in September)

Upper Sandusky

INDIAN MILL

Upper Sandusky - *State Route 23 and State Route 67 to Route 47 (along the banks of the Sandusky River) 43351. www.ohiohistory.org/places/indian. Phone: (419) 294-3349 or (800) 600-7147. Hours: Friday – Sunday 1:00 – 6:00pm (Memorial Day – Labor Day), weekends only in September and October. Admission: $1.00 Adult, $.50 Youth (6-12).*

In a scenic location along the Sandusky River, Indian Mill, built in 1861, is the nation's first educational museum of milling in its original structure. The restored three-story structure replaces the original one-story building that the U.S. government built in 1820 to reward the loyalty of local Wyandot Indians during the War of 1812. Many exhibits are placed around the original mill machinery. The restored miller's office displays the history of milling from prehistoric times to the present.

Vermilion

FESTIVAL OF THE FISH

Vermilion - Downtown. Victory Park. http://vermilionohioharbourtown.homestead. com/VermilionOhioFestivalOfTheFish.html. Walleye and perch sandwiches, "crazy" craft race, entertainment, crafts and a lighted boat parade. FREE. (Fathers Day Weekend)

WOOLLYBEAR FESTIVAL

Vermilion - Downtown. Main Street. www.vermilionohio.com. (440) 967-4477. An annual tribute to the weather "forecasting" woollybear caterpillar with a huge parade, caterpillar races, woollybear contests for kids, crafts and entertainment. FREE. (first Sunday in October)

INLAND SEAS MARITIME MUSEUM & LIGHTHOUSE

Vermillion - 480 Main Street (2 miles North of State Route 60 / OH 2 intersection) 44089. Phone: (440) 967-3467 or (800) 893-1485. www.inlandseas.org. Hours: Daily 10:00am-5:00pm (May-September). See website for hours remainder of year. Admission: $6.00 adult, $5.00 senior and child (6-12).

The museum celebrates adventures of the Great Lakes including models, photographs, instruments, a steam tug engine, and a 1905 pilothouse. Special artifacts are the timbers from the Niagara (Admiral Perry's 1812 ship) and an 1847 lighthouse built with a 400 foot catwalk to the mainland. Take the family on a unique underwater adventure as an interactive exhibit lets you dive the Great Lakes shipwreck of your choice. Nautical gift shop does not require admission.

Wellington

FINDLEY STATE PARK

Wellington - 25381 State Route 58 (3 miles South of Wellington on State Route 58) 44090. Phone: (440) 647-4490. www.dnr.state.oh.us.

Once a state forest, Findley State Park is heavily wooded with stately pines and various hardwoods. The scenic hiking trails allow nature lovers to view spectacular wildflowers and observe wildlife. One area of the park is set aside as a sanctuary for the Duke's skipper butterfly, an extremely rare insect. 931 acres of camping, hiking trails, bike rentals, nature programs, boating and rentals (paddles and electric only), fishing, swimming with beach and winter sports. 3 "Conestoga" camper cabins are available from April through October to overnight camp.

Willard

CELERYVILLE, BUURMA VEGETABLE FARMS

Willard - *4200 Broadway (Route 224 West to Route 103 South to Celeryville) 44890. Phone: (419) 935-3633. www.buurmafarms.com. Hours: Weekdays (June-September) just watching. Tours: 20+ people required.*

Judged one of the best industrial tours in the state, this is a 3000-acre organic "muck" vegetable garden. On tour you'll see greenhouses, celery and radish harvesting machines in

> Did you know each year this farm plants over 1 billion radish seeds, and if planted in a continuous row, would circumnavigate the world?

action, and vegetable processing (cleaning, pruning) and packaging. You'll love the facts and figures it takes to produce veggies. Although started with celery growing, the area now never grows celery (soil conditions prevent it).

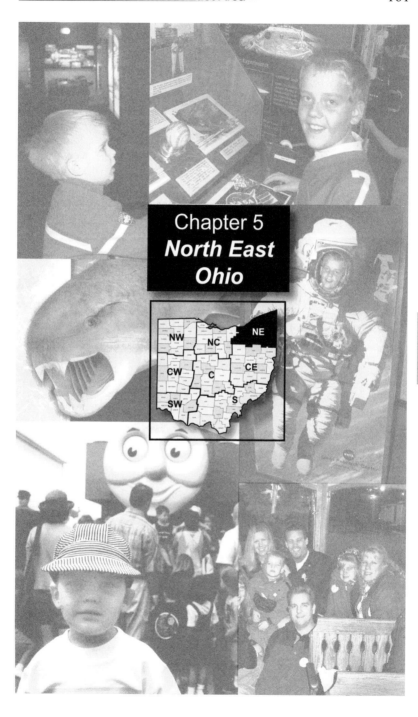

Chapter 5
*North East
Ohio*

Akron

- Akron Aeros
- Akron Symphony Orchestra
- Akron Zoo
- All American Soap Box Derby
- First Night Akron
- Goodyear World Of Rubber
- Portage Lakes State Park
- Stan Hywet Hall
- Weathervane Playhouse

Amherst

- Pumpkin Maze Playland

Andover

- Pymatuning State Park

Ashtabula

- Ashtabula Marine Museum
- Covered Bridge Pizza
- Hubbard House And Underground Railroad Museum

Aurora

- Wildwater Kingdom

Avon

- Duct Tape Festival

Bath

- Hale Farm And Village

Berlin Center

- Noah's Lost Ark Animal Sanctuary

Brecksville

- Cuyahoga Valley National Park

Brunswick

- Mapleside Farms
- Mapleside Farms Restaurant

Burton

- Century Village Museum & Store

Canfield

- Canfield Fair

Chardon

- Geauga County Maple Festival
- Pioneer Waterland And Dry Park

Cleveland

- A Christmas Story House
- Children's Museum Of Cleveland
- Cleveland Botanical Garden
- Cleveland Lakefront State Park
- Cleveland Metroparks Zoo & Rainforest
- Cleveland Museum Of Art
- Cleveland Museum Of Natural History
- Cleveland National Air Show
- Cleveland Orchestra
- Cleveland Playhouse
- Cleveland Sports
- Federal ReserVe Bank Learning Center And Money Museum
- Good Time III
- Grand Prix Of Cleveland
- Great Lakes Science Center
- Kidsfest, Cleveland
- Lolly The Trolley Tours
- Malley's Chocolates
- Memphis Kiddie Park
- Nasa Glenn Research Center
- Nautica Queen
- Rock And Roll Hall Of Fame Museum
- Steamship William G. Mather Museum
- U.S.S. Cod
- Western Reserve History Museum

Cleveland (Berea)

- Irish Cultural Festival

Cleveland (Brookpark)

- Cleveland Christmas Connection
- I-X Indoor Amusement Park

Cortland

- Mosquito Lake State Park

Cuyahoga Falls

- Festival Of Lights

Fairport Harbor

- Fairport Harbor Marine Museum

Geneva

- Geneva State Park
- Great Lakes Medieval Faire

Hinckley

- Buzzard Day

NE Area

Jefferson
- AC & J Scenic Railroad
- Ashtabula Covered Bridge Fest
- Jefferson Depot
- Victorian Perambulator Museum

Kirtland
- Holden Arboretum
- Lake Farmpark

Lake Milton
- Lake Milton State Park

Medina
- Elm Farm - Museum & Ice Cream
- Ice Festival

Mentor
- Lawnfield - Garfield Home Site

Middlefield
- Middlefield Cheese House
- Pumpkin Maze Playland

Newbury
- Punderson Manor House Resort
- Punderson State Park Resort
- Westwoods Park

Niles
- McKinley Birthplace & Museum

Painesville
- Headlands Beach State Park

Peninsula
- Cuyahoga Valley Scenic Railroad

Portage
- Tinker's Creek State Park

Ravenna
- West Branch State Park

Twinsburg
- Twins Days Festival

Vienna
- Wagon Trails Animal Park

Warren
- Most Magnificent McDonalds
- National Packard Museum

Youngstown
- Butler Institute Of American Art
- Children's Museum Of The Valley
- First Night Youngstown
- Gorant Candies
- Mill Creek Park
- Youngstown Historical Center Of Industry & Labor
- Youngstown Symphony

NE Area

A Quick Tour of our Hand-Picked Favorites Around...

North East Ohio

On your way to visit a major well-known attraction in the Cleveland/Akron area, you might not realize there are some very unique kid-friendly places hidden just around the corner. **Lake Farmpark** (Kirtland, far east side of Cleveland) – not really a farm – it's a park about farming - is a good example. Their focus is to discover where food and natural products come from so on any given day you might be able to milk a cow, card wool, watch honeybees at work or go down below the earth to see where plants get their start! On your way downtown, arrange a **Malleys Chocolate Factory** tour. Live the fantasy of making, molding, wrapping and boxing chocolates. Free samples, too.

Many folks know about Marblehead lighthouse but few have visited **Fairport Marine Museum** in Fairport Harbor, near Mentor. The highlight of this museum has to be the real lighthouse (and the inexpensive admission price)! After you proudly climb the 69 steps, catch your breath with a beautiful view of Lake Erie.

Still want more of the outdoors? Two favorite parks of ours are in this region of the state: **Cuyahoga Valley National Park** (south of Cleveland) and **Mill Creek Park** in Youngstown. Some of the best kept, cleanest parks you'll want to visit offer more than just great hikes – they also offer canals, gristmills, gardens or train rides and, best of all, seasonal festivals to engage little ones' sense of wonder.

You'll find some pretty old stuff around this area, too. Meet a mastodon or Dunk, a fearsome 16-foot long armored fish with huge self-sharpening jaws at the **Cleveland Museum of Natural History**. More "old stuff" and characters pretending like they're really from the old days is well-played out at **Hale Farm and Village** in Bath, near Peninsula.

Sites and attractions are listed in order by City, Zip Code, and Name. Symbols indicated represent:

 Festivals   Restaurants   Lodging

Akron

STAN HYWET HALL

Akron *- 714 North Portage Path (I-77 or I-71 to State Route 18, follow signs into town) 44303. Phone: (330) 836-5533. www.stanhywet.org. Hours: Wednesday-Sunday 10:00am-4:30pm, until 6:30pm on Thursdays (April-New Years). Closed January-March for maintenance. Admission: $12.00 adult, $6.00 child (6-17) - self guided. Add several dollars for a guided tour. Seniors and Military half off admission on Tuesdays. Miscellaneous: Family Members can also join the Kids Club. Museum Store, Carriage House Café. Special event Nooks and Crannies tour is more of an adventure into secret passages and doors (added cost). Family Friendly Days and Vintage Baseball games select weekends during the summer.*

Want to pretend you're visiting old rich relatives for tea? – this is the place. The long driveway up to the home is beautifully landscaped. You can park right next to the home and carriage house (vs. a block away) and are greeted as an invited guest. The actual family photographs of the Seiberling Family (Frank was the co-founder of the Goodyear Tire and Rubber Company) scattered throughout the home make you feel as if you know them. Stan Hywet means "stone quarry" referring to the stone quarry the house was built on and the stone that was supplied for building. Being an English Tudor, it is rather dark inside with an almost "castle-like" feeling (the detailed wood panels and crown molding are magnificent). Try to count the fireplaces (23) and discover concealed telephones behind the paneled walls. The Corbin Conservatory, a 7,600 square-foot Gothic replication of the original 1915 building, is a complimentary addition to the grounds. Track Butterflies in Flight (seasonally) or explore other garden exhibits.

STAN HYWET'S DECK THE HALL

Akron - The manor House is decorated for the holidays and the grounds and gardens offer a winter wonderland of lights. The Carriage House Museum Store is open with specially selected gift items, and the Café serves hot chocolate, cookies, and other holiday fare. (daily except Monday evenings late November thru December)

AKRON ZOO

Akron - 500 Edgewood Avenue (Perkins Woods Park, I-77 exit 21C, Route 59 east) 44307. Phone: (330) 375-2525. www.akronzoo.com. Hours: Daily 10:00am-5:00pm (May-October). Daily 11:00am-4:00pm (November-April). Closed New Year's Day, Thanksgiving, Christmas Eve and Christmas Day. Admission: $10.00 adult, $7.50 senior, $6.00 child (2-14). Small parking fee. Reduced winter admission. Miscellaneous: Concessions. You also are permitted to bring food into the zoo. There are several picnic areas available on a first come, first serve basis. Educators: click on "Our Animals" link for info and pics about each animal (great start for reports).

The 50-acre Akron Zoo is one of 214 accredited world conservation zoos. When you visit the zoo, you'll come nose-to-nose with more than 700 animals, including endangered Humboldt penguins, snow leopards, Sumatran tigers, jaguars and Komodo dragons. The zoo features Monkey Island, The River Otter Exhibit, and an Ohio Farmyard petting area. Visit the Asian Trail with Tiger Valley, the red pandas, and the barking deer. The exhibit "Wild Prairie" includes prairie dogs and black-footed ferrets. Check out the new Jellyfish exhibit and It's a Wild World Show.

SNACK WITH SANTA

Akron – Akron Zoo. Bring the kids and grandkids to the zoo to feed the penguins, decorate cookies, create a holiday craft and have a picture taken with Santa. Admission. (second & third weekend in December)

AKRON AEROS

Akron - Canal Park, downtown 44308. Phone: (330) 253-5151 or (800) 97-AEROS. www.akronaeros.com.

Minor league baseball with ticket prices ranging $5.00-10.00. AA affiliate of the Cleveland Indians. Special events like Little League Nights and fireworks. Orbit, the Akron Aeros loveable mascot, invites you to become a member of the Akron Aeros Kids Club that includes souvenirs, free game tickets and special parties.

NE Area

AKRON SYMPHONY ORCHESTRA

Akron - 17 N. Broadway, 44308. www.akronsymphony.org. Phone: (330) 535-8131.

Professional orchestra offers pops, classical and educational concerts. Performances at EJ Thomas Hall, Civic Theatre, and Lock 3. Family & Kids series like the Odyssey Series, Picnic Pops in the Park and Youth Symphony. (September – July)

WEATHERVANE PLAYHOUSE

Akron - 1301 Weathervane Lane 44313. www.weathervaneplayhouse.com. Phone: (330) 836-2626.

Offers mainstage and children's productions, Young Actors Series, Spring Puppet show (ex. Snow White, Sound of Music).

GOODYEAR WORLD OF RUBBER

Akron - 1144 East Market Street (Downtown, Goodyear Hall, 4th floor of headquarters) 44316. Phone: (330) 796-7117. www.goodyear.com. Hours: Monday-Friday 8:00am-4:30pm. Tour: Introductory film (by request) of tire production. 1 hour. Groups of 10 or more should call ahead for a reservation.

NE Area

Did you know Goodyear accidentally discovered weatherproof rubber from excitedly throwing a fistful of gum on a sizzling hot potbellied stove?

Discover how Charles Goodyear vulcanized rubber in his kitchen in a replica of his workshop. Other attractions include a simulated rubber plantation (hands on), Indy race cars, an artificial heart, a moon buggy, history of blimps, history of the trucking industry, and of course an array of Goodyear products. Everyone leaves knowing about at least one unusual new product made from rubber to tell his or her friends about.

PORTAGE LAKES STATE PARK

Akron - 5031 Manchester Road (SR 93) 44319. www.dnr.state.oh.us. Phone: (330) 644-2220.

The wetlands of the park attract thousands of geese and waterfowl during spring and fall migration periods. Mallards, wood ducks and Canada geese nest in the wetlands each year. Five miles of hiking trials lead visitors to the woodlands and marshes of the park. Turkeyfoot Lake offers a public swimming beach. 4,963 acres of camping, hiking trails, boating, fishing, swimming and winter sports.

ALL AMERICAN SOAP BOX DERBY

Akron - *Derby Downs, 1-77 & State Route 244 East. www.aasbd.org. The annual gravity "grand prix" of soap box derby racing is still run the same way since 1934. Youths from over 100 local competitions participate and learn workmanship, completing a project and competing. Parade at 10:00am. Admission. (late July weekend)*

FIRST NIGHT AKRON

Akron - *Downtown. A family oriented non-alcoholic event with indoor and outdoor activities such as kid's/parent's food, entertainment and crafts, and a countdown to midnight. Admission. www.firstnightakron.org. (New Years Eve)*

Amherst

PUMPKIN MAZE PLAYLAND

Amherst - *Hillcrest Orchard, 50336 Telegraph Road. Pumpkin Patches / Hayrides / Corn Mazes / Fall Playland - Admission (average $6.00). Plan on at least two hours playtime. Open weekends, some weekdays (by appointment) and weeknights. www.hillcrestfunfarm.com. (late September - late October).*

Andover

PYMATUNING STATE PARK

Andover - *Lake Road (6 miles Southeast of Andover off SR 85) 44003. Phone: (440) 293-6329. www.dnr.state.oh.us.*

In a setting that highlights the mystery of an old swamp forest and the excitement of a water recreation area, Pymatuning State Park invites outdoor lovers of all ages to enjoy one of the finest walleye and muskellunge lakes in the country. Camping, swimming and boating opportunities as well. Two miles of well-marked Hiking trails and an assortment of casual, furnished family cabins.

NE Area

Ashtabula

COVERED BRIDGE PIZZA

Ashtabula (North Kingsville or Andover) - SR 85 or US 20. (440) 969-1000 or (440) 293-6776. Open daily for lunch and dinner. Casual. Actual covered bridge (late 1800s) was cut in two and rebuilt into pizza parlors! Located in the heart of Ashtabula County (Ohio's populous of covered bridges), historical pictures of the history of the bridge are displayed on the walls of the shop.

ASHTABULA MARINE MUSEUM

Ashtabula - 1071 Walnut Blvd. (Point Park in Ashtabula Harbor) 44004. Phone: (440) 964-6847. www.ashtabulamarinemuseum.org. Hours: Friday-Sunday Noon-5:00pm (June-August). Weekends only (September). Admission: $3.00-$4.00 (age 6+).

Holds treasures of the Great Lakes. It is housed in the former residence of the Lighthouse Keepers and the Coast Guard Chief that was built in 1898. Contains models, paintings, marine artifacts, photos of early Ashtabula Harbor and ore boats and tugs, miniature hand-made brass tools that actually work, and the world's only working scale model of a Hulett ore unloading machine. Expansive view of the harbor from the hill. Feel like you're captain of the high seas in the actual pilothouse from the steamship.

HUBBARD HOUSE AND UNDERGROUND RAILROAD MUSEUM

Ashtabula - Walnut Boulevard and Lake Avenue (near the Ashtabula Harbor) 44004. Phone: (440) 964-8168. www.hubbardhouseugrrmuseum.org. Hours: Friday-Sunday 1:00-5:00pm (Memorial Day weekend-September). Closed on holidays. Admission: $3.00-$5.00 (age 6+).

The Hubbard House, known as Mother Hubbard's Cupboard, is the only Ohio Underground Railroad terminus, or endpoint, open to the public.

There are three distinct features of the Hubbard House: the circa 1841 home of William and Catharine Hubbard on the first

floor, the Underground Railroad exhibit area on the second floor; and the Civil War and Americana exhibit area in the basement. This is recognized as a northern terminal that was part of the pathway from slavery to freedom in the pre Civil War era. Ashtabula County was instrumental in John

Brown's famous attack on the Federal arsenal at Harper's Ferry, Virginia. Of the nineteen men who charged the arsenal with John Brown, Sr., thirteen were from Ashtabula County.

Aurora

WILDWATER KINGDOM

Aurora - 1060 Aurora Road, St. Rte. 43 (9 miles north of Turnpike Exit 13) 44202. Phone: (330) 562-8303 or (877) 989-3389. www.wildwaterfun.com. Hours: Generally 11:00am-7:00pm (Memorial Day weekend thru Labor Day). Admission: ~$26.00 general. ~$12.00 for kids (under 48" and Seniors (61+). Kids age 2 and under FREE. $5.00 for Parking   Miscellaneous: Lockers and changing rooms. Picnic area. Food service. Towel rental. Proper swimwear required. Swimwear available in gift shops. Restaurants.

After nearly 110 years of providing amusement thrill rides, Geauga Lake will no longer operate the amusement park side of the attraction but will open Wildwater Kingdom each summer season.

WATER PLAY AT WILDWATER KINGDOM: 2½ acre pool with waves, water chutes, lazy river, and Ohio's tallest water slide featuring three enclosed body slides, four inner tube (raft) slides, and one breathtaking view from the top. Liquid Lightning puts the fun in funnel - a liquid funnel ride. Little ones can splash in mini-waterfalls and slides, shoot cannons or get drenched by the tipping bucket (even a feeding area for babies) at Coral Cove & Splash Landing.

Avon

DUCT TAPE FESTIVAL

Avon - Veteran's Memorial Pk, I-90 to Rte. 254 Detroit Rd. The annual Avon Heritage Duct Tape Festival kicks off just in time to celebrate Father's Day. The festival is an all-weekend event. This three-day event celebrates duct tape, its enthusiasts and its wacky and fun uses. The festival also honors the history and heritage of the city that is proclaimed the "Duct Tape Capital" of the world—Avon, Ohio—the home of Duck brand duct tape. From sculptures and fashion to games and a parade, everything at the festival revolves around duct tape. FREE. www.avonducttapefestival.com. (Fathers Day Weekend in June)

Bath

HALE FARM AND VILLAGE

Bath - *2686 Oak Hill Road (I-77 exit 226 or I-271 exit 12 (Rte. 303), follow signs) 44210. Phone: (800) 589-9703 or (330) 666-3711. www.wrhs.org. Hours: Wednesday-Saturday 11:00am-5:00pm, Sunday and Holidays Noon-5:00pm. (Memorial Day - Labor Day). Weekends only (September/October). Special Weekends (November-March). Admission: $10.00 adult, $5.00 child (3-12). Miscellaneous: Museum Shop (you can purchase crafts made on site) and Cafe. Map and sample questions to ask towns people provided. Summer Family Fun days are old-fashioned fun geared towards kids. Remember, authentic dirt roads throughout the village.*

Jonathan Hale moved to the Western Reserve from Connecticut and prospered during the canal era building an elaborate brick home and farm typical of New England. The gate house prepares guests with an orientation movie, then

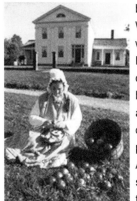

begin your adventure around the homestead area. Wheatfield Village is a small Ohio town struggling with the impact of the War Between the States. Period tools and machines provide wood- working demonstrations. Other barns serve as shops for a blacksmith, glass-blower, candle or broom-maker and basket maker. The Hale House (bricks made on site by Hale family and still made today) has pioneer cooking (and sampling!) demonstrations. Across the street, visit with mothers, daughters, sons and fathers (they are first person 1860s) as they share with you thoughts of the day. You will

feel like you're part of mid-1800's life as crops are planted and harvested, meetings attended, letters written, textiles spun, barters made, and church and school attended. Kids are asked to help with chores and schoolwork. Maybe you'll even get to "knead" the dough for bricks (with your feet!) or card wool or roll clay marbles. Samples of crafts worked on are given to the kids as souvenirs. We liked the mix of some buildings set in the present, some set in the Civil War era - it's amusing and interesting.

HOLIDAY LANTERN TOURS

Bath – Hale Farm & Village. Take a leisurely guided tour around the Village of Wheatfield, circa 1862. Visitors can enter the "homes" around the village green and see what holiday celebrations during the Civil War era were like. Admission. (Friday nights in December)

Berlin Center

NOAH'S LOST ARK ANIMAL SANCTUARY

Berlin Center - *8424 Bedell Road (off SR 224) 44401. Phone: (330) 584-7835. www.noahslostark.org. Hours: Tuesday-Sunday 10:00am-5:00pm (May-August). Weekends only until 4:00pm (September-October). Admission: $6.50 adult, $5.00 child (2-17).*

Tour the no-frills Exotic Animal Park. The facility is dedicated to providing a permanent safe haven for unwanted and abused Exotic animals. Hands-on interaction with unusual, uncommon international animals (camels, pot-bellied pigs, antelope). Wagon rides thru farm. The newly constructed large cat compound featuring Tigers, Lions, Ligers, Servals, Leopards, Caracals and Bobcats or the Primate Area are favorites.

Brecksville

CUYAHOGA VALLEY NATIONAL PARK

Brecksville - *15610 Vaughn Road (I-271 exit 12, Rte. 303) 44141. Phone: (216) 524-1497 or (800) 257-9477 or (800) 445-9667. www.nps.gov/cuva/index.htm or www.dayinthevalley.com. Hours: Visitor Center open at 10:00am-4:00pm. Park hours vary by season. Some smaller Visitors Centers scattered throughout the park have more restricted hours in the cooler months (non summer break) and are closed except weekends. Admission: FREE entrance fee. Educators: Online lesson plans for study of the Ohio & Erie Canal - click on For Teachers icon. NPS Junior Ranger programs. Miscellaneous: Hale Farm & Village & Cuyahoga Valley Scenic Railroad all within park. See separate listings in this chapter for details. No overnight camping within the park, however some is available near the perimeter.*

Visitors enjoy picnicking, hiking, bike trails, bridle trails, winter sports, golf, fishing, and ranger-guided programs. Some of the park attractions are:

CANAL VISITOR CENTER: Permanent exhibits illustrate 12,000 years of history in the valley, including the history of the Ohio & Erie Canal. The canal-era building once served canal boat passengers waiting to pass through Lock 38. A 20-minute slide program about the park is shown by request. Hours: 10:00am-4:00pm daily except winter holidays. (Canal Road 1.5 miles south of Rockside Road. Access off Hillside Road). Just down the street is the Frazee family home, typical of the era (only open summer weekends).

LOCK 38 DEMONSTRATIONS: Learn about the canal days in the museum and watch the canal lock demonstrations held afternoons every weekend during the summer and periodically in early fall. "Hoooooo!" is the command that mule drivers shouted as they approached Twelve-mile Lock. Step back in time and relive the canal era along the Ohio & Erie Canal. Imagine riding in a boat being raised or lowered in the old stone lock. Join volunteers and park rangers in 19th-century dress as they operate Lock 38.

Learning how a lock works...

OHIO & ERIE CANAL TOWPATH TRAIL: Once a mode of transportation of goods and people, the canal (dry and overgrown in places) makes for a nice path for over 19 miles of biking, hiking, running or walking. As you enjoy the Towpath Trail each summer, you may chance upon musicians playing banjo, harmonica, and other instruments.

BRANDYWINE FALLS: A boardwalk trail allows a close view of the roaring water (best after lots of rain).

THE LEDGES OVERLOOK: Hikers can climb to the top of the valley walls to view lots of greenspace.

BOSTON STORE: 1836 general store functions as a museum with exhibits on canal boat construction.

Brunswick

MAPLESIDE FARMS

Brunswick - *294 Pearl Road, US 42 (on US 42, between Rte. 82 and Rte 303 off I-71 exits) 44212. Phone: (330) 225-5577 store. www.mapleside.com. Tours: Scheduled. Minimum 12 people. $5.00-$8.00 per person. Teachers are FREE. Monday-Friday (Labor Day-October) Miscellaneous: Gift shop, bakery and ice cream parlor. See Suggested Lodging and Dining for Restaurant.*

They harvest over 20,000 bushels of apples each year from 5,000 apple trees. Many of the 20 different varieties are kept fresh in controlled atmosphere storage so they can be enjoyed year around (what's the secret?). Fall group tours of the orchards include sample apples (some picked, some from packing room); a tour of apple orchards and production areas with explanation of growing and processing apples; a cup of cider and bakery; a visit to Harvest Hideout playland; and a small pumpkin for each child. Everything you ever wanted to know or never knew about apples!

JOHNNY APPLESEED FESTIVAL

Brunswick – *Mapleside Farms. This event features homemade craft exhibits, a corn maze, live bands, horse-drawn wagon rides, bag your own apples, apple butter making, cloggers, apple products for sale and kids activities. Admission. (mid-September weekend)*

FALL FESTIVAL

Brunswick – *Mapleside Farms. Pumpkin patches, hayrides, corn mazes, fall playland. Admission. (late September-late October)*

MAPLESIDE FARMS RESTAURANT

Brunswick - *294 Pearl Road, US 42 44212. www.mapleside.com. Phone: (330) 225-5577. Hours: Open daily for lunch and dinner, closed Mondays (November-August). Mapleside Farms is more than just an apple farm - it's a destination that combines a view of the apple orchards in the valley, a great dining experience in a rustic country restaurant overlooking the orchards and unique shopping in the Farm Market, Bakery, Craft Shop and take out Deli & Cafe and Ice Cream Parlor. Try yummy apple fritters and dishes with pork and apples. Even their side dishes are "apple-related" like: Waldorf Salad, homemade applesauce or escalloped apples.*

SANTA FEST

Brunswick – *Mapleside Farms Restaurant. Breakfast with Santa, Kids Crafts, Face Painting, Wagon Rides.*

Burton

CENTURY VILLAGE MUSEUM AND COUNTRY STORE

Burton - *14653 E. Park Street (State Route 87 and State Route 700) 44021. Phone: (440) 834-1492. www.geaugahistorical.org. Admission: $7.00 adult, $4.00 child (6-12). Tours: Saturday, Sunday 1:00 and 3:00pm (mid-April to mid-November).*

Tour the magnificent century homes on the Village grounds, hear stories of early settlers, and view a collection of 9,000 toy soldiers. A restored community with 12 buildings (log cabin, church, barns, schoolhouse, marshal's office and train station) containing 19th Century historical antiques and a working farm. Best to attend during Festivals or Pioneer School Camp when the village comes alive with visiting "villagers."

MAPLE SYRUP FESTIVAL

Burton – *Century Village. The Log Cabin sells all types of Maple products! Choose from syrup, candy, maple spread and much more. They collect & boil sap at the log cabin during Maple Sugaring season (usually mid-February to mid-March depending on the weather)*

APPLE BUTTER FESTIVAL

Burton – *Century Village. Apples & cider. Apple pie eating contests. Apple peeling contests. Apple butter. Candy apples. Wagon/hayrides. Apple Dumplings, Fritters, Donuts, etc. Parades. Pioneer crafts. Admission. (second weekend in October)*

Canfield

CANFIELD FAIR

Canfield - *Canfield Fairgrounds, off Rtes. 46, 11, and 224. www.canfieldfair.com or (330) 533-4107. Grandstand headliners, the World's Largest Demolition Derby, Truck and Tractor Pull, agricultural displays, milk a cow, pet pigs, Elephant Encounter. Admission. (Wednesday - Sunday-Labor Day week)*

NE Area

Chardon

PIONEER WATERLAND AND DRY PARK

Chardon - 10661 Kile Road (off US 6 or SR 608/US 322) 44024. Phone: (440) 285-0910. www.pioneerwaterland.com. Hours: Daily 10:00am-7:00pm (Memorial Day-Labor Day). Extended weekend hours. Admission: $19.95 and up. Discount tickets available online. Dry activities are a few additional dollars each. Less than 40" tall FREE. Miscellaneous: Picnic Area, Food Service, and Video Arcade.

Little ones frequent the toddler play area and waterland. Others can explore the water slides, paddleboats, inner tube rides, volleyball nets, Indy raceway, batting cages, miniature golf or driving range. All adjoining a chlorinated crystal clear lake with beaches.

GEAUGA COUNTY MAPLE FESTIVAL

Chardon - Downtown, Chardon Square. I-90 exit to Rte. 44 south. (440) 286-3007 or www.maplefestival.com. Sap Run contest, midway, parades, bathtub races and maple syrup production and sales. (long third weekend in April)

Cleveland

CLEVELAND SPORTS

CLEVELAND BROWNS - Browns Stadium, lakefront. (440) 224-3361 tours. www.clevelandbrowns.com. NFL Football, New Dawg Pound. Largest scoreboard in NFL Football. Kids Club. Tours by appointment give you facts and figures plus a peek at locker rooms and press boxes. (September-December)

CLEVELAND CAVALIERS - Quicken Arena (The Q). (216) 420-2200 or www.nba.com/cavs. Professional Basketball. (September – April).

CLEVELAND INDIANS - Progressive Field. www.indians.com. (866) 48-TRIBE. Kids Club. $7.00-$27.00 tickets. (April – October). Tours (fee of $4.50-$6.50) include Kidsland, a press box, a suite, a dugout, a fun video…lasts one hour (Monday-Saturday 10:00am-2:00pm, some summer Sundays).

CHILDREN'S MUSEUM OF CLEVELAND

Cleveland - *10730 Euclid Avenue (University Circle, I-90 to MLK exit 177) 44106. Phone: (216) 791-KIDS. www.clevelandchildrensmuseum.org. Hours: Daily 10:00am-4:45pm, except Christmas and New Years. Admission: General admission (age 1yr -12yrs) is $7.00. Anyone 13 and over is $6.00.*

The Children's Museum of Cleveland offers innovative and educational exhibits for children. Splish! Splash! features a two-story climbing structure that is designed to teach basic principles of the water cycle (fun to climb into). Also in this area is the Kids' Forecast Center (predict weather, then present it before camera). Put on an apron & splash play in Water Works. Bridges to Our Community features areas that are joined together by bridges. Kids pretend to shop, bank, pump gas or drive a bus. Build with blocks or create art here, too. The Big Red Barn area is a child's book brought to life- infants & preschoolers play with lots of chutes and ladders. Temporary exhibits might be covering tools or trains or sand. Summer camps. Best for kids under 8.

CLEVELAND BOTANICAL GARDEN

Cleveland - *11030 East Blvd. (University Circle, I-90 to MLK exit) 44106. Phone: (216) 721-1600. www.cbgarden.org. Hours: Monday-Saturday 10:00am-5:00pm and Sunday Noon-5:00pm. Closed Mondays in winter. (Hershey Children's Garden closes all winter) Admission: $7.50 adult, $5.50 senior (60+), $3.00 child (3-12).*

Display gardens changing each season (best April-October for color). Most like the Knot Garden and the newer areas: the spiny desert of Madagascar and the cloud forest of Costa Rica. With its wheelchair-accessible tree house, dwarf forests, scrounger garden, worm bins and watery bog, Hershey Children's Garden is an exciting destination for families. Lots of adventure paths to explore and splash in water spouts. Flowers in a bathtub - oh my!

CLEVELAND MUSEUM OF ART

Cleveland - *11150 East Boulevard (University Circle, near the Botanical Gardens) 44106. Phone: (216) 421-7340 or (888) 262-0033. www.clevelandart.org. Hours: Tuesday, Thursday, Saturday & Sunday 10:00am-5:00pm. Wednesday & Friday 10:00am-9:00pm. Check website for updates on hours. Admission: FREE general admission. Miscellaneous: Café open daytime. Families Learning Together creation days each month. Educators: rent an Art to Go package. Online interactive In the Attic visual tour and learning site.*

New, renovated museum is open after almost a year of changes and improvements. See the large collection of objects from all cultures and periods including European and American paintings, medieval, Asian, Islamic,

NE Area

pre-Columbian, African masks, Egyptian mummies and Oceanic art. The kids really like the Armor Court (knights in shining armor).

CLEVELAND MUSEUM OF NATURAL HISTORY

Cleveland - 1 Wade Oval Drive (University Circle, I-90 and Martin Luther King Dr. exit) 44106. Phone: (216) 231-4600 or (800) 317-9155. www.cmnh.org. Hours: Monday-Saturday 10:00am-5:00pm, Sunday Noon-5:00pm. Also, Wednesdays open until 10:00pm (September-May only). Closed holidays. Admission: $9.00 adult, $7.00 youth (7-18) and senior (60+), $6.00 child (3-6). Miscellaneous: Gift shop. Modern Planetarium and interactive pre-show activities (extra fee) plus Observatory open Wednesday evenings. Live animal shows daily. Café lunch. Parking fee. Educators: thematic teaching kits are recently refreshed with new hands-on materials and updated teacher guides.

Meet "Happy" the 70 foot long dinosaur, "Jane" the teenage dino, or "Lucy" the oldest human fossil. Look for real dino eggs and touch real dino bones! Highlights of Ohio Natural History are: Johnstown Mastodon -- A long-ago Ohio resident and Dunk - this fearsome 16-foot-long armored fish with huge self-sharpening jaws is a native Clevelander found in the shale of the Rocky River Valley (look low, then look high - oh my!). The Ringler dugout is the oldest well-dated watercraft ever

Meet the famous "Dunk"

found in North America (found in 1976 in Ashland, OH). Also look for the Glacier that Covered Cleveland; the Diorama of Moundbuilders - shown in layers depicting what might be found (excellent examples-the most spectacular mounds were found in Ohio); or the Wildlife Center & Woods (outside, partially enclosed) where natural habitats are home to raptors (owls, hawks), songbirds, turkey, river otters, fox and many other species found in the state. The lower level of the museum has Ohio Botany, Ohio Birds & Insects and Ohio Ecology. In the Discovery Center, kids can use microscopes or view live insects and reptiles. Lots of touch and feel toys and games. "Planet e" is an interactive area featuring actual footage from NASA space missions projected onto a large viewing monitor. Your "spacecraft" can take you to planets and moons in the solar system and launch a probe. Or, experience an earthquake in Ohio - are we ready? Kids visiting here are first amazed at the large scale of the prehistoric skeletons and also love that many prehistoric artifacts came from

For updates & travel games visit: **www.KidsLoveTravel.com**

Ohio. As you might have guessed, you need several hours or many visits to explore every corner of this place!

CLEVELAND ORCHESTRA

Cleveland - *11001 Euclid Avenue 44106. Phone: (216) 231-1111 or (800) 686-1141. www.clevelandorchestra.com.*

Concerts in beautiful Severance Hall (September-May), outdoors at Blossom Music Center (Summer). The COYO (Cleveland Orchestra Youth Orchestra) performs concerts also. Family Concerts are specially designed for children 6 and older. These narrated concerts are structured around a theme and include collaborative artist such as young musicians, singers, dancers and actors.

CLEVELAND PLAYHOUSE

Cleveland - *8500 Euclid Avenue 44106. www.clevelandplayhouse.com. Phone: (216) 795-7000.*

America's longest running regional theatre presents contemporary and classical children's series plays during the school year. Classics include A Christmas Story or popular fairy tale themes.

FEDERAL RESERVE BANK LEARNING CENTER AND MONEY MUSEUM

Cleveland - *1455 East 6th Street (corner of Superior Ave. and East 6th St, downtown) 44106. www.clevelandfed.org/LearningCenter/Index.cfm. Phone: (216) 579-3188. Hours: Monday-Thursday 10:00am-2:00pm, closed holidays. Admission: FREE. Educators: Education, Curricula, and Classroom Activities online under Resources for Teachers. Money games under Online Activities.*

Does money grow on trees? Was paper money always used? The Museum and Learning Center includes exhibits of ancient currency such as tiny cowrie shells from Indian Ocean Islands and giant stones from the Pacific Island of Yap. Want to see what your face looks like on a dollar? Older kids may even learn a little about economics and money management.

WESTERN RESERVE HISTORY MUSEUM

Cleveland - *10825 East Boulevard, University Circle (I-90 to MLK exit 177) 44106. Phone: (216) 721-5722. www.wrhs.org. Hours: Tuesday-Saturday 10:00am-4:00pm. Sunday Noon – 4:00pm. Open Wednesday evenings until 9:00pm. Admission: $8.50 adult, $7.50 senior, $5.00 student (age 6+). Includes Mansion, History, Costume Wing and Crawford Museum. Check website for seasonal special offers. Miscellaneous: We strongly suggest hands-on programs and guided tours for*

families. Educators: their Education link has four wonderful links to interactive Cleveland history online programming.

Cleveland's oldest cultural institution boasts a tour of a grand mansion recreating the Western Reserve from pre-Revolution War to the 20th Century. The look (but mostly don't touch) displays include: farming tools, clothing and costumes (displayed with cute artifacts of the time) and over 200 classic automobiles (Cleveland built cars, oldest car, and heaviest car) and airplanes (Crawford Auto-Aviation Museum). Look for an original Morgan Traffic Signal (native Clevelander) or the Tinkerbelle - the smallest sailboat to cross the Atlantic.

MARTIN LUTHER KING PROGRAM

Cleveland – *Western Reserve History Museum. (216) 231-1111. In observance of the Martin Luther King Jr. Day holiday, many museums and attractions in University Circle offer free or discounted admission on that day…plus, Orchestra Concert. (Martin Luther King Day-January)*

UNIVERSITY CIRCLEFEST

Cleveland - *University Circle area. (216) 791-3900. FREE admission to University Circle museums plus holiday carolers and Santa. FREE. (first Sunday in December)*

CLEVELAND LAKEFRONT STATE PARK

Cleveland - 8701 Lakeshore Blvd., NE (off I-90, downtown) 44108. Phone: (216) 881-8141. www.dnr.state.oh.us.

Cleveland Lakefront State Park provides natural relief to the metropolitan skyline. Sand beaches, tree-lined picnic areas and panoramic views of the lake are found within the park along the Lake Erie shoreline. The annual Erie fish catch nearly equals the combined catches of all the other great lakes. Dominant species are perch, smallmouth and white bass, channel catfish, walleye and freshwater drum. Facilities include: Edgewater Park - This park is divided into upper and lower areas connected by a paved bicycle path and fitness course; East 55th Marina; Gordon Park; Euclid Beach - 650-foot swimming beach with shaded picnic areas and a scenic observation pier; Villa Angela; and Wildwood. 450 acres of boating and rentals, fishing, swimming, and winter sports.

FESTIVAL OF FREEDOM

Cleveland – Lakefront State Park, Edgewater Park. July 4th celebration including downtown parades, rides, entertainment and fireworks. Edgewater park.

A CHRISTMAS STORY HOUSE

Cleveland - 3159 W 11th Street (I-71 exit W. 14th St., around traffic circle and turn right onto Rowley Ave.) 44109. www.achristmasstoryhouse.com. Phone: (216) 298-4919. Hours: Thursday-Saturday 10:00am-5:00pm, Sunday Noon-5:00pm. Open Wednesdays 10:00am-5:00pm from November 26 to December 31. Tours every half hour. Closed all major holidays. Admission: $5.50-$7.50 Admission (age 7+). Miscellaneous: While we are personally not fans of the movie, over 35,000

people have visited the first year alone!

Purchased by a longtime fan, this is the very home where the movie was filmed. The house was returned to its Hollywood appearance and opened in celebration of the 1983 film. Across the street is a museum dedicated to the movie, with behind-the-scenes photos, items donated by actors and original props. Among the props and costumes are the toys from the Higbee's window, Randy's snowsuit and zeppelin, the chalkboard from Miss Shields' classroom and the family car.

CLEVELAND METROPARKS ZOO & RAINFOREST

Cleveland - 3900 Wildlife Way (I-71 exit Fulton Road or East 25th Street) 44109. Phone: (216) 661-6500. www.clemetzoo.com. Hours: Daily 10:00am-5:00pm. Until 7:00pm Weekends (Summer). Closed only Christmas and New Year's Day. Admission: $10.00 adult (12+), $7.00 child (2-11). Reduced admission (November-March). Free Parking. Free zoo only admission for local residents on non-holiday Mondays. Look online for Great Deals coupons and discounts. Miscellaneous: Outback railroad train ride, camel rides and adventure rides are $1.50-$3.00 extra. Concessions and cafes. Zoo trams run daily for FREE. Coolers and picnic baskets are allowed on Zoo grounds. Educators: Animal Fun and Games is located under the Education icon, then click Students or Families.

Discover animals from every corner of the world. A rainforest with animal and plant settings like the jungles of Africa, Asia, and South America is the most

NE
Area

popular exhibit to explore. The rainforest boasts a storm every 12 minutes, a 25-foot waterfall, and a walk-through aviary. Altogether, the whole zoo holds

thousands of animals from all continents including Africa and Australia. Wolf Wilderness is a popular educational study exhibit where you can view thru a giant window the wolves acting "naturally" in the day and night. Wolf Wilderness is part of Northern Trek, where everyone can learn about the Zoo's winter-loving animals including reindeer, Siberian tigers, polar bears and wolves. The Australian Adventure has a kookaburra station, wallaby walkabout and koala junction (55 ft. treehouse and play area with petting yard). The Center for Zoological Medicine allows zoo guests to view veterinary care through three observation windows. Cameras in the operating rooms allow procedures to be seen up close, and the vets don't shy away from letting people view every stage in an animal's life. New animals are born here often so check their website for who's new!

DECEMBER DAYS & BRUNCH WITH SANTA

Cleveland – *Cleveland Metroparks Zoo. December Days offers seasonal activities to enjoy including animal programs, seasonal music, eco-friendly crafts, holiday cookie decorating and more. And, Santa Claus will greet visitors daily through December 24. Stroll Zoo grounds on foot or ride aboard a complimentary heated shuttle, the Sleighbell Express, past monkeys. Hop off for a stop in the seasonal greenhouse or Pachyderm Building. Take an invigorating walk through Northern Trek to see many of the Zoo's winter-loving animals including reindeer, bears, tigers and wolves. (December long weekends 11:00am-3:00pm, reduced winter admission).*

NOON YEAR'S EVE

Cleveland – *Cleveland Metroparks Zoo. (11:00am-1:00pm on New Years Eve Day in December) The grown-ups can have their New Year's Eve fun at night, but kids get to celebrate the New Year's arrival during daylight hours. Watch a crew of charismatic critters in a special Noon Year's Eve Wild Animal Show; make New Year's ReZOOlutions and create eco-friendly crafts. The Noon Year's Eve celebration culminates at the stroke of noon with an alcohol-free toast and a traditional ball drop. Noon Year's Eve activities are FREE with regular Zoo admission.*

LOLLY THE TROLLEY TOURS

Cleveland - 1831 Columbus Road (Station: Powerhouse @ Nautica, west bank of Flats) 44113. Phone: (216) 771-4484 or (800) 848-0173. www.lollytrolley.com. Hours: Early morning or afternoon departures. More available on weekends (even early evening). Weekends only in winter. Admission: $8.00-$11.00 (1 hr.) or $12.00-$17.00 (2 hr.). Tours: 1 or 2 hours, Reservations Required. 1 hour tour is suggested for preschoolers. Miscellaneous: Lots of specialty tours and school group tours with educational themes or Holiday Tours.

"Lolly the Trolley", an old fashioned bright red trolley, clangs its bell as you take in over 100 sights around the downtown area. The tour includes Cleveland's North Coast Harbor featuring the world's only Rock & Roll Hall of

Fame and Museum and the Great Lakes Science Center; Downtown Cleveland; The Warehouse District, The Flats, a river port by day and a bustling entertainment center by night; Ohio City, with many Victorian homes and the county's oldest church; and the West Side Market, one of the world's largest indoor/outdoor food and produce markets; Playhouse Square and University Circle, a focal point for cultural educational and medical institutions. Your tour concludes with a brief stop at the Rockefeller Greenhouse and a drive along the Lake Erie shoreline back to the station. A great way to show off the city to visitors or get an overview of sites to decide which you want to visit.

TRAIN RIDES WITH SANTA

Cleveland – Lolley the Trolley. Train trip in decorated coaches with Santa. Songs and treats. Dress warmly. Weekends only. Admission. (December)

GOOD TIME III

Cleveland - 825 East 9th Street Pier (Behind Rock & Roll Hall of Fame) 44114. Phone: (216) 861-5110. www.goodtimeiii.com. Admission: $15.00 adult, $14.00 senior, $9.00 child (age 2+-11). Add $10.00 extra for lunch. Tours: Tuesday-Saturday, Noon and 3:00pm, Sunday times vary (mid-June to Labor Day). Weekends (Friday-Sunday) only in May and September. Miscellaneous: Food Service Available. Lower deck is air-conditioned and heated. Parking on the pier. They sail rain or shine.

GOOD TIME III *(cont.)*

The quadruple-deck, 1000 passenger boat takes a two hour excursion of city sights along the Cuyahoga River and Lake Erie. The word Cuyahoga is Indian for "crooked". You'll see tugboats and the largest yellow crane boats in the country. See all the industry in the Flats including concrete, pipe, transportation, limestone, and coke businesses. Collision Bend used to be so narrow that many boats got tangled up. Since then, they have dredged the curve and it's now very wide.

GREAT LAKES SCIENCE CENTER

Cleveland - 601 Erieside Avenue (E 9th Street and I-90, North Coast Harbor, Downtown) 44114. Phone: (216) 694-2000. www.glsc.org. Hours: Daily 10:00am-5:00pm. Only closed Thanksgiving and Christmas. Admission: $7.50-$9.50. Memberships Available. Omnimax additional $7.50-$9.50. Discount combo tickets. Miscellaneous: Gift Shop OmniMax Theater – 6 story domed screen image and sound. Bytes sandwich restaurant on location. Educators: Printer Projects are found under the icon "Think!" online.

Located on the shores of Lake Erie is one of America's largest interactive science museums. You can't miss the iconic wind turbine and solar panel canopy at the entrance. Over 400 interactive exhibits – especially fun on the second floor. Pilot a blimp, test your batting skills, or bounce off the walls in the Polymer Funhouse. The science playground museum focuses on the Great Lakes region and its environment (Sick Earth, Cloud Maker, Nitrogen Fixation). Young lab scientists (guests) can create a tornado or create light. Here, visitors can touch an indoor tornado, watch the power of lightning and learn about the environment all within several feet of each other. Virtual Sports, Electric Shows & one of the largest video walls east of the Rockies.

NAUTICA QUEEN

Cleveland - 1153 Main Avenue (West Bank Flats) 44114. Phone: (216) 696-8888 or (800) 837-0604. www.nauticaqueen.com. Hours: Monday – Thursday Noon, 7:00pm; Friday Noon, 7:30pm; Saturday 11:00am, 7:30pm; Sunday 1:00pm (April-December). Reservation Required. Admission: $14.00-$23.00 child (Adult prices are about double).

Experience the excitement of the Nautica Queen, Cleveland's luxury cruise dining ship, offering a unique adventure in lakefront and river cruise dining for people of all ages. 3 Hour Dinner Cruise or 2 hour Lunch/Brunch Cruise. Many cruises include entertainment with special themes like pirates or shipwrecks (ex. Capt'n Willie Family Lunch Pirate Cruise - Capt'n Willie and first mate Zap the Pirate enthrall you and your children with tales of pirates, ghost stories, music, trivia, balloon twisting, a little magic, and even some Cleveland history; or Easter Bunny Egg Hunt).

ROCK AND ROLL HALL OF FAME MUSEUM

Cleveland - One Key Plaza, 1100 Rock and Roll Blvd. (9th Street exit north, downtown waterfront) 44114. www.rockhall.com. Phone: (216) 781-ROCK or (800) 493-ROLL. Hours: Daily 10:00am - 5:30pm (open until 9:00pm on Wednesdays). Closed Thanksgiving and Christmas. Admission: $22.00 adult, $17.00 senior (65+), $13.00 youth (9-12). Free Museum admission for children 8 and under with the purchase of an adult admission.

Visit Cleveland's own Rock and Roll Hall of Fame, the world's only museum celebrating the soundtrack of your life. New exhibits, new programs, live performances and of course, the world's largest single collection of rock and roll memorabilia. Each level has interactive listening exhibits. As parents reminisce, kids will probably giggle, at most of the many exhibits including: Rock & Roll in the 50s, The Music of Ohio, Cinema (documentary films), Induction Videos, Radio Station and the Hall of Fame. Please check in with Visitor's Services before you explore here - they'll let you know which areas have PG and above ratings - you'll know which areas to overlook.

STEAMSHIP WILLIAM G. MATHER MUSEUM

Cleveland - Docked at 305 Old Erieside Avenue (Dock 32 at Northcoast Harbor Park, just north of Science Center) 44114. http://little.nhlink.net/wgm/wgmhome.html. Phone: (216) 574-6262. Hours: Daily 10:00am-5:00pm (summer). Weekends Only (Friday-Sunday - May, September, October). Admission: $6.00 adult, $5.00 senior (60+), $4.00 youth (5-18 and college w/ID). Educators: New, complete Teachers Packets are downloadable and printable online. They cover history, vocabulary, projects, geography and a scavenger hunt. Miscellaneous: Best for preschoolers and older because of dangerous spots while walking. Films play continuously. After your visit, have lunch or dinner at Hornblowers Restaurant (216-363-1151). An actual barge restaurant on the water.

The floating Mather is an iron freighter once used to carry ore, coal and grain along the Great Lakes. Little eyes will open wide in the 4 story engine room and they will have fun pretending to be the crew (or maybe guests) in the cozy sleeping quarters or the elegant dining room. Group tours are treated to programmed learning fun in the Interactive Cargo Hold area. Make a sailor hat or a boat made from silly putty (why does

a boat float?). Learn to tie sailors' knots with real rope or pretend you're at sea as you move the ship's wheel. In the pilothouse area, kids use navigation charts, working radar, and a marine radio to plan a trip. Already visited before? Try the July 4th Rock and Boom fireworks or the Air Show Deck Party each Labor Day weekend for some added festive fun.

The stately wheelhouse...

U.S.S. COD

Cleveland - *1809 East 9th Street (North Marginal Road next to Burke Lakefront) 44114. Phone: (216) 566-8770. www.usscod.org. Hours: Daily 10:00am-5:00pm (May-September). Admission: $6.00 adult, $5.00 senior (62+), $3.00 student (under 6 Free). FREE for military in uniform. Miscellaneous: Recommend airport parking lot. PLEASE NOTE: Because the COD has not been altered from her wartime configuration, visitors must enter and exit through the original hatchways and climb up and down ladders. Caution must be exercised by persons with small children, the elderly and the handicapped. Educators: dozens of links on their Homepage lead to websites for research papers.*

We started our visit at the Aristotle periscope on shore that gives you a view of Lake Erie and puts you in the mood to explore the WW II submarine that sank

enemy shipping boats. The ninety-man crew lived in cramped quarters - an amazing reminder of the price of freedom. The eight separate compartments, tight quarters, ladders to climb and plenty of knobs to play with give an authentic feeling of submarine life. The best part of this tour is the fact that the sub was actually used in wartime and still remains pretty much the same as during wartime…very authentic presentation.

MALLEY'S CHOCOLATES

Cleveland - *13400 Brookpark Road (I-480 and West 130th street) 44135. Phone: (216) 362-8700 or (800) 835-5684. www.malleys.com. Admission: FREE. Tours: Monday-Friday 9:30am-4:00pm excluding holidays. Summer hours vary. Strollers allowed, No cameras. 60 minute guided tour available with reservations, 15-50 person limit.*

See and hear about the story of chocolate from a professional at Malley's family business (since 1935). We learned it takes 400 cocoa beans to make one pound of chocolate. You'll watch them roast nuts, dip chocolates, and wrap goodies along with samples at the end of the tour - if you ask nicely. They sell one half million pounds per year with the most sales at Easter, then Christmas, then Valentine's Day. Allow time to shop in their factory store.

NASA GLENN RESEARCH CENTER

Cleveland - *21000 Brookpark Road (I-480 to Exit 9, next to Cleveland Hopkins Airport, Lewis Field) 44135. Phone: (216) 433-2000. www.grc.nasa.gov. Hours: Weekdays 9:00am-4:00pm. Saturday & Holidays 10:00am-3:00pm, Sunday 1:00-5:00pm. Closed major winter holidays. Admission: FREE. Tours: Available, call for details. Family programs and tours are offered most Saturdays. On special family days, look to take the free "pop-in" picture op as an Astronaut.*

Astronaut Daniel

The interactive exhibit space called the Aero Adventures houses displays on a space shuttle, satellites, zero gravity chamber, wind tunnels, and space environmental tanks. The Apollo Command Module (used on Skylab 3) is the most popular area. Look for the moon rock, major league baseball, and space suit used by astronauts (audio explanation) or tribute to John Glenn. The Launch Control Center allows you to conduct a countdown sequence towards a simulated launch of a rocket. You can perform some of the steps that the astronauts performed when working with the Combustion Module.

After following the steps, actual footage is played from one of the experiments conducted in space. Other areas allow kids to operate a wind tunnel or a DropTower - Boom! The ACTS satellite control room and the space shuttle live broadcasts are a great reason for frequent visits.

MEMPHIS KIDDIE PARK

Cleveland - 10340 Memphis Avenue (I-71 to West 117th/Memphis Avenue Exit) 44144. Phone: (216) 941-5995. www.memphiskiddiepark.com. Hours and Admission: 10:00am-8:00pm, seasonal. Pay per ride (~$1.40 each). Discounts for books of tickets. RIDERS MUST BE UNDER 50 INCHES TALL FOR MOST RIDES.

With many of the original rides still in place, Memphis Kiddie Park is truly a landmark of the Cleveland area which has thrilled generations of children. Memphis Kiddie Park consists of eleven miniature amusement rides, a concession stand, an arcade, and an eighteen hole miniature golf course. The park is mainly for youngsters anywhere from about a year old on up to around eight. Little tots rides like a ferris wheel, roller coaster (our little girl's first!) and carousel.

GRAND PRIX OF CLEVELAND

Cleveland - Burke Lakefront Airport, Downtown. www.grandprixofcleveland.com. (800) 498-RACE or The world's top Indy Car drivers compete on the 213 miles of racing. Also a Grand Prix Parade on Friday. Admission. (last weekend in June)

KIDSFEST, CLEVELAND

Cleveland - Downtown, Tower City Amphitheater. www.cleveland.com/kidsfest/. Playground World Pavilion, Circus, Robots, animal acts, kid-friendly music and great kids' entertainment. Admission. (second or third weekend in July)

CLEVELAND NATIONAL AIR SHOW

*Cleveland - Burke Lakefront Airport, downtown. www.clevelandairshow.com. (216) 781-7747. One of the nation's top air shows featuring the best in military jet demonstrations and civilian aerobatics performers. Thunderbirds and Blue Angels Flybys. Admission. (Labor Day weekend). Tour the **INTERNATIONAL WOMEN'S AIR & SPACE MUSEUM** on premises (the museum is open during normal airport hours year-round). Discover the achievements of women in aviation and space through exhibits that include an aerobatic plane, a flight simulator and a hands-on mission control console. Learn about life in space in the new exhibit, "Living & Working in Space". This hands-on exhibit* lets visitors exercise, get into a vertical sleeping bag, and work with space gloves. See the "Pretty Purple Puddy Tat", a Smith Mini-plane built and flown by Tracy Pilurs. Learn about the women pilots who underwent secret astronaut testing in 1961.

IRISH CULTURAL FESTIVAL

Cleveland (Berea) - Cuyahoga County Fairgrounds, 164 Eastland Blvd. Irish culture at its best with dancing, music, arts & crafts, storytelling and workshops. Admission. www.clevelandirish.org. (third weekend in July)

I-X CENTER INDOOR AMUSEMENT PARK

Cleveland (Brookpark) - 6200 Riverside Drive, next to airport. (800) 897-3942 or www.ixamusementpark.com. Hours vary daily (Call for details). Admission: $13.00-$16.00 (age 3+), Seniors (60+) FREE. Food service. After riding the World's Tallest Indoor Ferris Wheel (10 stories high) you can SCREAM through 150 rides! Also features a video arcade, miniature golf, laser karaoke, Kidzville, and live entertainment. (month-long most of April)

NE Area

CLEVELAND CHRISTMAS CONNECTION

Cleveland (Brookpark) - IX Center, near Hopkins Airport. (216) 676-6000. Gifts, arts and crafts, regional entertainment, Santa, train rides, giant indoor ferris wheel rides, nice free gift craft area for kids, variety of ethnic food. www.christmasconnections.com. Admission. (long weekend before Thanksgiving)

Cortland

MOSQUITO LAKE STATE PARK

Cortland - 1439 SR 305 (10 miles North of Warren off State Route 305) 44410. Phone: (330) 637-2856. www.dnr.state.oh.us.

Several hiking trails allow visitors to explore the woodlands and scenic shoreline of the park. Ten miles of bridle trails give horsemen access to the park's interior. Snowmobilers have access to 14 miles of shoreline and 15 miles of wooded trails. Mountain biking is permitted on 5 miles of multiple-use trails. 11,811 acres of camping, boating and rentals, fishing, swimming at sandy beach and winter sports. Near the lake, look for the 12 bald eagles that reside in the area.

Cuyahoga Falls

BLOSSOM HOLIDAY LIGHTING FESTIVAL

Cuyahoga Falls - *Blossom Music Center , I-77 exit 143, SR 176. Hundreds of thousands of lights & holiday / storybook characters. www.blossomlightingfestival.com. Two miles with 300+ light displays and 2 million lights with 35 different scenes. Daily, evenings. Admission. (mid-November thru first week of January)*

Fairport Harbor

FAIRPORT HARBOR MARINE MUSEUM

Fairport Harbor - *129 Second Street (I-90 to SR 44 north to SR 2) 44077. Phone: (440) 354-4825. www.ncweb.com/org/fhlh. Hours: Wednesday, Saturday, Sunday and Holidays. 1:00 – 6:00pm (Memorial Weekend – Labor Day) Admission: $3.00 adult, $2.00 senior and $1.00 child (6-12).*

Pretend you're on a sea voyage as you explore an old pilothouse with navigation instruments, maps and charts and a large ship's wheel. Find out what number of whistles you use to indicate the ship's direction. This room is large enough to really romp around. The highlight of this museum has to be the real lighthouse (although it's a steep climb up and out to the

A fun lighthouse that's worth the climb...

deck). After you proudly climb the 69 steps, catch your breath with a beautiful view of Lake Erie. Our favorite lighthouse & museum combo!

Geneva

GENEVA STATE PARK

Geneva - *4499 Padanarum Road (Shore of Lake Erie, I-90 to Geneva Exit 218) 44041. Phone: (440) 466-8400 or (800) 801-9982 lodge. www.dnr.state.oh.us. Miscellaneous: ERIEVIEW PARK - www.erieviewpark.com. Located on the "strip" with 20 old-fashioned classic rides, kiddie rides, bumper cars and water slides. Food service and picnic areas. Ride or day pass admissions. No fee to wander park area.*

Located on Ohio's northeastern shoreline, Geneva State Park reflects the charisma of Lake Erie. Vacationers enjoy fishing and boating, swimmers love the beautiful sand beach, while nature enthusiasts retreat to the park's freshwater marshes and estuaries. Three miles of multi-use trails traverse the park. They are used by hikers and cross-country skiers. 698 acres of camping, boating and jet ski rentals, and large cottages for rentals.

The **LODGE & CONFERENCE CENTER** at Geneva State Park (www. thelodgeatgeneva.com) is a newer upscale resort with a spectacular view of Lake Erie. The resort includes 109 guest rooms, a restaurant, indoor pool, outdoor pool, fitness center, game room and gift shop. Bicycle rentals are available for guests who would like to experience the NorthCoast from atop a bike. In addition, direct access to Lake Erie is available at the beach and marina located in the State Park.

GREAT LAKES MEDIEVAL FAIRE

Geneva - *3033 State Route 534. www.medievalfaire.com. The Great Lakes Medieval Faire is a shaded, 13th century family fun theme park filled with fine continuous entertainment, juried crafts and artisans, jugglers, jesters, musicians, rides and interactive games, and foods fit for a King. Step back in time to an age of romance and chivalry, where brave knights battle on the open jousting field for the favor of the Queen, fair damsels, and the roaring crowd. Join King Arthur, Queen Guinevere, and the Knights of the Round Table as they visit the village of Avaloch for a day of Celebration and Festivities! Admission. (weekends July to mid-August)*

Hinckley

BUZZARD DAY

Hinckley - *Cleveland Metroparks Reservation. (440) 351-6300. www.clemetparks.com/ events/buzzards_sun.asp. Annual migration of the buzzard with breakfast watch. Those most famous residents of Hinckley will return and the Buzzard Roost will be a-flutter with turkey vulture fans from all over the country. Cleveland Metroparks naturalists will be on-hand to talk about the natural history of the birds and why they return to this same spot year after year. Buzzard Sunday! activities include: Naturalist-led Hikes (including an "Early Bird" hike at 9:00am); Shuttle Hikes (to Top'O Ledges and Worden's Ledges); An Official Buzzard Scoreboard; EarthWords Nature Shop - with buzzard merchandise; Live Musical Entertainment; Buzzard Bingo; Children's Craft; Storytelling; Live Animal Programs; Historical Bus Tours of Hinckley; and an Exhibit Area. FREE. (mid-March Sunday)*

Jefferson

AC & J SCENIC RAILROAD

Jefferson - *State Route 46 to East Jefferson Street (Rte. 11 north, exit @ Rte. 307 west) 44047. Phone: (440) 576-6346. www.acjrscenic.net. Hours: Weekends departing 1:00 or 3:00pm (mid-June - October). Only Sundays in September. One is a former long-distance car with air-conditioning. Two others are commuter cars having windows that open and ceiling fans. Several can be heated for cooler weather. There is one on-board lavatory. Admission: $10.00 adult, $9.00 senior (60+), $7.00 child (3-12). Miscellaneous: Look for the Santa Train in December.*

Ride on a 1951 Nickel Plate train with a bright red caboose on a one hour ride through woodlands and farmland. Stop halfway at a staging yard for coal and iron ore in Ashtabula Harbor. Gift shop / concessions.

CIVIL WAR TRAIN RAID

Jefferson – AC&J Scenic Railroad. Watch as the Union and Confederate soldiers' battle for control of the railroad from the safety of your coach. Visit free Civil War encampment and shop at period merchants adjacent to the tracks at Jefferson. Optional stagecoach rides. Fares slightly higher than normal. Advance paid reservations highly suggested. (second weekend in July)

WILD WEST WEEKEND

Jefferson – AC&J Scenic Railroad. Meet some of the better known "outlaws" and "heroes" of the old west. Be part of a train hold-up and witness justice being served western style. Free admission to western town shop with period merchants, witness street gunfights and a jail break. Optional stagecoach rides. Fares slightly higher than normal. Advance paid reservations highly suggested. (third weekend of August)

KIDS PUMPKIN TRAIN

Jefferson – AC&J Scenic Railroad. Come and enjoy the antics of Freddie the HoBo or the Great Brad and receive a pumpkin to take home. Free kids popcorn w/ child fare. Admission. (second and third weekends in October)

TRAIN RIDES WITH SANTA

Jefferson – *AC&J Scenic Railroad. Train trip in decorated coaches with Santa. Songs & treats. Dress warmly. Admission. (Saturday after Thanksgiving until mid-December)*

JEFFERSON DEPOT

Jefferson - 147 E. Jefferson Street (SR 46 and downtown) 44047. Phone: (440) 293-5532. www.jeffersondepotvillage.org. Admission: $2.00 donation accepted. Tours: Guided Tours every Sunday, 1:00-4:00pm during June, July, August and September. School tours are early fall and late spring with hands-on activities and themes.

Travel back in time to the 1800's. Costumed kinfolk will let you peek back into the past! See the ornate 1872 LS&Ms Railroad Station on the National Register, the quaint 1848 "Church in the Wildwood," 1849 Church barn, 1918 Caboose, 1838 Spafford One-Room School House, Hohn's General Store, Early Pharmacy and 1888 House. The Blacksmith shop and Post Office are newer buildings on the property.

CHILDREN'S OLD-FASHIONED WILLIAMSBURG CHRISTMAS & CANDLELIGHT WALK

Jefferson – *Jefferson Depot. (second Sunday in December)*

VICTORIAN PERAMBULATOR MUSEUM

Jefferson - 26 East Cedar Street (off State Route 46) 44047. Phone: (440) 576-9588. www.webspawner.com/users/carriage/. Hours: Wednesday and Saturday 11:00am-5:00pm (Summer Only). Saturdays only (September-December). Admission: $4.00-$5.00.

First of all, do you know what a perambulator is? If you were like us, we just had to know! Answer…a baby carriage. Two sisters have collected and displayed almost 140 carriages dating from the mid-1800's to the early 1900's. Some are shaped like swans, gondolas, seahorses, and antique cars (made from wicker, which was the Victorian style). This is the nation's only baby carriage museum.

ASHTABULA COUNTY COVERED BRIDGE FESTIVAL

Jefferson - Ashtabula County Fairgrounds, 25 West Jefferson Street. (440) 576-3769 or www.coveredbridgefestival.org. Ashtabula is known as the working covered bridge capital of the Western Reserve. Enjoy a tour of 16 covered bridges during the beautiful fall season, plus entertainment, crafts, and draft horse contests. Admission. (second weekend in October)

Kirtland

HOLDEN ARBORETUM

Kirtland - 9500 Sperry Road 44094. Phone: (440) 946-4400. www.holdenarb.org. Hours: Daily 9:00am-5:00pm. Closed Christmas and Thanksgiving. Admission: $6.00 adult, $3.00 child (6-12).

Tour the many trails, which offer a variety of lengths and difficulty, from easy to rugged; something for everyone. Walk through gardens, fields and woods, past ponds and down into the valley. Guided hikes are available year-round. 3000 acres of gardens and walking trails (focus on woody plants). Holden Butterfly Garden is directly behind the Visitor Center. This fabulous garden is over two acres and home to two ponds, a waterfall and a profusion of plantings geared to attract caterpillars, butterflies and hummingbirds. Guided or self-guided hikes begin at Visitors Center. $2.00 Tram Tour, by reservation.

LAKE FARMPARK

Kirtland - 8800 Chardon Road (I-90 to SR 306 south to SR 6 east) 44094. Phone: (800) 366-FARM. www.lakemetroparks.com. Hours: Daily 9:00am-5:00pm. Closed Mondays (January-March) and all major holidays. Admission: $6.00 adult, $5.00 senior (60+), $4.00 child (2-11) Miscellaneous: Gift Shop. Restaurant. Comfortable walking or tennis shoes are best to wear on the farm. Wagon rides throughout the park are included. Wagon rentals are available. Barnyard - ostriches, poultry,

sheep petting. Pony rides are $2.00. Seasonal events are fantastic!

Not really a farm - it's a park about farming (and the cleanest farm you'll ever visit!).   Most of their focus is to discover where food and natural products come from. In the Dairy Parlor, you can milk a real cow and make ice cream from the cow's milk. Wander over to the Arena and watch the sheep show or a horse show. What products can be made with the help of sheep? How about feta cheese from their milk and yarn from their wool coats. Use special brushes to clean their wool and then spin some by hand. Some of the cutest exhibits are the babies...look for them all around the Arena. Exhibits are ready to be played with all day in the Great Tomato Works. A giant tomato plant (6 feet wide with 12-ft. leaves) greets you and once inside the greenhouse, you can go down below the earth in the dirt to see where plants get their start. Sneak up on a real honeybee comb, but mind the words on the sign, "DO NOT DISTURB - HONEYBEES AT WORK". This visit generates lots of questions about the food you eat. Great learning!

MAPLE SUGARING WEEKEND

Kirtland – *Lake Farmpark. Syrup making demos. Pancake dinners/breakfasts. Sugarbush tours by foot or by wagon or by train. (second weekend in March)*

VILLAGE PEDDLER & PUMPKIN HARVEST WEEKENDS

Kirtland – *Lake Farmpark. Pumpkin patches, hayrides, corn mazes, fall playlands, festive foods and crops. Admission. (select long weekends in October)*

COUNTRY LIGHTS

Kirtland – *Lake Farmpark. Horse-drawn sleighbell rides through the light show; live entertainment; baby calves, chicks and pigs; miniature railroad displays; delightful holiday horse shows; and, best of all, the life-like Toy Workshop where elves help kids make an old-fashioned wooden toy to take home. Your kids hammer, drill and paint their own creations. Holiday food served at the Visitor's Center, too. By reservation only! $1.00 extra admission over normal prices. (select days in December)*

Lake Milton

LAKE MILTON STATE PARK

Lake Milton - *16801 Mahoning Avenue (1 mile South of I-76 off State Route 534) 44429. Phone: (330) 654-4989. www.dnr.state.oh.us.*

Lake Milton's reservoir offers the best in water-related recreation. Boating, swimming and fishing are popular. A new 600-foot beach has restrooms,

NE Area

change booths, showers, playground, basketball court and sand volleyball court. The scenic shoreline provides a habitat for waterfowls and shorebirds for visitors to enjoy. 2,856 acres of boating (unlimited horsepower), fishing, swimming and winter sports.

Medina

ELM FARM - AMERICAS ICE CREAM & DAIRY MUSEUM & PARLOR

Medina - *1050 Lafayette Road (I-71 to SR 18 exit to town square, then US 42, 2 miles south of the Square, near the water tower) 44258. Phone: (330) 722-3839. www.elmfarm.com. Hours: Monday-Saturday 11:00am-6:00pm, Sunday Noon-5:00pm. Extended hours for parlor. Fewer hours in the winter. Admission: $2.00-3.50 (age 6+).*

The dairy farm dates back to the early 1900's. They started manufacturing ice cream in the 50's. The parlor serves the treats and light lunch foods in a soda fountain theme. In the back, they have a museum that features displays showing the way dairies used to operate and lots of dairy inventions through the years (i.e.. Jack Frost freezer, 20's & 30's Popsicle molds). The interactive areas and collection of full-size rare trucks and milk bottles demonstrates a great deal about the history behind Elm Farm and the dairy industry.

ICE FESTIVAL

Medina - *Downtown. Uptown Square. (800) 463-3462. www.elegantice.com. Cash prizes and medals for an ice carving competition. Sculpting demos and a "parade" of ice sculptures in front of uptown merchants' businesses. FREE. (mid-February long weekend)*

Mentor

LAWNFIELD - GARFIELD NATIONAL HISTORIC SITE, JAMES A.

Mentor - *8095 Mentor Avenue (I-90 exit Rte. 306, turn right 2 miles East on US 20) 44060. Phone: (440) 255-8722. www.nps.gov/jaga. Hours: Monday-Saturday 10:00am-5:00pm, Sunday Noon-5:00pm (May-October). Weekends only (November-April). Admission: $5.00 per person (age 16+). Educators: online biography for research papers. Miscellaneous: Gift Shop. Summer Fun Programs (weekdays at 2:00pm) are recommended for hands-on. If touring with school-aged kids, ask for the Young People's club worksheet of puzzles & games. Not recommended for preschoolers. Garfield Birthplace Site & Monument east of Cleveland (440-248-1188 & 216-421-2665).*

The Victorian farmhouse mansion was the home of President James A. Garfield. Notice the tiles in the dining room fireplace were painted by family as a craft project. The walk-in safe is neat (contains the wreath sent to his funeral by the Queen of England). Like to drape your legs over the side of a chair? See Garfield's office Reading Chair. Who killed him and why? A great museum explains his politics and death. Shortly after his election, an opponent at a railroad station in Washington D.C. assassinated him. See the video showing his life as a preacher (he strongly believed in Divine Providence), teacher

Did You Know?

The wallpaper in James A. Garfield's home and a side table in the Memorial Library have a spider web motif. Victorians believed that house spiders brought good luck and good fortune to the inhabitants.

and lawyer plus Garfield's campaign on the front porch of his home in 1880. Journalists standing on the lawn covering the campaign nicknamed the property "Lawnfield". Other structures on the 7.82 acre site include the carriage house (visitor center), the campaign office, the 75-foot tall pump house/windmill and barn. Be sure to spend as much time in the Visitors Center as on tour.

PRESIDENTS DAY AT THE GARFIELD NATIONAL HISTORIC SITE

Mentor – *Lawnfield. Join their annual President's Day program and take part in a new game, Presidential Squares. Join Presidents Lincoln and Garfield, along with several other presidents and their first ladies, in an interactive game of trivia tic-tac-toe for all ages. Crafts and activities in the afternoon. Small fee for each craft and discounted tickets for tours of the Garfield Home will be sold in honor of the event. (President's Day in February)*

CHRISTMAS OPEN HOUSE

Mentor – *Lawnfield. Buildings decorated for holidays, Santa visit, entertainment and light refreshments served. Great way to expose younger ones to historical homes that might be boring otherwise. Admission. (winter break at 2:00pm)*

Middlefield

NE Area

MIDDLEFIELD CHEESE HOUSE

Middlefield - *State Route 608 (north of Rte. 87) 44062. Phone: (440) 632-5228 or (800) 32-SWISS. www.middlefieldcheese.com. Hours: Monday – Saturday 8:00am – 5:30pm.*

Approximately 25 million pounds of Swiss cheese are produced here each year. Did you know that it takes nearly 6 quarts of fresh milk to make one pound of Swiss Cheese? Your tour begins with the film "Faith and Teamwork" describing the cheese-making process. Then wander through the Cheese House Museum with Swiss cheese carvings, antique cheese-making equipment, and Amish memorabilia. Lastly, sample some cheese before you buy homemade cheese, sausage and bread for a homemade snack on the way home.

PUMPKIN MAZE PLAYLAND

Middlefield - *Ridgeview Farm (SR 87, west of SR 45). Pumpkin Patches / Hayrides / Corn Mazes / Fall Playland - http://experienceridgeviewfarm.com. Admission (average $6.00). Plan on at least two hours playtime. Open weekends, some weekdays (by appointment) and weeknights. (late September - late October).*

Newbury

PUNDERSON MANOR HOUSE RESORT

Newbury - *Punderson State Park, (440) 564-9144 or www.atapark.com. Become a royal guest in an English Tudor-style mansion.* The charming rooms (not stuffy),

modernized indoor and outdoor pools and cozy cabins combine enchantment with relaxation (Rooms run ~$100+ and Cabins run ~$120.00+). They have board games and videos to check out at the front desk. There are sport courts (including horseshoes and volleyball) and a playground or two. The restaurant is upscale English/American for dinner, but lunch offers a more casual, moderately-priced fare (ever tried Welsh Rarebit?). Weekly summer activities for kids include: playing tag, Storytime, sand art, chalk art, nature walks, and a variety show. The resort has indoor/outdoor pools, tennis, basketball, toboggan and winter chalet.

PUNDERSON STATE PARK RESORT

Newbury - *(2 miles East of Newbury off State Route 87) 44065. Phone: (440) 564-2279. www.pundersonmanorresort.com.*

Nature programs. Tennis. 996 acres of camping, hiking trails, boating and rentals, fishing, swimming and winter sports. Family cabins with A/C and fireplaces. Just the right size for small family getaways in the woods. Activities abound year-round in this beautiful setting. Enjoy the tranquility of relaxing at the indoor and outdoor pools. Wade a while at the sandy beach, play tennis, volleyball, basketball. Combine that with 15 miles of natural hiking trails (some are nature walks with signs) that wind past deer, squirrel, beaver, giant maples, and scented pine trees. You might even catch a wink of a busy beaver working on his dam. When winter comes, you can snowmobile, cross-country ski, ice fish or race downhill on a giant grooved sled hill. And when it's time for sleep, you can hideaway in your room, the tower library or lounge by a fire. Lots of seasonal getaway packages are available.

NE Area

SLED DOG CLASSIC

Newbury – Punderson State Park. Dog sled racing in Ohio? Yes! See sled dog racers mush their teams through challenging race courses. Fee for racers. Spectators are admitted FREE. (one weekend in January, depending on weather)

WESTWOODS PARK

Newbury - 9465 Kinsman Road (Route 87) (I-90 to Route 306. Travel south on Route 306 for approximately 12.7 miles to Route 87. Turn east on Route 87) 44065. Phone: (440) 286-9516. www.geaugaparkdistrict.org/nature/westwoods.htm. Miscellaneous: Geauga County Parks are nearby.

They had an excellent Ice Age exhibit that has left, but the Ice Age theme continues throughout the year through outdoor adventures. Take home a souvenir glacier rock. Other exhibits highlight the geology, hydrology, and diverse ecology of the county's lands. More than 5 miles of trails traverse through woodlands, across streams and past outcroppings of conglomerate sandstone. Other trails lead past "black swamp" pools, past Sunset Overlook, or to Ansel's Cave. This is a one-stop place for studying glaciers in northeast Ohio.

Niles

MCKINLEY BIRTHPLACE MEMORIAL AND MUSEUM

Niles - 40 North Main Street (SR 46 to downtown) 44446. Phone: (330) 652-1704. www.mckinley.lib.oh.us. Hours: Monday-Thursday 9:00am-8:00pm. Friday and Saturday 9:00am - 5:30pm, Sunday 1:00 - 5:00pm (September - May Only)

The classic Greek structure with Georgian marble which houses a museum of McKinley memorabilia. Also see artifacts from the Civil War and Spanish-American War. McKinley was the 25th President and the first to use campaign buttons. He was assassinated in office.

Painesville

HEADLANDS BEACH STATE PARK

Painesville - State Route 44 (2 miles Northwest of Painesville) 44060. Phone: (440) 881-8141. www.dnr.state.oh.us.

The trademark of Headlands Beach State Park is its mile-long natural sand beach, the largest in the state. In addition to its popularity during the summer season with picnickers and swimmers, the area is home to many plant species

NE Area

typically found only along the Atlantic Coast. 125 acres of hiking trails (adjacent nature preserve), fishing, swimming and winter sports. **HEADLANDS DUNES STATE NATURE PRESERVE** - is located on the east end of the park, and one of the last remaining examples of Lake Erie beach and dunes. Preserve open daylight hours.

Peninsula

CUYAHOGA VALLEY SCENIC RAILROAD

Peninsula - *Cuyahoga Valley National Recreation Area (Independence Depot is off I-77 exit 155, follow signs) 44264. Phone: (330) 657-2000 or (800) 468-4070. www.cvsr.com. Hours: Departs Wednesday-Sunday, Morning and early Afternoon (June-October). Weekends, Morning and early Afternoon (Rest of the Year) Admission: $10.00-$15.00 per person (age 3+). Reservations are highly recommended. Educators: the wonderful Underground Railroad excursions are an immersion experience for students to become a slave escaping to freedom by foot and train. Miscellaneous: Gift Shop Car/Concession Car, Park Ranger/ Volunteer available for transportation or nature information. Main train trips depart from Independence, Peninsula & Akron. Bring a picnic lunch to eat in transit or at a stopover. Wheelchair car available.*

Ride in climate controlled coaches built between 1939 and 1940 on the very scenic 2 - 6½ hour ride to many exciting round trip destinations. Meadowlands,

The conductor punches Daniel & Jenny's train ride tickets...

pinery, marsh, rivers, ravines, and woods pass by as you travel to Hale Farm and Village, Quaker Square, Akron Zoo, Canal Visitor Center, Stan Hywet Hall or just a basic scenic tour (best if small kids take shorter trips or ones with layovers). Narration of views and history of changes in the area included. The Canal Limited is the only excursion which begins at the depot in Peninsula on a trip north to Canal Visitor Center. The center is a restored house on the Ohio & Erie Canal. Learn about the canal days in the museum and watch the canal lock demonstrations held every weekend during the summer and periodically in early fall. This is a fun way to spend the day family style (grandparents too!) and see one other attraction along the way. Be sure your little engineers get a blue or pink cap to wear along the trip as a memory of their first train ride! Preschoolers look forward to the summer special rides on the "Little Engine that Could". All kids love the holiday themed train rides.

MAPLE SUGAR EXPRESS

Peninsula – *Cuyahoga Valley Scenic Railroad. Departure is from Rockside Station. Ride the train to Hale Farm & Village. Travel to the year 1814 to meet a pioneer family who will share the ancient process of maple sugar production including tree tapping, sap collecting and syrup tasting. Admission. (first two weekends in March)*

EASTER BUNNY EXPRESS

Peninsula – *Cuyahoga Valley Scenic Railroad. Easter Bunny appearance, treat stations, egg hunts, and kids' entertainment and crafts. Admission. (Usually held Easter weekend and/or the weekend before)*

DAY OUT WITH THOMAS THE TANK ENGINE

Peninsula - *Cuyahoga Valley Railroad, Boston Mills Ski Resort, 7100 Riverview Road. (800) 468-4070 or www.cvsr.com. Four day event offering 20 minute rides onboard coaches pulled by a real-live 55 ton steam engine Thomas. Play games, watch Thomas videos, interact with exhibits, clowns, magic shows, food and Sir Topham Hatt. Admission, reservations suggested. (last two long weekends in May)*

PUMPKIN TRAIN

Peninsula – *Cuyahoga Valley Scenic Railroad. CVSR train excursions to Heritage Farm maze and pumpkin patch. Admission. www.heritagefarms.com. (October weekends)*

HOLIDAY EXPRESS, CHRISTMAS TREE ADVENTURE OR POLAR EXPRESS

Peninsula – *Cuyahoga Valley Scenic Railroad. Train Trip in decorated coaches with Santa. Songs and Treats. Some are pick your own tree or ride in pajamas. Dress warmly. Advance tickets necessary. Weekends and some weekdays.*

NE Area

Portage

TINKER'S CREEK STATE PARK

Portage - *10303 Aurora Hudson Rd. (2 miles West of State Route 43) 44266. Phone: (330) 296-3239. www.dnr.state.oh.us.*

Herons, ducks, geese and beaver can be found in the spring-fed waters, while cattail, buttonbush and swamp white oak line the shores of this beautiful park. Tinker's Creek State Nature Preserve is located adjacent to the state park and features extensive marshes. A 1.5-mile trail, known as the Seven Ponds Trail, features a boardwalk through the wetlands. An observation deck has been constructed to allow visitors excellent views of waterfowl. The preserve is open during daylight hours and is accessible only on foot. Parking is available on Old Mill Road in Aurora. 60 acres of fishing trails, swimming and winter sports.

Ravenna

WEST BRANCH STATE PARK

Ravenna - *5708 Esworthy Road (5 miles East of Ravenna off State Route 5) 44266. Phone: (330) 296-3239. www.dnr.state.oh.us.*

West Branch State Park's large lake with its many forks and coves is extremely popular with fishermen, boaters and swimmers. The park's meadows and woodlots provide an excellent backdrop for camping, hiking and horseback riding. Nature programs. More than twelve miles of hiking trails provide access to a portion of the state's Buckeye Trail passing through the park and is linked to the campground by a two-mile spur trail. The park offers extensive snowmobile trails when conditions permit. Mountain biking is permitted on trails in the snowmobile area.

Twinsburg

TWINS DAYS FESTIVAL

Twinsburg - *I-80/90 to SR-91, follow signs. www.twinsdays.org. The largest gathering of twins in the world (usually over 2500) includes twins contests, entertainment, fireworks and the nationally televised "Double Take" parade. Small fee for non-twins. Twinsburg was originally named by the Wilcox twins in the early 1800s. Admission. (first weekend in August)*

Vienna

WAGON TRAILS ANIMAL PARK

Vienna - *907 Youngstown-Kingsville Road (SR 193) 44473. Phone: (330) 539-4494. www.wagontrails.com. Hours: Daily, except Tuesday 10:00am-4:00pm (May-October). Admission: $14.00 adult, $11.00 senior (65+), $10.00 child (2-12). Coupon online. Tours: Include wagon ride, bucket of feed and petting zoo. Wagon and zoo are wheelchair and stroller accessible.*

From horse-drawn wagons, you'll see and feed animals from the farm to the Outback. Your safari will now take you over a bridge where you will feed colorful koi fish in the pond. Then your safari will go to new heights as your safari truck takes you up the new "mountain" where you'll get a view of the animals. Knowledgeable safari guides narrate your tour through 60 acres of woods, ponds and animals. Zoo food included with your admission. Get up close and personal as you feed the animals. Don't forget your camera!

Warren

NE Area

NATIONAL PACKARD MUSEUM

Warren - *1899 Mahoning Avenue NW 44482. www.packardmuseum.org. Phone: (330) 394-1899. Hours: Tuesday-Saturday Noon-5:00pm, Sunday 1:00-5:00pm. Admission: $5.00 adult, $3.00 senior (65+), $3.00 child (7-12).*

Watch a video about Packard's family of vehicles and personal family stories. See memorabilia about the manufacturer's history from 1899 – 1958. Look for vehicles named "Wingfoot", "Caribbean" or "flying". Also Packard Electric history display.

MOST MAGNIFICENT MCDONALDS IN AMERICA

Warren - *162 North Road SE 44484. Phone: (330) 856-3611.*

The 3-story building (mostly glass) complete with brass and marble fixtures, a glass elevator and even a baby grand piano. Open daily for breakfast, lunch and dinner with typical menu served. Closed Christmas Day.

Youngstown

MILL CREEK PARK

Youngstown - *(South of Mahoning Avenue off Glenwood Avenue) 44406. Phone: (330) 740-7115 (Lanterman's Mill). (330) 740-7107 (Ford Nature Center) or (330) 740-7109 (Winter). www.millcreekmetroparks.com. Hours: Tuesday-Friday 10:00am-5:00pm, Saturday and Sunday 11:00am-6:00pm (Center/Mill). Miscellaneous: Gift Shop. Lanterman's Mill (May - October), small admission.*

This park has your basic scenic trails, lakes, falls, gorges, gardens and covered bridges but it also has more.

FORD NATURE CENTER is a stone house with live reptiles and hands-on exhibits about nature. Recorded messages are available for the different stations along the trail beginning outside the Center.

LANTERMAN'S MILL is a restored 1845 water-powered gristmill with a 14-foot oak wheel. While in the mill, observe the pioneer ingenuity involved in the early production of meal and flour. Smell the aroma of freshly ground grains. Hear the gentle trickle of water as it flows toward the wheel. Feel the rumblings of the stones as they whirl, grinding the various grains. Later, if you would like, try baking some Johnny Cakes, a staple of an early American diet made with stone-ground corn meal.

The famous Mary Poppins-like Silver Bridge

As you travel through the park, be on the look out for the Silver Bridge (reminiscent of Old England and Mary Poppins). Fellowship Riverside Gardens is a colorful mixture of greens and flowers. The best community park system (and very well kept) you'll find anywhere!

CHILDREN'S MUSEUM OF THE VALLEY

Youngstown - *139 E. Boardman Street (corner of East Boardman St. & Walnut Street, across from the main Post Office, downtown) 44501. Phone: (330) 744-5914. www.valleykids.org. Hours: Tuesday-Friday 10:00am-4:30pm, Saturday Noon-4:00pm. Admission: $5.00 (age 3+).*

The Children's Museum of the Valley provides regional educational opportunities for hands-on interaction. Activities and exhibits explore the culture, art, drama, construction, science, and natural history connected to the Mahoning Valley. Be a mad scientist and perform real science experiments yourself. Visit the Science Laboratory to assist and view science demonstrations. The Phenomenal Puzzle Place is where you test your puzzle prowess as your try to solve the wide variety of puzzles. Come and learn more about your world, region, and state with giant maps. Test your navigation and mapping skills about your community. Visit Culture Central and live the culture of one of the more than one hundred countries from which people came to the Valley. Or, be a television or stage star and play with art and writing displays.

BUTLER INSTITUTE OF AMERICAN ART

Youngstown - 524 Wick Ave. 44502. Phone: (330) 743-1711. www.butlerart.com. Hours: Tuesday – Saturday 11:00am - 4:00pm, Sunday Noon - 4:00pm. Open Wednesday evenings until 8:00pm.

Showcases American art from colonial times to the present. Children's Gallery (hands on) and American Sports Art Gallery. FREE Sunday Family Programs and FEE paid "gift art" classes available.

YOUNGSTOWN HISTORICAL CENTER OF INDUSTRY & LABOR

Youngstown - 151 West Wood Street (Wood Street is off of Market Street two blocks north of downtown) 44503. www.ohiohistory.org/places/youngst/. Phone: (330) 743-5934 or (800) 262-6137. Hours: Wednesday-Saturday 9:30am-5:00pm, Sunday & Holidays Noon-5:00pm. Closed winter holidays. Admission: $7.00 adult, $3.00 student (all ages). Educators: the link to ohiohistoryteachers.org provides background info before you tour and a brief history, activities, word search and a puzzle.

If your family has a heritage of steelworkers in the family, then this is the place to explain their hard work. The history of the iron and steel industry in the Mahoning Valley area can be viewed easily looking at the life-sized dioramas titled, "By the Sweat of Their Brow" or from the numerous videos shown throughout the building. Rooms are set up like typical steel mill locker rooms, company houses, and a blooming room. They certainly give you the "feel" of the treacherous work at the mill.

YOUNGSTOWN SYMPHONY

Youngstown - *260 Federal Plaza West 44503. www.youngstownsymphony.com. Phone: (330) 744-4264.*

Performs Pops Concerts with guest artists in Powers Auditorium (tours). Community site Storytyme concerts provide opportunities for the Symphony to engage young people in programs on their common ground. Youngstown Symphony Youth Orchestra and Youngstown Symphony Symphonette programs.

GORANT CANDIES

Youngstown - *8301 Market Street (State Route 7, Boardman) 44512. Phone: (800) 572-4139 Ext.1236. Tours: Tuesday-Thursday until 1:30pm (usually March only). Maximum 50 people. 1st grade and above. Miscellaneous: Candy store. Displays of chocolate history. Hair net (provided) must be worn.*

Put on your paper hat and watch up to 375,000 pieces of chocolate candy being made each day. See the 2000-pound chocolate melting vats and color-coded rooms. The brown walls are the molding room where chocolate is poured and shook on vibrating tables (takes out the air bubbles). The yellow room is the coating room. A personalized hand dipper (only one) dips 3600 candies a day. Receive a free candy bar at the end of the tour.

FIRST NIGHT YOUNGSTOWN

Youngstown - *Downtown. A family oriented non-alcoholic event with indoor and outdoor activities such as kid's/parent's food, entertainment and crafts, and a countdown to midnight. Admission. www.firstnightyoungstown.org. (New Years Eve)*

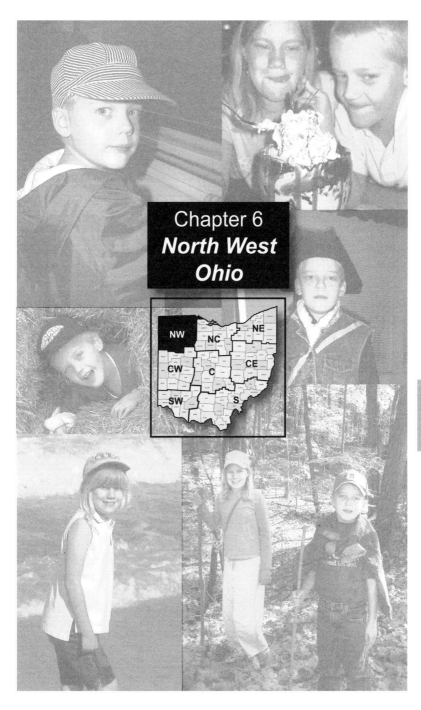

Chapter 6
North West Ohio

Archbold
- Sauder Village

Attica
- Oak Ridge Festival

Bluffton
- Bluffton Blaze Of Lights

Bowling Green
- American Civil War Museum Of Ohio
- Bg Wind Farm
- Snooks Dream Cars Museum

Bryan
- Spangler Candy Factory (Dum Dum Pops Candy)

Defiance
- Auglaize Village Farm Museum
- Independence Dam State Park

Delphos
- Museum Of Postal History

Fayette
- Harrison Lake State Park

Findlay
- Dietsch Brothers Fine Chocolates & Ice Cream
- Mazza Collection Museum
- Northwest Ohio Railroad Preservation

Grand Rapids
- Canal Experience
- Mary Jane ThurstOn State Park

Lima
- Allen County Museum
- Apple Festival

Sylvania
- Fossil Park

Toledo
- Lagrange Street Polish Festival
- Sandpiper Canal Boat
- SS Willis B Boyer
- Toledo Botanical Gardens
- Toledo Firefighters Museum
- Toledo Mud Hens Baseball
- Toledo Museum Of Art
- Toledo Symphony Orchestra
- Toledo Zoo
- Tony Packo's Café
- Wolcott House Museum Complex

Toledo (Maumee)
- Children's Wonderland
- Splash Bay Resort

Toledo (Oregon)
- Maumee Bay State Park

Toledo (Perrysburg)
- Fort Meigs

Van Buren
- Van Buren Lake State Park

Van Wert
- Kernel Coopers Corn Maze

Waterville
- Bluebird Passenger Train

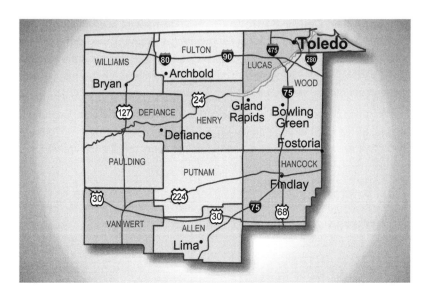

A Quick Tour of our Hand-Picked Favorites Around...

North West Ohio

Giant freighters pour into the Toledo harbor and you can even tour one. The most kid-friendly fort in the Midwest is located down the road at **Fort Meigs** - with plenty of dress up clothes to try on and green space to run on. Built up an appetite for some crazy food? Stop by the original **Tony Packo's** and take a bite of a Packo's Hungarian Hot Dog while viewing framed hot dog buns signed by celebrities. We told you - crazy stuff...

Do your kids love candy? What about spending the day sampling chocolates, ice cream and hard candies? You're in the right place! This region of the state has **Dietsch Brothers** (Findlay) old-fashioned ice cream and chocolates and **Spangler Candy Factory** (Bryan), the makers of Dum Dum Pops suckers. Tours are not too hard to coordinate (weekdays) or tag along on. Try wacky flavors like Cream Soda, Cotton Candy, "Everything but the Kitchen Sink," or "Snick-a-Ripple" flavors. You can't miss on these visits – just be sure to brush your teeth soon after!

After lunch it's time to take a trip back in time at **Sauder Village**. Costumed guides will lead you through hands-on activities and more. Hope you're there on a day the marble maker is around but most every day the ice cream shop is open.

Sites and attractions are listed in order by City, Zip Code, and Name. Symbols indicated represent:

 Festivals   Restaurants   Lodging

Archbold

SAUDER VILLAGE

Archbold - *22611 State Route 2 (off SR 66, 2 miles Northeast on State Route 2 or off turnpike exit 25) 43502. www.saudervillage.org. Phone: (419) 446-2541 or (800) 590-9755. Hours: Tuesday-Saturday 10:00am-5:00pm. Sunday & Holidays Noon–4:00pm (Late-April – October). Closed 60-90 min. early in the spring and fall. Admission: $12.50 adult, $6.25 child (6-16). $1.00 Carriage, Train or Wagon rides - Group Rates available for 25+. Educators: Wonderful, easy-to-follow study guides and suggested activities for all grades are on the Teacher Resources Page online. Miscellaneous: The Barn Restaurant serves wonderful home-style food with a children's menu ($3.00-5.00). Meals served buffet or family style. Gift Shop. Bakery. Sauder Store & Outlet - featuring all of the ready-to-assemble furniture made right here in Archbold. Heritage Inn w/ indoor pool with waterfall and hot tub adjacent to the "Great Oak Tree", new game and exercise rooms. Campground - new this year, campers can use the pool, hot tub and game room at the Inn.*

Like to get inside the mind of a successful entrepreneur? Learn the history of Sauder Woodworking & Erie Sauder. He started from using wood scraps (his teenage woodworking shop is open for touring). Meet famous & very talented glass, pottery and wood crafters (you'll flip over the beautiful giant marbles!). Maybe get locked in jail, trade furs or take a lick from an old-fashioned ice cream cone. In the Homestead (1910), look for baby animals, an old baby walker, a Mother's Bench Rocker or a baby bottle warmer. Walk along the craft village where you can meet a weaver, broom maker, tinsmith or blacksmith all dressed in early 20th Century clothing. "Erie Express" is a new train that

takes guests on a 1 1/2 mile ride around the perimeter of the Historic Village. The Natives & Newcomers: Ohio in Transition area is a living-history experience telling the story of Northwest Ohio from 1803 to 1839. Covered with swamps and thick forests, this region of the state was one of the last to be settled by Europeans. The settlement also depicts the family lives of the many Native American nations who called this area home. Lastly, the Pioneer Settlement area is being developed and they conduct programs and hold events in that space every so often (worth checking out). While focusing on Northwest Ohio, the Pioneer Settlement stories mirror our national story of immigration, community building and technological changes. Workers here love what they do!

DAIRY DAYS

Archbold – Sauder Village. June is National Dairy Month – a time to celebrate America's great bounty of dairy products. Activities vary from day-to-day. Some of the special dairy demonstrations during the week-long celebration include making buttermilk biscuits, buttermilk pie, bread pudding and schmearcase, which is like cottage cheese. Costumed guides make buttermilk salad, cheese pie, ice cream and homemade cheese. Guests are able to try their hand at making butter, rolling out homemade biscuits, and hand-cranking the ice cream. There are also be historic recipes for guests to pick up and try at home.

OLD FASHIONED 4TH OF JULY AT SAUDER VILLAGE

Archbold – Sauder Village. What better place to celebrate Independence Day than at Ohio's largest living-history village! Join them for a day filled with special activities from hand-cranked ice cream and old-fashioned games, to a reading of the Declaration of Independence and patriotic songs being played on the reed organ. Admission. (July 4th)

APPLE BUTTER MAKING WEEK

Archbold – *Sauder Village. Guests can watch the boiling of the cider, the adding of the thinly sliced apples and the cooking of the apples in the copper kettles over an open fire. Admission. (last full week in September)*

HOLIDAY LANTERN TOURS

Archbold – *Sauder Village. (By Reservation Only). Time: Tours last roughly 90 minutes and will be repeated every half hour from 4:00 – 8:30pm. An opportunity to experience a turn-of-the-century Christmas at Sauder Village! The flicker of a candle-lit lantern lights the way as a costumed interpreter, through a personalized, guided lantern tour, takes small groups on a journey to meet historical characters in the 1910 Homestead, the District 16 Schoolhouse, Villages' St. Mark's Church and the Train Depot. Guests are invited to experience the holiday customs and celebrations of the 1900s in Northwest Ohio as along the way, your guide shares stories about Christmas' past and the history of Northwest Ohio. (Saturday after Thanksgiving, first Saturday in December, and second weekend in December)*

Attica

OAK RIDGE FESTIVAL

Attica - *SR 4 & US 224, on Township Road 104. www.oakridgefestival.com. Early 1800's frontier life & Indian village. Re-enactors, craft demonstrations, authentic open fire, wood cooked food and folk entertainment. (mid-October weekend)*

Bluffton

BLUFFTON BLAZE OF LIGHTS

Bluffton - *Downtown. Hundreds of thousands of lights & holiday / storybook characters. Wagon rides. www.allencvb.lima.oh.us/events.asp. Daily, evenings. Admission. (Thanksgiving - January 1)*

Bowling Green

AMERICAN CIVIL WAR MUSEUM OF OHIO

Bowling Green - *123 East Court Street (I-75 exit 181 west on SR 25) 43402. Phone: (419) 352-0209. www.acwmo.org. Hours: Tuesday, Thursday, Friday 11:00am-5:00pm, Saturday 10:00am-5:00pm and Sunday Noon-4:00pm. Admission: $5.00 adult, $4.00 senior (55+) and $2.50 student. $13.00 family. A new cell phone audio tour is included free with paid admission.*

The Civil War exhibits feature dioramas, mannequins, audio visual tools and display boards to focus on different aspects of a soldier's life. The exhibits include "The Soldier's Life" - helps the visitor understand the daily routine and hardships endured. "Medicine" - focuses on the inadequate medical care, as well as sickness and battlefield casualties. "Prisoners of War" discusses the POW experience and how it influenced the outcome of the war. "Ohio in the Civil War" explores Ohio's role in the Civil War (20 minute video) and "Put it On" allows children to dress in reproduction Civil War clothing and gear.

BG WIND FARM

Bowling Green - *Corner of Route 6 & Tontogany Rds. (I-75 exit 179) 43402. Phone: (419) 354-6246.*

Visit the only wind farm in the state of Ohio (Daily from 9:00am-6:00pm). Four wind turbines swirl through the air to generate electricity to BG and its electric co-op. An informational computerized kiosk is available for visitors to see how these towering turbines were erected.

SNOOKS DREAM CARS MUSEUM

Bowling Green - *13920 County Home Road, Twp 172 (I-75 exit 179, east on US 6) 43402. Phone: (419) 353-8338. www.snooksdreamcars.com. Hours: Daily 11:00am-4:00pm. Admission: $3.00-$5.00 per person.*

Begin in a 1940's era Texaco filling station, featuring "automobilia" - everything from hood ornaments to backseat games to seat covers. Operational mechanics area leads to coin-operated amusement games (even a Model T kiddie ride). Remember pedal cars? The showroom has dream cars showcased in themed rooms from the 30's-60's. "We like to consider this a living museum," says Jeff, co-owner, "since all the cars on display are in working condition. My father and I drive one or another of them around town on a regular basis."

Bryan

SPANGLER CANDY FACTORY (DUM DUM POPS CANDY)

Bryan - *400 N. Portland Street (10 miles south of 80/90 Toll Road, exit 13, SR 15 south to town, right on Mulberry Street) 43506. Phone: (419) 636-4221 or (888) 636-4221. www.spanglercandy.com. Hours: Wednesday - Friday Noon-5:00pm (winter). Tuesday-Friday Noon-5:00pm (summer). Factory tour prices are: Adults $5.00, Children 6-18 years $3.00, Children 5 & Under Free with paid Adult, Seniors $4.00. There is no admission charge for the store/museum. Tours: Public tours of the factory are available on the Dum Dum Trolley Tuesday or Wednesday through Friday 12 Noon to 4:30pm. There are no reservations. Tours are on a first come,*

first served basis. Tours will not be offered on any day that is a holiday for the factory.

If you are in northwest Ohio please stop by to see them. The Spangler Store & Museum is located at the corner of Portland and Mulberry Streets, next to the world-famous Dum Dum Pop factory! Due to safety and FDA regulations, the trolley tour will not go through the main kitchen areas, but does go through the candy pack-out and warehouse areas (similar to what the Jelly Belly tours do). Candy cooking and forming in the kitchen areas are shown via a DVD player while on the trolley tour. The small, ball-shaped treats are famous for their array of great-tasting flavors, from Cream Soda to Cotton Candy and Butterscotch, which rotate in part based on consumer voting. Consumers can go to www. dumdumpops.com and vote for their favorite Dum Dum flavor, weigh in on newly introduced flavors, and submit suggestions for new flavors.

The museum features historical information in a timeline fashion, along with samples of products and other artifacts from years past. A video history of the company runs continuously in the museum. Through the museum experience visitors will learn how their company grew from one man and some baking powder to the world-class hard candy company it is today.

NW Area

Defiance

AUGLAIZE VILLAGE FARM MUSEUM

Defiance - *12290 Krouse Road (3 miles SW of Defiance - follow signs. Off US 24, west of town) 43512. Phone: (419) 784-0107. http://historicalauglaizevillage.com/. Hours: Event Weekends Only 9:00am-5:00pm (April-October).*

A recreated late 19th Century village - 17 new, restored or reconstructed buildings that serve as museums. The Red Barn with the Street of Shops and Hall of Appliances is probably the most interesting - especially the old-fashioned appliances and authentic period food they serve. Best to visit during festivals or special events when there is an abundance of costumed guides. For example, they have an Old West Shoot-out the third Sunday of each month.

BLACK SWAMP STEAM & GAS SHOW

Defiance - *Auglaize Village. Working gas tractors and over 30 operating steam engines on the sawmill, threshing wheat and plowing machines. Admission. (second weekend in June)*

JOHNNY APPLESEED FESTIVAL

Defiance - *Auglaize Village. The historic village is busy with crafts, apple butter, cider and molasses making, and harvest demonstrations. Tractor pulls and train rides. 1840 Encampment. Admission. (first weekend in October)*

INDEPENDENCE DAM STATE PARK

Defiance - *State Route 424 (4 miles East of Defiance) 43512. Phone: (419) 784-3263. www.dnr.state.oh.us.*

Independence Dam State Park is situated along the banks of the beautiful Maumee River. The river is ideal for boating, fishing or a scenic canoe trip. A three-mile hiking trail, once the towpath of the Miami and Erie Canal, offers the hiker a glimpse into the colorful past of Ohio's canal era. The trail meanders between the canal and the river through a dense hardwood forest. The three-mile access road through the park offers a scenic ride for bicyclists. The park offers the perfect setting for a picnic or overnight camping experience.

NW Area

Delphos

MUSEUM OF POSTAL HISTORY

Delphos - *339 North Main Street (Lower Level of Post Office) 45833. Phone: (419) 695-2811. www.postalhistorymuseum.org. Hours: Monday, Wednesday, Friday 1:30-3:30pm. Admission: FREE.*

7000 square feet of displays plus media presentations that show development of American history and the influences of the U.S. Mail. See the progress of mail processing, development of the letter, stamps, postmarks and the idea of a post office. You can actually sit in a 1906 rural mail coach.

Fayette

HARRISON LAKE STATE PARK

Fayette - *26246 Harrison Lake Road (4 miles South of Fayette off State Route 66) 43521. Phone: (419) 237-2593. www.dnr.state.oh.us.*

A green island of scenic woodlands in a rich agricultural region. A 3.5-mile hiking trail circles the lake and provides the opportunity to explore the scenic lakeshore and woodlands. Harrison Lake is popular for swimming, fishing, camping and canoeing. 249 acres of camping, hiking trails, boating (no power), fishing, swimming, and winter sports.

Findlay

DIETSCH BROTHERS FINE CHOCOLATES & ICE CREAM

Findlay - *400 W. Main Cross Street (I-75 exit 157, State Route 12) 45839. Phone: (419) 422-4474. http://dietschs.com/. Hours: Store open daily except Mondays. Tours: Wednesday & Thursday mornings (1st grade & up). (Fall & Spring). ½ hour long, 20 people maximum. Reservations required.*

Three brothers (2nd generation) run an original 1937's candy and ice cream shop. In the summer, see ice cream made with real cream. They make 1500 gallons per week. Fall, heading into the holidays, is the best time to see 500 pounds of chocolate treats made daily. Try some wacky flavors like "Everything but the Kitchen Sink" or "Snick-a-Ripple."

MAZZA COLLECTION MUSEUM

**Findlay - *1000 North Main Street (University of Findlay Campus, I-75 EXIT 159
SR 224) 45840. www.mazzacollection.org. Phone: (419) 424-4777 or (800) 472-
9502. Hours: Wednesday-Friday Noon-5:00pm, Sunday 1:00-4:00pm. Closed all
holidays. Admission: FREE. Tours: Tuesday-Thursday between 9:00am-2:00pm
and Friday 9:00am-Noon. $2.00 per student, $1.00 extra for craft. Educators:
Illustration kits - free.***

This is the world's first and largest teaching museum devoted to literacy and
the art of children's picture books. All the artwork here is based on children's
storybooks and the teaching units include such exhibits as printmaking,
the Mother Goose Corner, a borders section, the book-making process, an
historical art gallery, and an art media exhibit. After a tour, some groups opt
to have an art activity where the students get to use the ideas they saw in the
galleria to produce their own artwork.

NORTHWEST OHIO RAILROAD
PRESERVATION

**Findlay - *11600 County Rd. 99 (northeast corner of I-75 exit #161 east and
County Rd. 99, north end of Findlay) 45840. www.nworrp.org. Phone: (419) 423-
2995. Hours: Generally weekends 1:00-4:00pm (April-December) plus evenings
during peak seasonal excursions. Diesel on Saturdays and Steam on Sundays.
Admission: $1.00-$2.00 per person.***

Experience the thrill of a coal-burning steam train ride on the nearly 1/2 mile
of 15" gauge track layout. Special events, such as Tracks To The Past in
September, the Pumpkin Train in October & Christmas' North Pole Express
in December are best times to visit. Tours of their B&O caboose are the first
Sunday of each month, April-September. Kids eyes gleem at the Lionel Toy
Train layout.

TRACKS TO THE PAST

Findlay *– NW Ohio Railroad Preservation. Gas engines, tractors, steam engines,
operating sawmill, antique cars, firetrucks, quarter-scale live steam Train Rides, B&O
caboose tours, HO Model Trains, Wood carvers, Alpacas, Birds of Prey, Infantry
Reenactments, Blacksmithing, Kiddie tractor pull and all-you-can-eat breakfasts. Small
admission. (weekend after Labor Day)*

PUMPKIN TRAIN

Findlay – *NW Ohio Railroad Preservation. Take your little ones on a delightful train ride to the Pumpkin Patch where they can choose their special pumpkin to be transported back to the station on the flatbed car attached to the train. Small admission fee for ride and for pumpkin. (October weekends)*

SANTA TRAIN

Findlay – *NW Ohio Railroad Preservation. Train trip in decorated coaches with Santa. Songs and treats. Dress warmly. Admission. (Thanksgiving weekend)*

Grand Rapids

CANAL EXPERIENCE

Grand Rapids - *Mill Road in Providence Metro Park (I-475 exit 45, US 24 and State Route 578) 43522. www.metroparkstoledo.com/metroparks. Phone: (419) 535-3050 mill or (419) 407-9741canal. Hours: Wednesday-Friday 10:00am-2:00pm, Weekends & Holidays Noon-4:00pm (May-October). Extended weekday hours in the summer. Admission: FREE demonstrations of mill. Canal boat tickets: $6.00 adult, $5.00 senior (60 and over), $3.00 child (3 to 12). Tours: 45 minute mule drawn canal boat rides leave every hour until 4:00pm. Narrated. Miscellaneous: Fishing below the roller dam, hiking/biking on 8-mile towpath (once occupied by canal mules). Educators: Discovery Walks.*

CANAL BOAT: It's always 1876 at Providence, where people and goods still travel by mule-drawn canal boat at 4 MPH. Grain is still ground in a gristmill and water still powers saws that slice logs. Visitors to the Metropark step back in time to become passengers on the Miami & Erie Canal aboard the "The Volunteer," with a crew of costumed interpreters in character for the first half of a 45-minute, narrated journey.

ISAAC LUDWIG MILL: At the mill, the saw whirls in the background as interpreters explain how people lived and worked in the former canal town of Providence, Ohio, on the Maumee River opposite the current canal town of Grand Rapids. One of the few mills left in Ohio, this 19th century mill sits on the Maumee River and demonstrates how a flour mill, sawmill and electric generator can be powered by water from the old canal below.

NW Area

MARY JANE THURSTON STATE PARK

Grand Rapids - *State Route 65 (2 miles West of Grand Rapids) 43534. Phone: (419) 832-7662. www.dnr.state.oh.us.*

The Maumee is not only scenic, but also provides some of the best stream fishing in Ohio. Boaters have access to the river while history buffs may explore the remnants of the old canal. A one-mile portion of the Buckeye Trail passes through the park following the side cut canal. The trail continues on to the Village of Grand Rapids. A one-mile loop trail winds through the floodplain forest while an easy half-mile trail circles the day use area. Six miles of trails in the North Turkeyfoot Area may be used for backpacking, horseback riding or mountain biking.

Lima

ALLEN COUNTY MUSEUM

Lima - *620 West Market Street (I-75 exit 125 on SR117/309) 45801. Phone: (419) 222-9426. www.allencountymuseum.org. Hours: Tuesday-Friday 1:00-5:00pm. Saturday & Sunday, 1:00-4:00pm. Closed holidays & Mondays. Children's Museum only open in summer and by appointment in the school year. Admission: Suggested donation of $5.00 per adult. Miscellaneous: While in town, stop for lunch or dinner at the Old Barn Out Back (3175 W. Elm St - www.oldbarnoutback. com) serving country-style food in the "Chicken Coop" or "Pig Pen" - known for their fried chicken and cinnamon rolls.*

Indian and pioneer artifacts. Antique automobiles and bicycles. Barber Shop, Doctor's office, country store, log house on grounds. Next door is MacDonell House (wall of purses). Lincoln Park Railroad exhibit locomotive and Shay Locomotive (huge train) is something the kids will love. The most unusual display is a collection of objects that people have swallowed (ex. Bolts, diaper pins). Try your hand at various trivia games and puzzles located throughout the Children's Center. Each year, they present a new theme in the Children's Discovery Center where kids can assemble and operate exhibit interactives based on relevant themes (ex. Railroads). Experiment with other means of communication. Try your hand at sign language. Learn how to read and write Braille. Play checkers blindfolded. Send signals with flags. Write with hieroglyphs like an ancient Egyptian. Try to decipher a secret code. Make a craft or art project to take home with you.

NW Area

APPLE FESTIVAL

Lima - *Allen City Farm Park, 1582 Slabtown Road. www.jampd.com. Apples & cider. Apple pie eating contests. Apple peeling contests. Apple butter. Candy apples. Wagon/ hayrides. Apple Dumplings, Fritters, Donuts, etc. Parades. Pioneer crafts. Petting Zoo. (first weekend in October)*

Sylvania

FOSSIL PARK

Sylvania - *5705 Centennial Road (I-75 exit 210 west on SR 184) 43560. Phone: (419) 882-8313. Hours: Saturday 10:00am-6:00pm, Sunday 11:00am-6:00pm (Memorial Day -late October).*

Fossil Park, located in an abandoned quarry is an unusual destination for travelers who are interested in rocks, quarries or mines. The park contains some of the best fossils from the Devonian period in the world; even little tyke diggers can easily find corals, brachiopods, echinoderms and trilobites . Visitors are allowed to break the fossils from the soft shale and keep any fossils that they find...but, no tools are allowed. FREE Admission.

Toledo

WOLCOTT HOUSE MUSEUM COMPLEX

Toledo - *1031 River Road (I-475/23 to exit 4, Rte. 24 east) 43537. Phone: (419) 893-9602. www.maumee.org/recreation/wolcott.htm. Hours: Thursday-Sunday Noon-4:30pm (April-December). Admission: $5.00 adult, $4.00 senior (60+), $2.50 student. Educators: Teacher Tour Activities online.*

Life in the mid-1800's in the Maumee Valley. Costumed guides lead you through a building complex of a log home, depot, church and gift shop.

TOLEDO MUD HENS BASEBALL

Toledo - *Fifth Third Field, Warehouse District (I-75 exit 202A or 201 B) 43604. Phone: (419) 725-HENS. www.mudhens.com.*

AAA Semi-professional baseball (farm team for the Detroit Tigers) played in a newly built classic ballpark. See "Muddy" the mascot or sit in "The Roost" bleachers. Also, playground and picnic areas. Tickets $6.00-$8.00. (April-September).

NW Area

SS WILLIS B BOYER

Toledo - 26 Main Street, International Park (East side of Maumee River – Downtown. I-75 exit 201A) 43605. Phone: (419) 936-3070. www.willisbboyer.org. Hours: Monday-Saturday 10:00am-5:00pm, Sunday Noon-5:00pm (May-October). Admission: $6.00 adult, $5.00 senior (60+), $4.00 student.

The 617-foot freighter depicts how ships of the Great Lakes worked in the early to mid-1900's. It was the biggest, most modern ship on the Great Lakes (in its day) and as you drive up, it takes up your whole panoramic view. Visitors

are awed by the massive engine room, posh officer's dining room, stainless steel galley and the captain's quarters. A nautical museum of Lake Erie resides inside with photographs, artifacts and best of all for kids, hands-on exhibits. Have your picture taken "at the wheel". Ask for the "child-oriented" tours.

TONY PACKO'S CAFÉ

Toledo - 1902 Front Street (I-280 exit 9) 43605. www.tonypackos.com. Phone: (419) 691-6054. Built up an appetite for some crazy food? After seeing the "macho" life of "shipsmen" near the Toledo port, try some fiery or authentic ethnic Hungarian food at Tony Packo's Café. The original restaurant is part dining, part museum. Sample a Packo's Hungarian Hot Dog, made famous by Corporal Klinger on the TV show "M.A.S.H." Be sure to look for the 100's of hot dog buns signed by TV stars that have visited the café. Other unique dishes are a Chili Sundae (chili and toppings served in a sundae glass with chips); Fried Pickles; Cabbage Rolls; and Chicken Paprikas.

SANDPIPER CANAL BOAT

Toledo - 2144 Fordway, Riverfront (Jefferson Street Docks, I-75 exit 201B or 202A) 43606. Phone: (419) 537-1212. www.sandpiperboat.com. Admission:

Range of $7.00-$15.00. Basically double the price for lunch cruises.

Replica of a Miami and Erie Canal boat. Educational or historical Cruise up river past riverside estates, downtown or down river. See busy ports, shipyards

and dry docks. Public and group tours average 2-4 hours. Mostly weekends (morning/lunchtime). Some evening cruises. Seasonal Fireworks and Fall Cruises. Bring a picnic. Reservations suggested. (May-October)

TOLEDO ZOO

Toledo - *2700 Broadway (I-75 to US 25 - 3 miles South of downtown) 43609. Phone: (419) 385-5721. www.toledozoo.org. Hours: Daily 10:00am-5:00pm (May - Labor Day). Daily, 10:00am-4:00 pm (Rest of the Year). Admission: $11.00 adult, $8.00 senior (60+) and child (2-11). Parking fee $5.00. Military, County residents and special promotion discounts updated seasonally on the website. Miscellaneous: Carnivore Cafe (dine in actual cages once used to house big cats!). Children's Zoo - petting zoo and hands on exhibits. Wagon/stroller rentals. Educators: The Kids Corner online page has coloring sheets and games for grades pre-K thru 6th. The Zoo's Discovery Boxes contain books, activities, posters and games that bring the wonders of nature right to your classroom or living room for a small fee.*

They have areas typical of a zoo but they are known for their Hippoquarium (the world's first underwater viewing of the hippopotamus) along with a well-defined interpretive center and hands-on exhibits. The Kingdom of Apes and African Savanna are other popular exhibits. The zoo established a milestone in polar bear history when it welcomed three cubs in 2006. For fans of Animal Planet's hit show, "Meerkat Manor," be sure to check out the zoo's meerkat mob. The renovated Aviary, Primate Forest and Arctic Encounter (a nose-to-nose view thru a cabin window to observe gray wolves and an underwater view of seals) are hot spots, too.

LIGHTS BEFORE CHRISTMAS

Toledo – Toldeo Zoo. Hundreds of thousands of lights & holiday / storybook characters. Daily, evenings (unless noted). Admission. (begins third weekend of November thru most of December)

TOLEDO FIREFIGHTERS MUSEUM

Toledo - *918 Sylvania Avenue (I-75 exit 206) 43612. www.toledofiremuseum.com. Phone: (419) 478-FIRE. Hours: Saturday Noon-4:00pm. Admission: FREE.*

Feel what 150 years of history of fire-fighting must have meant to the fireman. Learn fire safety tips. In Jed's Bedroom, children are taught how to roll out of bed, keep low in case of smoke, and feel the door for heat with the back of their hand. See actual vintage pumpers, uniforms, and equipment used that trace the growth of the Toledo Fire Department. Located in the former No. 18 Fire Station.

TOLEDO BOTANICAL GARDENS

Toledo - *5403 Elmer Drive (I-475/US23 exit 13, off North Reynolds Road) 43615. Phone: (419) 936-2986. www.toledogarden.org. Hours: Open 8:30am-5:30pm.*

Fifty-seven acres of meadows and gardens. The outdoor sculpture and storybook garden appeal to kids. A scavenger hunt can be picked up at the Administrative Office for families to enjoy while discovering the Garden. Gallery and gift store. FREE except for special events. Family Nights are held each season (fee).

TOLEDO MUSEUM OF ART

Toledo - *2445 Monroe at Scottwood (off I-75) 43620. Phone: (419) 255-8000. www.toledomuseum.org. Hours: Tuesday-Saturday 10:00am-4:00pm, Sunday 11:00am-5:00pm. Open Friday evening til 10:00pm.*

Discover treasures from the riches of the medieval, the splendors of a French chateau, and the tombs of Egypt. Also glass, sculpture, paintings. Visit the extensive collection, including works of art from ancient to contemporary, a sculpture garden, a medieval cloister, a room from a French chateau and much more. The Family Center - Free, fun, and open to everyone! The TMA Family Center is the perfect place for our youngest Museum visitors to make and take memories with their parents and caregivers. Drop in for themed activities that enliven the world of art for kids of all ages (even those in grown-up guise). Check the calendar for upcoming projects. TMA is open late on Fridays and admission is always FREE!

TOLEDO SYMPHONY ORCHESTRA

Toledo - *1838 Parkwood Avenue 43697. Phone: (800) 348-1253 or (419) 246-8000. www.toledosymphony.com.*

Regional symphony performs orchestral masterpieces with guest artists, chamber, contemporary, pops, youth and summer concerts. Their Young People's concerts combine other forms of art with classical music (September-May)

LAGRANGE STREET POLISH FESTIVAL

Toledo - *Lagrange Street between Central & Mettler Sts. www.polishfestival.org. All kinds of Polish foods, polish bands, dancers, a polka contest, rides and craft area. Free. (first full weekend in July, after the 4th)*

SPLASH BAY RESORT

Toledo (Maumee) - *1705 Tollgate Drive 43537. www.splashbaymaumee.com. Phone: (419) 897-5555. Hours: Vary by season. Generally open most evenings from 3:00pm until dark. Closed on Tuesday and Wednesdays. Extended weekend hours (all day). Admission: Day Passes are $20.00-$25.00 per person. Spectator Passes $6.00. Overnight packages begin around $179.00 / night with waterpark passes included that work on the day of check in and check out.*

In Northern Ohio, Splash Bay opened in October of 2007. The 35,000 square foot domed waterpark features a kiddy pool, lazy river, a giant playspace with bucket, and water slides that weave in and out of the building (still covered while outside, of course). The tube slides and body bowl are favorites with many kids. Cute, local names for rides like: Fort Meigs Deck Top and Walleye River Run add to the fun. There is also an arcade to satisfy your dry time gaming urges and a snack bar in the park.

CHILDREN'S WONDERLAND

Toledo (Maumee) - *Lucas County Recreation Center, 2901 Key Street. (419) 213-2200. Children's Wonderland has received national recognition as the only display of its kind in the nation. The entire 22,000 square feet is turned into a fantasyland filled with animated displays, colorful lighting, and holiday music. Children can ride the North Pole train, visit with Talking Tree, and see over 40 holiday displays. Small Admission. (entire month of December)*

MAUMEE BAY STATE PARK

Toledo (Oregon) - *1400 Park Road #1 (I-280 exit 7 - 8 miles East of Toledo, then 3 miles North off State Route 2) 43618. Phone: (419) 836-7758 park, (419) 836-1466 Lodge or 836-9117 Nature Center. www.dnr.state.oh.us.*

Resort cottages and rooms, golf, racquetball, sauna, whirlpool, fitness, tennis, volleyball and basketball are available. The lodge, cottages and golf course are nestled among the scenic meadows, wet woods and lush marshes teeming with wildlife. The park boasts two sand beaches -- on the Lake Erie shore while the other lines the park's inland lake. Developed hiking trails in the park include the Mouse Trail, a 3-mile diverse trail winding through meadows and young woodlands, and several miles of paved combination trails for bicycling and cross-country skiing. Hikers will discover acres of meadow, marshland and woodland. A 2-mile boardwalk traversing swamp and marsh wetlands has interpretive signs, an observation blind and tower, and wheelchair accessible loop. 1,845 acres of camping, hiking trails, boating, fishing, swimming and winter sports.

For updates & travel games visit: **www.KidsLoveTravel.com**

NW Area

FORT MEIGS

Toledo (Perrysburg) - *29100 West River Road (1 mile Southwest of State Route 25, I-475 to exit 2) 43552. www.fortmeigs.org. Phone: (419) 874-4121 or (800) 283-8916. Hours: Wednesday-Saturday 9:30am-5:00pm. Sunday & Holidays Noon-5:00pm (April-October). Visitor Center ONLY remains open year-round. Admission: $8.00 adult, $7.00 senior (60+), $4.00 child (6-12). Miscellaneous: Military History Center with Gift Shop at the stone shutterhouse describes role of Ohioans at War. Monthly summer weekend reenactments. Educators: Printable activity sheets (word search and scavenger hunts) are online under Education link. Occasional Miniature War Gaming days held where mini warfare is re-created on tabletop battlefields (separate admission).*

A War of 1812 era authentic castle-like log and earth fort with seven blockhouses that played an important role in guarding the Western frontier against the British. William Henry Harrison built Fort Meigs on the Maumee River in 1813 to protect northwest Ohio and Indiana from British invasion. The remodeled museum with authentically restored fort is a child's dream! The

museum has many unique artifacts, easily displayed with a large gift shop attached. But, the fort's blockhouses, earthen mounds and cannon holes are major "role-playing" spaces! Each blockhouse exhibits a "theme" and the re-enactors add flare to the scene.

March like a soldier or try the "Wheel of Disease". The walls of the blockhouses are 2 feet thick with 4-inch deep windows with cannon hole ports on the second floor. See actual cannons fired as the air fills with smoke. Notice how much manpower was needed to "run" a fort. Our favorite fort in the Midwest!

1813 INDEPENDENCE CELEBRATION

Toledo (Perrysburg) - The 4th of July at Fort Meigs is celebrated with cannon firings, toasts, music, and a day of leisure. War of 1812 soldiers and civilians recreate this day through cannon firings, demonstrations, and hands-on activities for children. The highlight of the day is the eighteen-gun National Salute accompanied by toasts, and fife and drum music starting at 2:00pm on July 4th. A War of 1812 living history encampment, weapons demonstrations, and more take place throughout the weekend. Admission. (July 4th weekend)

FORT MEIGS HOLIDAY OPEN HOUSE

Toledo (Perrysburg) - *War of 1812 soldiers and civilians will be on hand to provide demonstrations and answer questions about the War of 1812 and camp life. Enjoy holiday music, hot cider and cookies and hands-on activities. Try your hand at period dancing. No partner or experience is necessary. Shop the museum store for holiday gifts. New this year is tin-smithing demonstrations. Admission. (second Saturday in December)*

Van Buren

VAN BUREN LAKE STATE PARK

Van Buren - *State Route 613 (1 mile East of Van Buren, I-75 exit 164) 45889. Phone: (419) 832-7662. www.dnr.state.oh.us.*

Hiking trails circle the lake. Hikers, horseback riders, and mountain bikers are welcome on 6 miles of multiple-use trails traversing steep ravines and gentler terrain in scenic woodlands. 296 acres of camping, hiking trails, boating, fishing, and winter sports.

Van Wert

KERNEL COOPERS CORN MAZE

Van Wert - *Cooper's Amazements, 9867 Mendon Road. Pumpkin Patches / Hayrides / Corn Mazes / Fall Playland. www.kernelcoopers.com. Admission (average $6.00). Plan on at least two hours playtime. Open weekends, some weekdays (by appointment) and weeknights. (late September - late October).*

Waterville

BLUEBIRD PASSENGER TRAIN

Waterville - 49 North 6th Street (3rd and Mill Street - Grand Rapids Depot - departures) 43566. Phone: (419) 878-2177. www.tlew.org. Hours: Wednesday & Thursday, Saturday, Sunday and Holidays- Afternoon Departures (Summer). Weekends and Holidays Only (May, September, October). Visit website for updated departure/arrival schedule. Admission: $11.00 adult, $10.00 senior (65+), $7.50 child (3-12). Round trip.

Can you guess why they call it "Bluebird"? Answer: The bluebirds come back to Ohio in the spring and leave in the early fall. That's when the train runs. The 45-minute trip (each way) on a 1930's era passenger train includes a spectacular view from a 900-foot long bridge over the Maumee River and Miami & Erie Canal (now the millrace for Isaac Ludwig Mill).

NW Area

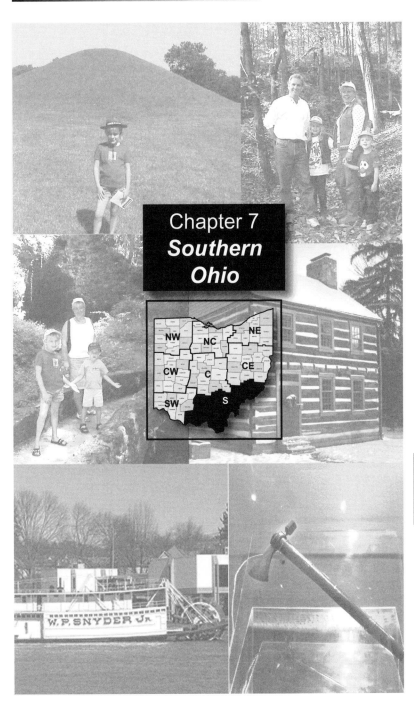

Chapter 7
Southern Ohio

Athens
- Stroud's Run State Park

Bainbridge
- Cave Canyon (7 Caves)
- Magic Waters Theatre
- Paint Creek State Park
- Pike Lake State Park

Belpre
- Lee Middleton Doll Factory

Chillicothe
- Adena
- Apple Festival
- Feast Of The Flowering Moon
- Great Seal State Park
- Hopewell Culture National Historical Park
- Ross County Heritage Center
- Scioto Trail State Park
- Sumburger Restaurant
- Tecumseh
- Telephone Museum, James M. Thomas

Glouster
- Burr Oak State Park
- Smoke Rise Ranch Resort

Laurelville
- Tar Hollow State Park

Logan
- Hocking Hills STate Park
- Lake Logan State Park
- Washboard Music Festival

Marietta
- Campus Martius
- Marietta Soda Museum
- Marietta Trolley Tours
- Ohio River Museum
- Pumpkin Maze Playland
- Red, White And Blues

Marietta (cont.)
- Rossi Pasta
- The Castle
- Valley Gem Sternwheeler

McArthur
- Lake Hope State Park

Nelsonville
- Hocking Valley Scenic Railway
- Paul Bunyan Show

Oak Hill
- Jackson Lake State Park

Peebles
- Serpent Mound

Portsmouth
- Portsmouth Murals

Reedsville
- Forked Run State Park

Rio Grande
- Bob Evans Farm

Rockbridge
- Hocking Hills Canopy Tours

Waverly
- Lake White State Park

Wellston
- Buckeye Furnace
- Lake Alma State Park

West Portsmouth
- Shawnee State Park

S Area

A Quick Tour of
our Hand-Picked
Favorites Around...

Southern
Ohio

Grab your cameras and backpacks and head for southeast Ohio in time
to hear the conductor of the **Hocking Hills** Scenic Railway in Nelsonville
beckon "all aboard" the old-time passenger train. The cave and trail system
(near Logan or Glouster) here attracts visitors from hundreds of miles away
but the beauty of the different southern Ohio seasons is really why they came.
If you don't have "sure foots" in your crowd, a nice leisurely ride on the train
may suit your family best.

Ancient Indians are the name of the game in Chillicothe. Curious? Try to
answer these questions: Why did Ancient Hopewell Indians build Mounds?
Where did they get seashells and copper from? At **Hopewell Indian**

Mounds you may just be able to piece the clues together. To keep with the Indian theme, purchase tickets for your older elementary kids to the **Tecumseh** drama or just catch his tomahawk at **Adena**.

Wear layered clothing and comfortable walking shoes because your family is going on an adventure! **Cave Canyon** (formerly **7 Caves**) is an absolutely wonderful way to spend almost the entire day in nature as you explore a series of small caves you actually peer into. But first, you have to traverse the 100 foot deep canyon surrounded by an enchanting rock-walled gorge. Don't worry, clear paths lead the way...

Have you ever looked at an ugly wall and thought – how can I cover this up? Paint, of course, is the answer. But what if that wall is 2,200 feet long and 20 feet high? About 10 years ago, in the river town of Portsmouth, a committee was formed to begin a project that would take a 20 foot floodwall that protected its city from the Ohio River and transform it into 2,200 feet of magnificent art. Each **Portsmouth Mural** tells the story of the history of Ohio and its people - beginning in the year 1730 and ending in 2002. Which one is your favorite?

At the very tip of the southern region of Ohio is a town that still has an air of the first settlement in the Northwest Territory. The whole downtown Marietta area is one of our favorites to visit during the summer months (festival season) but your family might especially like seeing artifacts from really old Ohio at **Campus Martius**. Things like the oldest house, farm or musical instruments. Some of their murals are so big, you feel you're actually walking into them. Plenty of videos and interactive voices make this old place pretty interesting. Afterwards, lighten the scene by popping into a pasta factory or soda shop and museum.

How many states can boast of having a doll factory that is open to tour? Well, Ohio can! Going west from Marietta along the Ohio River is the cutest factory you'll ever find – **Lee Middleton Doll Factory**. On your tour you'll discover how they make those little babies look and feel real. Even guys like to watch them "pop" the eyeballs in. Warning: prepare to fall in love with these "babies" and want one for your own.

Sites and attractions are listed in order by City, Zip Code, and Name. Symbols indicated represent:

 Festivals   Restaurants   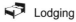 Lodging

---

Athens

STROUD'S RUN STATE PARK

Athens - *11661 State Park Road (8 miles Northeast of Athens off US 50A, Cty Road 20) 45701. Phone: (740) 592-2302. www.dnr.state.oh.us.*

The first settlers arrived in the Athens County region in 1796. Two townships of land in the area had been apportioned by the Ohio Company in 1795 for the benefit of a university. Settlers were encouraged to settle on these college lands to make them attractive, productive and to form a fund for the institution. The park derives its name from the Strouds family who settled in the area in the early 1800s. Fifteen miles of hiking trails meander through the wooded hills of Strouds Run leading to scenic vistas throughout the park. Excellent bird-watching and nature study can be done along the trail. An 8½ mile bridle trail has been constructed. A 900-foot sand beach on the east side of the lake is open during the summer months from sunrise to sunset. 2,767 acres of camping, hiking trails, boating and rentals, fishing, swimming and winter sports.

Bainbridge

CAVE CANYON (7 CAVES)

Bainbridge - *7660 Cave Road (US 50, 4 miles Northwest, follow signs) 45612. Phone: (937) 365-1935. www.highlandssanctuary.org. Hours: Daily (except Wednesday) 10:30am-4:00pm (June-August). Weekends only (April, May, September, October). Admission: $10.00 adult, $5.00 child. Includes Museum facilities, orientation slide presentation, and three trails available for hiking on one's own. Group reservations throughout the week by appointment. (March-November). Miscellaneous: Many stairs - not stroller accessible. Shelter house. They have plans to create a Natural History Center in the Gift Shop Welcome Center area.*

The Grotto trails are so much fun!

Wear layered clothing and comfortable walking shoes because your family is going on an adventure! An absolutely wonderful way to spend almost the entire day in nature as you explore a series of small caves you actually peer into. The region abounds with cliffs and canyons, seeps and springs, sinkholes and small caves. An imposing 100 foot deep vertical canyon carved by the Rocky Fork Creek winds through the heart of the preserve, presenting an enchanting rock-walled gorge. Naturalist-led tours include a forest walk and candle-lit cave tours (led Tom Sawyer style - with old-fashioned candle lanterns). Guided tours allow for the kids to learn about the unusual structures as they walk along. Cute, clever names are given to each naturally carved figure. Some areas require following "corkscrew" paths to deep dungeons or grottos. Three different trails lead to caves with cemented walkways, handrails, and lighting showing specific formations. See cliffs, canyons, and waterfalls. About a hundred kinds of birds inhabit The Seven Caves, the Pileated Woodpecker is the rarest. It's a beautiful and humbling experience. A hidden treasure here!

MAGIC WATERS THEATRE

Bainbridge - *7757 Cave Road 45612. www.highland-ohio.com/magicwaters. Phone: (937) 365-1388. Performances: Friday-Saturday 8:00pm, Sunday 7:00pm (mid-June through Labor Day). Pre show picnics available with reservations and additional fee. Admission: $7.00 adult, $4.00 senior, $3.50 child.*

Live outdoor drama in a rustic amphitheater featuring magic shows and kid's theatre (i.e. The Wizard of Oz). Christmas at the Cabin (October through December 25) and pre-show dinners are wonderful additions to the regular lineup.

PAINT CREEK STATE PARK

Bainbridge - *14265 US 50 (17 miles East of Hillsboro on US 50) 45612. Phone: (937) 365-1401. www.dnr.state.oh.us.*

Located amid the scenery of the Paint Creek Valley, Paint Creek State Park features a large lake with fine fishing, boating and swimming opportunities. A modern campground and meandering hiking trails invite outdoor enthusiasts to explore the rolling hills and streams of this area. Nature programs. On the west side of the lake is Paint Creek Pioneer Farm. The pioneer farm includes a log house, collection of log buildings, livestock, gardens and fields which represent a typical farm of the early 1800's. A walk through Pioneer Farm provides further insight into the settlers' lives. Boating rentals and winter sports. Bicycle rental is available and miniature golf can be enjoyed for a small fee.

PIKE LAKE STATE PARK

Bainbridge - *1847 Pike Lake Road (6 miles Southeast of Bainbridge) 45612.*
Phone: (740) 493-2212. www.dnr.state.oh.us.

The surrounding state forest is known for its variety of ferns, mosses, lichens and fungi. The wildflowers are diverse, creating spectacular displays--spring through autumn. The park features 12 standard cottages and 12 family cottages. Six miles of hiking trails provide strenuous and/or casual walks to scenic locations. The adjacent state forest has several miles of bridle trails. Horses are not provided by the park or forest. Nature programs. 613 acres of camping, hiking trails, boating and rentals, fishing, swimming and winter sports.

Belpre

LEE MIDDLETON DOLL FACTORY

Belpre - *1301 Washington Boulevard (I-77 to SR 50/618) 45714. Phone: (740) 423-1481 or (800) 233-7479. www.leemiddleton.com. Tours: Monday – Friday 9:00am – 2:00pm (Hourly). March – December. Approximately 20 minutes. Reservations Suggested. FREE. Educators: the whole tour is a giant physics and chemistry lesson - moving parts, perfectly tempered vinyl heads, non-toxic paint techniques. Miscellaneous: Factory Store with bargain buys and Nursery where you can adopt a life-sized Middleton infant baby doll complete with papers, promises and pictures. You can also visit a Newborn Nursery at many locations in the nation to adopt a baby.*

Lee Middleton started making dolls at her kitchen table in 1978 and modeled them after her children and children she knew. Take a brief walk through the Legacy Dollhouse Museum where you'll see some actual artifacts from Lee's beginnings and how the giant factory came about. On tour a guide shows you techniques critical to the distinctiveness of these high-quality collectable dolls that look and feel almost real. One machine makes feet, hands and heads out of liquid vinyl cured in molds. Watch them put eyes in by blowing up the mold head like a balloon (with an air compressor) and popping in the eyes. Then, they release the air and the eye is set in place (this is the part the guys like!). See the artists hand paint each doll's face using stencils and paint makeup. What a fun "girl's place" to visit - include lunch at their cafe. Hopefully during your visit you'll get

S Area

to experience a little girl adopting her first Middleton baby. It's so real, you'll swell with emotion as you see the new "Mom" promise the nursery worker to care for her baby properly. Prepare to fall in love with a doll and want one for your own!

Chillicothe

ADENA

Chillicothe - *(West of State Route 104 off Adena Road) 45601. Phone: (740) 772-1500 or (800) 319-7249. www.friendsofadena.org. Hours: Wednesday-Saturday 9:30am-5:00pm, Sundays and Holidays Noon-5:00pm (April-October). Admission: $8.00 adult, $4.00 student (all ages). Tours: Tours of the mansion begin on the hour, from 10:00am-4:00pm, with no tour at noon. Educators: Adena to Go glossary, word search, and bios are on the link: www.ohiohistoryteachers.org.*

View the overlook of the hillside that was used to paint the picture for the Ohio State Seal. Looking east from the north lawn, one can see across the Scioto River Valley to the Mount Logan range of hills (the Seal view). Adena was the 2000-acre estate of Thomas Worthington (1773-1827), sixth governor of Ohio and one of the state's first United States Senators. The mansion house, completed in 1806-1807, has been restored to look much as it did when the Worthington family lived there, including many original Worthington family furnishings. Look for Thomas Jefferson's invention, a giant dumb waiter - why was it called that? Adena is an important site

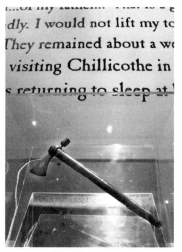

Tecumseh's tomahawk

for many reasons. It is the only plantation-type complex of its kind in the state and the stone mansion was built by the Father of our Statehood. Also visit a tenant house, smoke house, wash house, barn and spring house. Begin at the Visitors Center for an overview. Then, play games in two interactive areas, one dress-up, the other running a supply boat successfully in the early 1800s computer game area. A good area to study early Ohio statehood.

GREAT SEAL STATE PARK

Chillicothe - *Marietta Pike (3 miles Northeast of Chillicothe) 45601. Phone: (740) 773-2726. www.dnr.state.oh.us.*

Great Seal State Park is dedicated to the wilderness spirit of Ohio. The history of the Shawnee nation and Ohio's early statehood is in these hills. Rugged trails take visitors to scenic vistas of distant ridge tops and the Scioto Valley below. The Sugarloaf Mountain Trail (yellow), 2.1 miles, climbs through dense maple-dominated forests to the crest of Sugarloaf. This loop is short and rises almost 500 feet in less than a quarter mile. These very hills are depicted on the Great Seal of the State of Ohio, from which the park gets its name.

HOPEWELL CULTURE NATIONAL HISTORICAL PARK

Chillicothe - *16062 State Route 104 (two miles north of the intersection of US 35 and SR 104) 45601. Phone: (740) 774-1126. www.nps.gov/hocu. Hours: Daily 8:30am-5:00pm. Extended closing at 6:00pm in the summer. Closed Thanksgiving, Christmas and New Year's Day, and on Monday/Tuesday during December-February. Grounds open daily dawn till dusk. Admission: FREE. Educators: Before your visit, click on Teachers, then Curriculum Materials for a guide to*

print. There is popular activity booklet for kids that come to the park. Along with this they also offer Native American games and pottery making for kids. Junior Ranger program.

A Jr. Ranger tells us about the mounds...

The 120-acre park with 13-acre earthwall enclosure is home to 23 prehistoric burial and ceremonial mounds of the Hopewell Indians. The center presents the story of the prehistoric Hopewell culture with exhibits, brochures and the 17-minute video "Legacy of the Mound Builders." The park is a cool place for kids to learn about what happened in Ohio during the last 2000 years. Just wander through the park's museum, watch the short movie about the

S Area

Hopewell culture, or stroll around the mounds. Kids can also learn about the plants and animals that live in the park by walking the trails around the Mound City Group Visitor Center. Question: How did they make so many trinkets from materials like copper, seashells and mica (materials not found in Ohio)? After viewing many effigy (animal-shaped) pipes, maybe purchase a reproduction (inexpensively) as a souvenir.

ROSS COUNTY HERITAGE CENTER

Chillicothe - *45 W. Fifth Street (near Paint Street, downtown) 45601. Phone: (740) 772-1936. www.rosscountyhistorical.org. Hours: Tuesday-Sunday Noon-5:00pm (April-December). Friday & Saturday only (January-March). Admission: $4.00 adult, $2.00 senior & student.*

See the table upon which Ohio's Constitution was signed and Thomas Worthington's sea chest! See exhibits on early Chillicothe (diorama of town in 1803) and Ohio, Civil War (Camp Sherman -- "Ohio's World War I Soldier Factory,"), World War I and the Mound Builders. Also the McKell Library, the Knoles Log House Museum (everyday life in early 1800's Chillicothe) and Franklin House Women's Museum. Kids will be intrigued by the stories of olden times like: No garbage pickup? Just throw it in the streets and let roving animals eat the "slop". Or, how did the saying: Peas, Porridge Hot...Peas, Porridge Cold...Nine Days Old" come about (something to do with leftovers!). And, why didn't they use forks? Learn the real "scoop" about Conestoga wagons and how kids used miniature wagons to train their "pets". Look through an authentic old-fashioned ViewMaster (Megalethoscope). Because this complex showcases the first capital of Ohio, it has early Ohio historical value hidden in every corner!

SCIOTO TRAIL STATE PARK

Chillicothe - *144 Lake Road (10 miles South of Chillicothe off US 23) 45601. Phone: (740) 663-2125. www.dnr.state.oh.us.*

A small, quiet park nestled in beautiful 9,000-acre Scioto Trail State Forest, this state park is an undisturbed wooded refuge. Twelve miles of hiking trails and 17 miles of bridle trails lead to scenic overlooks and breathtaking vistas. 248 acres of camping, hiking, boating, canoeing, fishing and winter sports.

SUMBURGER RESTAURANT

Chillicothe - *1487 North Bridge Street 45601. Phone: (740) 772-1055. www.sumburger.com. To add to your "telephone" experience in town (Telephone Museum listing), eat a casual lunch or dinner (ordered from table telephones) at Sumburger Restaurant on the retail strip. If you want an even more authentic 50s experience, drive your auto into a covered spot, order from the menu into the intercom and soon your order is delivered and set on a tray next to your driver window. The house specialty is of course the Sumburger, "a jumbo all beef patty served up on a hot bun with melted cheese, lettuce, and our own special sauce."*

TECUMSEH

Chillicothe - *Sugarloaf Mountain Amphitheater (US 23 to Bridge St. exit, left on SR 159, right on Delano Road) 45601. Phone: (740) 775-0700 or (866) 775-0700. www.tecumsehdrama.com. Hours: Monday-Saturday, Show time 8:00pm. Show ends around 10:45pm. Reservations please. (early June to Labor Day weekend) Admission: $22.95 General (slightly reduced Monday-Thursday), $7.00 discount for children (under 10). Backstage Tours 4:00 or 5:00pm ($3.00-$4.00). Free Prehistoric Indian Mini-Museum. Backstage Tour - highly recommended for all*

ages. The stuntmen of TECUMSEH! give a dazzling display of stage-combat and flintlock firing, then pitch headfirst from a twenty-one foot cliff, get up, and explain how they did it. Tours last approximately one hour and also include make-up demonstrations (including mock "yummy" blood bags & Native "tanning" products) and detailed historical information on the drama and area. Necessary to understand storyline and not be frightened by savage conflicts. Miscellaneous: Gift Shop & Restaurant with buffet (good food & entertainment - $7.50 - $11.95 per person) served a few hours before the show. Warning: We recommend the Drama for 4th graders and older who have studied Ohio History and understand the savage, violent conflicts.

The backstage tour was great to learn about the many special effects, such as the safe "high fall"...

S Area

TECUMSEH *(cont.)*

This production has received national attention. Witness the epic life story of the legendary Shawnee leader as he struggles to defend his sacred homelands in the Ohio country during the late 1700's (before Ohio was a state). Fast action horses, loud firearms and speeding arrows make the audience part of the action especially when costumed actors enter the scene from right, left and behind. Lots of lessons learned about courage, honor, wisdom and greed…for kids and adults. We left quietly sobbing. As the actor playing Tecumseh said to us afterwards, "we got it."

TELEPHONE MUSEUM, JAMES M. THOMAS

Chillicothe - *68 East Main Street 45601. Phone: (740) 772-8200. Hours: Monday-Friday 8:30am-4:30pm. Closed holidays. Suggested $1.00 donation.*

Run by the Chillicothe Telephone Company, it shows the telephone from its invention stages to modern times. The museum features telephone equipment and paraphernalia dating back to 1895. Included are telephone instruments, early local directories, wooden underground conduit and a working section of electro-mechanical "step-by-step" switching equipment. Free tours by appointment.

FEAST OF THE FLOWERING MOON

Chillicothe *- Yoctangee City Park, just north of Main Street near the Railroad tracks. www.feastofthefloweringmoon.com. (800) 413-4118. This three-day themed event features Native-American dancing, crafts and village as well as a mountain-man encampment depicting pioneer life in the early 1800's. Extensive quality arts and crafts displays, food, entertainment, and a variety of activities to see and do. Free. (Memorial Day Weekend – Friday thru Sunday)*

APPLE FESTIVAL

Chillicothe *- Hirsch Fruit Farm, 12846 State Route 772. Apples & cider. Apple pie eating contests. Apple peeling contests. Apple butter. Candy apples. Wagon/hayrides. Apple Dumplings, Fritters, Donuts, etc. Parades. Pioneer crafts. Petting Zoo. Orchard tours, pick-your-own apples. www.hirschfruitfarm.com. (third weekend in September)*

Glouster

BURR OAK STATE PARK

Glouster - *10220 Burr Oak Lodge Road (6 miles Northeast of Glouster off State Route 13) 45732. www.dnr.state.oh.us. Phone: (740) 767-3570 or (740) 767-2112 Lodge.*

Located in southeast Ohio, quiet and remote Burr Oak State Park has a rustic country charm in its scenery of wooded hills and valley farms. Twenty-eight miles of hiking trails, including a portion of the state's Buckeye Trail, take hikers to scenic vistas and unique rock outcroppings. There are 30 family cottages with air conditioning and cable TV situated near the lodge in the wooded hills overlooking the lake. A public swimming beach offers enjoyment for swimmers and sunbathers. Nature programs, Bridle trails, Guest rooms in the Lodge with an indoor pool, tennis and basketball courts are highlights of this park. Also camping, hiking trails, low power boating and rentals, fishing, swimming, and winter sports.

SMOKE RISE RANCH RESORT

Glouster - *6751 Hunterdon Road (US 33 to SR 78 to CR 92) 45732. Phone: (740) 767-2624 or (800) 292-1732. www.smokeriseranch.com.*

Saddle up and get ready to discover your inner cowboy. Full service campground or cabins. Working Cattle Ranch (Ridin' & Ropin'), Riding Arenas, Trail riding. Activities Include: Round Up Rides , Pool and Hot Tub Parties, Hay Rides, BBQ's , Team Ropings and Team Pennings, Music Events and Dances.

Laurelville

TAR HOLLOW STATE PARK

Laurelville - *16396 Tar Hollow Road (10 miles South of Adelphi off State Route 540) 43135. Phone: (740) 887-4818. www.dnr.state.oh.us.*

Dense woodlands of scattered shortleaf and pitch pines growing on the ridges were once a source of pine tar for early settlers, hence the name Tar Hollow. Dogwoods, redbuds and a variety of wildflowers color the hillsides in the springtime. The 2-mile Pine Run mountain bike trail begins at the general store. 634 acres of camping, hiking trails, boating, fishing, swimming.

S Area

Logan

HOCKING HILLS STATE PARK

Logan - 19852 St. Rt. 664 South (Route 33 south to Route 664, follow signs) 43138. Phone: (740) 385-6841 or (800) HOCKING. www.dnr.state.oh.us/parks/. Hours: 6:00am-Sunset (Summer), 8:00am (Winter).

The hiking trails lead to awesome scenery around every corner....

In the mid 1700's, several Indian tribes traveled through or lived here including the Wyandot, Delaware and Shawnee. Their name for the river, from which the park gets its name, was Hock hocking or "bottle river." Nature trails are found throughout the park, many of them lead to obscure, out-of-the-way natural creations. The park includes: Ash Cave (an 80 acre cave and stream), Cantwell Cliffs, Cedar Falls, Conkle's Hollow, Rock House, and the most popular, Old Man's Cave (a wooded, winding ravine of waterfalls and caves). The recess caves at Ash Cave, Old Man's Cave and Cantwell Cliffs are all carved in the softer middle rock. Weathering and erosion widened cracks found in the middle layer of sandstone at the Rock House to create that unusual formation. Overnight accommodations, bed and breakfasts, camping, cabins with A/C, heat and fireplaces, recreation, picnic grounds, and hiking. Your children's sense of adventure will soar! Concessions available at Old Man's Cave or dining in the Lodge, seasonally (with outdoor pool). We recommend close supervision on the hiking trails for your child's safety.

HOCKING HILLS STATE FOREST: 9,267 acres in Hocking County. Hiking trails (9 miles), Bridle trails (40 miles), horse campground, see a former fire lookout tower, rock climbing a rappelling area, and state nature preserves. Hocking Hills State Park is adjacent.

S Area

MAPLE SUGARING IN THE HILLS

Logan – *Hocking Hills State Park. Meet at Old Man's Cave Naturalist Cabin behind the Visitors Center. Discover the many methods used to make this tasty treat from maple sap. Free samples available. Pancake breakfast is offered at the dining lodge for a fee. (first weekend in March)*

HOCKING FALL COLOR TOUR

Logan – *Rockbridge, Hocking State Forest. Enjoy a guided tour at Cedar Falls and a hayride through the fall colors, along with a bean dinner. FREE. (October)*

LAKE LOGAN STATE PARK

Logan - *30443 Lake Logan Road (4 miles West of Logan off State Route 664) 43138. Phone: (740) 385-3444. www.dnr.state.oh.us.*

One of the best fishing lakes in Ohio, the lake sports northern pike, bass, bluegill, crappie, catfish and saugeye. Across Lake Logan Road from the beach, the one-mile Pine Vista Hiking Trail circles a hilltop, providing opportunities for nature study and wildlife observation. 527-foot public swimming beach is located on the north shore of the lake on Lake Logan Road (CR 3). 717 acres of hiking, boating and rentals, fishing, swimming and winter sports for day-use only.

WASHBOARD MUSIC FESTIVAL

Logan - *Town Center (Main, Market, Spring Streets). (740) 390-3828. Home to the World's Largest Washboard. Fun filled weekend event for the whole family. Free tours of the Columbus Washboard Company, the only washboard factory left in the United States. Continuous music, factory tours, quilt show and food. FREE. (Father's Day weekend in June)*

Marietta

CAMPUS MARTIUS

Marietta - *601 2nd Street (2nd and Washington Street ,Downtown) 45750. Phone: (740) 373-3750 or (800) 860-0145. www.ohiohistory.org/places/campus. Hours: Wednesday-Saturday 9:30am-5:00pm and Sundays and Holidays Noon-5:00pm (March-October) Admission: $8.00 adult, $4.00 student (6-12). Educators: Treasure hunts and Vocabulary enhanced self-guided tours about settlement, migration, production and pioneer living are online at the ohiohistoryteachers.org link.*

CAMPUS MARTIUS *(cont.)*

Campus recreates early development of Marietta as the first settlement in the Northwest Territory (kids, you may need to know that on your proficiency test). The Putnam House is the oldest residence in Ohio. The home and land office display replicas of the hardships of early pioneer life including old surgical and musical instruments. An exhibit titled "Paradise Found and Lost: Migration in the Ohio Valley" highlights migration from farms to cities and from Appalachia to industry. See the stage jacket worn by Appalachian born Country Singer, Dwight Yoakum. Videos and interactive computer games on migration. You can actually create a feeling of being taken back in time by walking through the train passenger car and listening to actual stories of passengers taking a trip to the "big city" for business or jobs (Stories are told on telephone handsets). See actual huge photographs of downtown Columbus and Marietta in the early 1900's that take up an entire wall - you'll feel as if you're walking into them!

MARIETTA SODA MUSEUM

Marietta - *109-111 Maple Street, Harmar Village (across the pedestrian bridge from downtown) 45750. Phone: (740) 376-COKE. www.mariettasodamuseum.com. Hours: Thursday–Saturday 11:00am–3:00pm, Sunday Noon-5:00pm (Spring-Fall). Friday and Saturday 10:00am-4:30pm (Winter). Admission: FREE. Miscellaneous: Down the street is the Children's Toy & Doll Museum open Friday & Saturday afternoons (740-373-0799).*

Memorabilia from 1900 to the present traces the history of this beverage and its marketing. Buy a bottle of Coke or Sarsaparilla (vanilla Root Beer) and sip it while you browse. Although rusted, you can still see the Coca-Cola logo on the front of many old dispensers and metal signs. The soda fountain features 10 cent cokes and serves lunch items. The building has hundreds of soda collectibles (both on display and for sale).

MARIETTA TROLLEY TOURS

Marietta - *127 Ohio Street (Levee House Café, I-77 exit 6 towards downtown) 45750. Phone: (740) 374-2233. http://mariettaohio.org/directory/trolley_tours. Hours: Friday & Saturday Afternoon 10:30am and 12:30 pm (July-October). Other weekdays and Sundays at 12:30pm only. Schedule can vary. Call or visit website for details. Admission: $5.00-$7.50 (ages 5+).*

Narrated one-hour tours describing and viewing historic architecture, shops along Front Street, Marietta College and more. Start with this tour as soon as you get into town as a relaxing orientation. Then, you'll know which Museums are worth the price of your time and money without having to feel like you have to visit them all. While in town, park once and then walk the rest of the day - everything is packed into their quaint downtown.

OHIO RIVER MUSEUM

Marietta - *601 Second Street (St. Clair & Front Street, Downtown) 45750. Phone: (740) 373-3717 or (800) 860-0145. www.ohiohistory.org/places/ohriver. Hours: Saturday 9:30am-5:00pm. Sunday Noon-5:00pm (Memorial Day weekend - Labor Day). Admission: $7.00 adult, $3.00 student (all ages). Educators: find a scavenger hunt worksheet, "turkey" or mussels workshop, or River Explorers workshop online at ohiohistoryteachers.org link. Also, note group tours are early fall and early spring, even though the museum is not open to the public.*

The Ohio River Museum consists of three exhibit buildings, the first of which houses displays depicting the origins and natural history of the Ohio River. The golden age of the steamboat is featured in the second building, along with a video presentation on river steamboats. The last building features displays about boat building, mussels inn the Ohio River system, and tool and equipment from the steamboat era. The WP Snyder, Jr. moored along the museum is the last surviving stern-wheeled towboat in America. Also, see a model of a flat boat and other scale models of many riverboats. A video titled, "Fire on the Water" describes dangerous early times when boilers might explode, killing many. Diorama (full scale) of wildlife along the Ohio River.

OHIO RIVER STERNWHEEL FESTIVAL

Marietta - *Ohio River Levee. (800) 288-2577. Thirty plus sternwheelers dock for the weekend, some for commercial and some for residential use. Continuous musical entertainment, fireworks and grand finale sternwheeler races. FREE. (weekend after Labor Day)*

ROSSI PASTA

Marietta - *114 Greene Street (Downtown) 45750. Phone: (740) 376-2065 or (800) 227-6774. www.rossipasta.com. Hours: Monday - Saturday 9:00 am - 6:00pm, Sunday Noon - 5:00pm. Pasta making times vary, best weekdays before 3:00 pm.*

Call ahead for best times to tour. Tours: Group tours of the Rossi Pasta factory are offered Monday - Friday.

A retail store where they show a production video and have many archived pictures about Rossi Pasta. They hand roll dough adding fresh flavor ingredients as they "turn" the dough. Their secret is using spring wheat flour instead of highly manufactured semolina flour. Cooking is all about chemistry, you know. A machine cuts the pasta into very long and wide strips (linguini) or thin soup noodles. Teardrop shapes are stamped out. Next, the cut pasta goes into one of two large drying chambers which are precisely regulated to insure even temperatures. Finally, the pasta is packaged in clear Rossi-labeled bags. Be sure you invite your favorite gourmet cook along for this visit - it's a new level of pasta to experience. Take some Curry, Chocolato, or very Chili pasta home to try.

THE CASTLE

Marietta - *418 Fourth St. 45750. Phone: (740) 373-4180. www.mariettacastle.org. Hours: Daily (Summer); Thursday - Monday (April, May, September-December). Weekdays 10:00am-4:00pm. Weekends 1:00-4:00pm. Admission: $3.00-$6.00 (age 6+).*

Historic area furnishings. Impressive parlor and chandelier. Video. CHRISTMAS OPEN HOUSE - castle is decorated for the holidays and Santa's visit, entertainment and light refreshments. (generally first weekend in December)

VALLEY GEM STERNWHEELER

Marietta - *601 Front Street, under Washington Street Bridge (State Route 60 and State Route 7) (Docks next to the Ohio River Museum under the Washington Street Bridge) 45750. www.valleygemsternwheeler.com. Phone: (740) 373-7862. Admission: $5.00-$11.00 (ages 3+). Tours: Narrated Public Sightseeing Cruises are available at 2:30pm Daily (July, August), plus most days in June. Saturdays only in May & September. Monday Morning Muffin Cruises. Miscellaneous: Gift and snack area on board. Heated or A/C main cabin.*

The gentle splash of the paddlewheel reminds you of a bygone era, but this modern-day sternwheeler has all the amenities to make your sentimental journey tranquil and relaxing. Take the 300 passenger, 60 minute cruise on the Valley Gem where the captain points out historic interests. See who can find the large stone blocks spelling "Marietta" on the landing welcoming steamboats. Why was the boat named after a piano company?

RED, WHITE AND BLUES

Marietta - *Downtown. www.mariettaohio.org. A full day of parades, rides, entertainment & fireworks. (July 4th)*

PUMPKIN MAZE PLAYLAND

Marietta - *Sweetapple Farm, CR 805. Pumpkin Patches / Hayrides / Corn Mazes / Fall Playland - Admission (average $6.00). Plan on at least two hours playtime. Open weekends, some weekdays (by appointment) & weeknights. www.sweetapplefarm.com (September - early November).*

McArthur

LAKE HOPE STATE PARK

McArthur - *27331 SR 278 (12 miles Northeast of McArthur on State Route 278) 45651. Phone: (740) 596-5253 or (740) 596-0400 restaurant. www.dnr.state.oh.us.*

Lake Hope State Park lies entirely within the 24,000-acre Zaleski State Forest in the valley of Big Sandy Run. It is a rugged, heavily forested region traversed by steep gorges, narrow ridges, abandoned mines, ancient mounds and beautiful scenery. The dining lodge features The Stone Terrace Restaurant, meeting room, General Store, as well as lodge and cottage reservation office. A fine swimming beach is located near the dam. Nature programs. 3,223 acres of camping, family cabins, hiking, boating and rentals, fishing, swimming.

ZALESKI STATE FOREST: The Zaleski State Forest Sawmill is Ohio's only publicly owned and operated sawmill. It began operation in 1967. The "low-tech" approach taken at Zaleski gives the mill an almost historical significance. It is an efficient functioning mill that turns out specialty orders for many public works projects. Additionally, demonstrations and training activities (for example, grading workshops) are held every year at Zaleski. 26,827 acres in Vinton and Athens counties. Bridle trails (50 miles), 3 walk-in camp areas (self-registration permit - no fee) and sawmill. Lake Hope State Park is adjacent.

HOLIDAY LIGHTS

McArthur – Lake Hope State Park. www.1800hocking.com/whattodo/holiday_trail_ of_lights_at_lake_hope_state_park.htm. Hundreds of thousands of lights & holiday / storybook characters. Walk thru. (daily, all month of December)

Nelsonville

HOCKING VALLEY SCENIC RAILWAY

Nelsonville - 33 Canal Street (Off US 33) 45764. Phone: (740) 470-1300 or (800) HOCKING. (513) 753-9531 (Saturday and Sunday).   www.hvsry.com.   Hours: Weekends Noon and 2:30 pm, (Memorial Day weekend-early November). Special Holiday Schedule.   Admission: $11.00-$15.00 adult, $8.00-$10.00 child (2-11). Discounts for seniors. Upgrade at the depot to first class seating, in newly-restored luxury coach with toilet and air conditioning, by paying $2.00 more per person.

Ride through the hills of scenic Hocking Valley on an authentic 1916 steam locomotive or a 1950 diesel locomotive (trips are 14 & 22 miles roundtrip). Hear about Hocking Valley history as you pass the remains of industries, canal locks and other historic landmarks. Both rides include a 30-minute stop over at Robbins Crossing Visitor's Center (small 1850's settler village). Enjoy the blooming dogwood trees in the spring, summertime fun, nature's spectacular fall foliage or a special winter ride with Santa (heated cars). Most kids absolutely love the Robbery Train or the Caboose Only Train rides. No A/C or restrooms on train (except first class upgrade).

EASTER EGG HUNTS

Nelsonville – *Hocking Valley Scenic Railway. Easter Bunny appearance, treat stations, egg hunts, and kids entertainment and crafts. Admission. (usually held the Saturday before Easter)*

SANTA TRAIN

Nelsonville – *Hocking Valley Scenic Railway. Train trip in decorated coaches with Santa. Songs and treats. Dress warmly. Admission. (select weekend dates in December)*

PAUL BUNYAN SHOW

Nelsonville - *Hocking College Campus. (740) 753-3591 or www.ohioforest.org. Ohio's largest forestry exposition features lumberjack competitions, forestry displays, guitar pickers championship and chainsaw sculpting. Admission. (first weekend in October)*

Oak Hill

JACKSON LAKE STATE PARK

Oak Hill - *35 Tommy Been Road (2 miles West of Oak Hill on State Route 279) 45656. Phone: (740) 682-6197. www.dnr.state.oh.us.*

The park's serene lake is a focal point for excellent fishing and provides the ideal setting for a peaceful walks. 200 foot sand beach provides recreation for swimmers and sunbathers. 335 acres of camping, boating, fishing, swimming and winter sports.

S Area

Peebles

SERPENT MOUND

Peebles - 3850 State Route 73 (six miles north of State Route 32) 45660. Phone: (937) 587-2796 or (800)752-2757.   http://ohsweb.ohiohistory.org/places/sw16/. Hours: Museum open Friday-Sunday 10:00am-5:00pm (summer). Park open year-round 10:00am-5:00pm. Admission: $7.00 per car.   Miscellaneous: Profile of the "cyptoexplosion" doughnut shape can be seen off State Route 770 - East of Serpent Mound.

The largest earthwork in the United States, it measures 1335 feet from head to tail and is about 15 feet high. The mound appears as a giant serpent uncoiling in seven deep curves. The oval doughnut at one end probably represents the open mouth of the snake as it strikes. The museum contains exhibits on the effigy mound and the geology of the surrounding area.

Portsmouth

PORTSMOUTH MURALS

Portsmouth - State Route 23 South, Front Street (Washington Street to Ohio River - follow green mural signs) 45662. www.ohiorivertourism.org. Educators: although the murals keep the attention of the kids best, you may consider adding a tour of the <u>SOUTHERN OHIO MUSEUM</u>*, the* <u>1810 HOUSE MUSEUM</u>*, or the* <u>STONE HOUSE</u>*. Visitors come in close contact with the past by walking through an actual home where residents lived for decades instead of looking through glass panes and roped-off areas.*

About 10 years ago, a committee was formed to begin a project that would take a 20 foot floodwall that protected its city from the Ohio River and transform it into 2,200 feet of magnificent art. Each mural tells the story of the history of Ohio and its people - beginning in the year 1730 and ending in 2002. Artist Robert Dafford (internationally known muralist) for years could be seen working on new murals. Our two favorites were Chillicothe Street 1940's (a very

The murals are incredible. Each tells a story that you feel you can "walk into".

colorful, tremendously detailed, cartoon-like mural) and Twilight (a modern day view of the bridge over the river, looks like a photograph). What talent to be able to see a picture and then paint it to scale on a rough outdoor surface!

Reedsville

FORKED RUN STATE PARK

Reedsville - *63300 State Route 124 (3 miles Southwest of Reedsville off State Route 124) 45772. Phone: (740) 378-6206. www.dnr.state.oh.us.*

Located in the heart of Appalachia, colorful history, riverboats, scenic vistas and abundant wildlife give the park its rural charm. 400-foot sand beach offers enjoyment for swimmers and sunbathers. 817 acres of camping, hiking, low power boating and rentals, fishing, swimming, winter sports and food service. A disc golf course is on the property. Shade River State Forest (hiking trails) is adjacent (740) 554-3177.

Rio Grande

BOB EVANS FARM

Rio Grande - *State Route 588, 791 Farmview Drive (off US 35 to State Route 325 South) 45614. Phone: (800) 994-FARM. www.bobevans.com. Hours: Daily 10:30am-5:30pm (April-late December). Admission: FREE for tour - Activities additional.*

Begin or end your visit at the restaurant, once named "The Sausage Shop" - Bob's first restaurant. Then, wander 'round to visit the Farm (implements of yesteryear farms) and small animal barn yard, plus the Homestead (an old stagecoach stop and former home of Bob and Jewel Evans). At the Homestead Museum, sit at the reconstructed counter of the original Steak House owned by Bob Evans, view (on an old television console) commercials that were hosted by Bob and Jewell Evans in their own kitchen,

> To make the bean soup for each Farm Festival, it takes 3.2 million beans (2,000 pounds)

see through the lens of an actual television camera of the era a setting of Bob and Jewell "at work" filming the ads and tour many other displays which form a life-sized "scrapbook of the business." Nearby in Bidwell (State Route 50/35) is Jewel Evan's Mill where you can view millstones grinding flour. Also in the area are good horseback riding stables and canoe liveries.

FARM FESTIVAL

Rio Grande - Bob Evans Farm. Down on the farm feeling with over 100 craftspeople, country music, square dancers, homestyle foods and contests such as apple peeling, cornshelling, cow chip throwing and hog calling. Admission. (mid-October weekend)

Rockbridge

HOCKING HILLS CANOPY TOURS

Rockbridge - *10714 Jackson Street 43139. www.hockinghillscanopytours.com. Phone: (740) 385-9477. Tours: Scheduled in advance - daily April thru October. Hours change seasonally due to available light. Course fee: $75.00.*

Ohio's first Zipline Canopy Tour!. Nature-Lover meets Thrill-Seeker in this exciting tree-top adventure. Professional guides lead you along 10 ziplines and 4 Sky Bridges that offer a never-before-seen perspective of the beautiful Hocking Hills. You'll soar nearly 3/4 of a mile over a natural cave/waterfall, along the Hocking River, past fern-covered rock formations, and finally land in a "Garden of Eden". The tour lasts over two hours. This experience will leave you floating on air!

Waverly

LAKE WHITE STATE PARK

Waverly - *2767 State Route 551 (4 miles Southwest of Waverly on State Route 104) 45690. Phone: (740) 947-4059. www.dnr.state.oh.us.*

Part of Lake White State Park includes the remains of the old canal channel. 358 acres of camping, unlimited power boating, fishing, swimming/beach and wintersports.

Wellston

BUCKEYE FURNACE

Wellston - *123 Buckeye Park Road (two miles south of SR 124 on Buckeye Furnace Road in Jackson County) 45692. www.ohiohistory.org/places/buckeye. Phone: (740) 384-3537. Hours: Park is open daylight hours. Museum is only open weekends from Noon-5:00pm (June - October). Group tours may make an appointment for weekdays. Admission: $3.00-$4.00 per person. Educators: Excellent gradeschool aged lesson plans (self guided tour) are linked to ohiohistoryteachers.org site. Miscellaneous: The stone remnant of the old Richland iron furnace still stands on private property just north of Richland Furnace State Forest and is adjacent to Vinton Township Road 6. The required iron ore was mined by oxen from the underlying sandstone and limestone. The trees were cut and burned to produce charcoal to fire the furnace. The old ore pits are still noticeable near the ridges throughout the state forest. With the development of the ore fields in Missouri and the Lake Superior region at the end*

S Area

of the 19th century, the Hanging Rock iron industry quickly faded away. 2,448 acres in Jackson and Vinton counties. APV trails (7 miles).

Visit Ohio's only restored charcoal furnace which remains from the original 80 furnaces in Ohio. In the mid – 1800's, this industry took root as large trees were converted into charcoal to make iron for railroads and ammunition. The self-guided tour of the furnace shows you where raw materials (charcoal, iron ore, etc.) were brought to the top of the hill and poured into the furnace to be heated to 2700 degrees F. Impurities (slag) stayed on the top while liquid iron (which is heavier) flowed to the base. The reconstructed company store serves as a visitor orientation area. There are two nature trails.

LAKE ALMA STATE PARK

Wellston - *Rte. 1 (3 miles Northeast of Wellston on SR 349) 45692. Phone: (740) 384-4474. www.dnr.state.oh.us.*

A quiet lake and a gentle creek meandering through a wooded valley provide a restful setting for park visitors. 2 public beaches are located on the north side of the lake. Approximately 3.5 miles of trail traverse hilltops and valleys offering hikers a scenic view of the park. A 1-mile paved walkway/bicycle path begins at the park entrance and ends at the park exit. 279 acres of camping, hiking, boating, fishing and swimming.

West Portsmouth

SHAWNEE STATE PARK

West Portsmouth - *4404 State Route 125 (8 miles West of Portsmouth on State Route 125) 45663. Phone: (740) 858-6652. www.ShawneeLodgeResort.com. Miscellaneous: Watch out for thousands of ladybugs visiting each mid-October.*

Lodge rooms are furnished with American Indian and Appalachian furnishings and the restaurant serves an extensive children's menu (even steak), plus many good sandwiches and entrees (good food, slower service). Weekends, the restaurant has a guitar player. Many seasonal events include hayrides, hikes, campouts and cookouts (Autumn: Cornbread and Beans Black Pot Supper Days). Their one mile hiking trails are unpaved and just right for families. Public beaches are situated on Roosevelt Lake and Turkey Creek Lake, which offers vending machines. Nature programs, acres of camping, boating and rentals, fishing, swimming, winter sports and food service. Family cabins, lodge with indoor/outdoor pools, sauna, whirlpool, fitness center, tennis and basketball.

SHAWNEE STATE FOREST: 62,583 acres in Scioto and Adams counties. Ohio's largest state forest. Backpack trails (60 miles) with 8 walk-in camp areas (self-registration permit - no fee), Bridle trails (75 miles), horse campground (no fee), 5 small forest lakes, 8000 acre wilderness area. Shawnee State Park is adjacent.

S Area

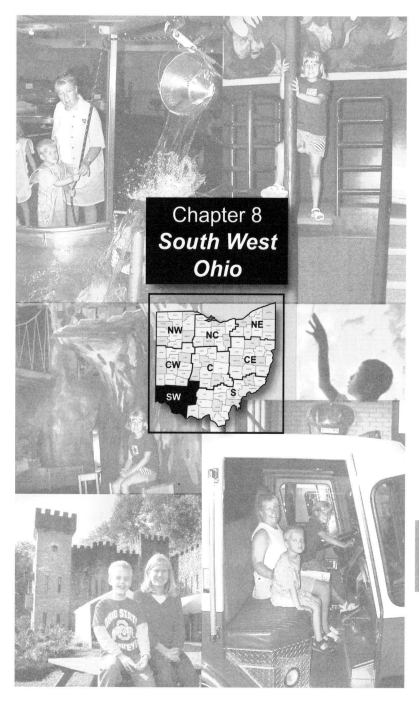

Chapter 8
South West Ohio

Bethel
- East Fork State Park

Cincinnati
- All American Birthday Party
- Carew Tower
- Cincinnati Art Museum
- Cincinnati Fire Museum
- Cincinnati History Museum
- Cincinnati Sports
- Cincinnati Symphony Orchestra
- Cincinnati Zoo And Botanical Gardens
- Coco Key Water Resort
- Coney Island
- Covedale Center For The Performing Arts
- Duke Energy Children's Museum
- Krohn Conservatory
- Museum Of Natural History And Science
- National Underground Railroad Freedom Center
- Oktoberfest-Zinzinnati
- Parky's Farm
- Stowe House, Harriet Beecher
- Taft Museum Of Art
- Taft National Historic Site, William Howard
- United Dairy Farmers

Cincinnati (Covington, Ky)
- BB Riverboats

Cincinnati (Fairfield)
- Jungle Jim's International Market

Cincinnati (Loveland)
- Loveland Castle

Cincinnati (Milford)
- Cincinnati Nature Center
- Pumpkin Maze Playland

Cincinnati (Newport, Ky)
- Ride The Ducks Newport

Cincinnati (Sharonville)
- Heritage Village Museum
- Homewood Suites By Hilton

Cincinnati (West Chester)
- Entertrainment Junction

Clarksville
- Pumpkin Maze Playland

College Corner
- Hueston Woods State Park

Corwin
- Little Miami State Park

Georgetown
- Glass Refactory
- Grant Boyhood Home

Hamilton
- Pumpkin Maze Playland
- Pyramid Hill Sculpture Park

Harveysburg
- Ohio Renaissance Festival

Hillsboro
- Rocky Fork State Park
- Thunder In The Hills Race

Kings Mills
- Kings Island & Boomerang Bay

Lebanon
- Lebanon Mason Monroe Railroad
- Pumpkin Maze Playland
- Warren County Historical Society Museum

Mason
- Great Wolf Lodge
- The Beach Waterpark

Middletown
- Light Up
- Middfest International

Okeana
- Governor Bebb Preserve

Oregonia
- Fort Ancient

Oxford
- McGuffey Museum

Pleasant Plain
- Stonelick State Park

Point Pleasant
- Grant Birthplace

Ripley
- Rankin House

Trenton
- Pumpkin Maze Playland

Waynesville
- Caesar Creek State Park

Wilmington
- Banana Split Festival
- Cowan Lake State Park

A Quick Tour of
our Hand-Picked
Favorites Around...

South West
Ohio

The first major-league pro baseball team was the Cincinnati Red Stockings, but the Cincinnati area has many more "major-league" attractions to offer. Spend the weekend exploring four great places in one historic building at the **Cincinnati Museum Center** at Union Terminal. Walk through the Ice

Age and a recreated limestone cave at the **Museum of Natural History and Science** or let kids explore The Woods, an interactive adventure in the wilderness, at the Duke Energy **Children's Museum**. A Hands-on History Museum and an IMAX theatre are located here, too.

But that's not all there is to do for family fun. In the city you can climb down a real fire pole (**Cincinnati Fire Museum**). On the water you can **Ride the Ducks** and get Quacky with it. In the water, the greater Cincinnati area has two indoor waterparks and two outdoor waterparks.

There are some pretty neat places just a little ways north of downtown Cincinnati that are so worth fitting into your next trip. A small pioneer village bustles with activity most every weekend at **Heritage Village** in Sharonville. Try your hand at churning butter or marching a Civil War battle drill at special events throughout the year. A hidden gem is **Loveland Castle** – a real castle over the spring and in the woods – that you can play like a knight or princess. You can pretend to be an engineer or a taste tester on tour at the giant **United Dairy Farmers** ice cream and milk factory. The reward for your icy cold adventure tour is freshly made ice cream sundaes at the end! Off the northern tip of the outerbelt you'll find a grocery store adventure at **Jungle Jim's**. This store is a supermarket that's a tourist attraction in Fairfield. Foodies and kids love the animals that greet you outside and the whimsical dioramas inside. Look for the Amish buggy, a shrimp boat, the Big Cheese, Elvis, a fire truck and even a walk through Sherwood Forest.

Finally, if you want to get away from the big city and wander a while in the woods, head for **Hueston Woods State Park Resort** in Oxford (home of Miami University). Stay overnight at the lodge or in a cozy cabin and in the morning head over to the Nature Center with programs including nature crafts, movies, fossils and animals – especially raptors in the rehab center.

Sites and attractions are listed in order by City, Zip Code, and Name. Symbols indicated represent:

 Festivals   Restaurants   Lodging

Bethel

EAST FORK STATE PARK

Bethel - *3294 Elklick Road (4 miles Southeast of Amelia off SR 125, I-275 exit 63 or 65) 45106. Phone: (513) 734-4323. www.dnr.state.oh.us.*

East Fork offers a great diversity of recreational opportunities and natural history only 25 miles from Cincinnati. The park's terrain includes both rugged hills and open meadows. There are 2,160 acres of water and unlimited horsepower boating with access available at six launch ramps. A 1,200-foot swimming beach features change boots with showers, restrooms and a vending area. 32-mile Steven Newman Worldwalker Perimeter Trail circles the park and is available for hikers, backpackers, and horsemen. 10,580 acres of camping, hiking, boating, fishing, swimming and winter sports.

CINCINNATI SPORTS

Cincinnati

When you're in the birthplace of professional baseball, you know you're in a place where sports are special. Have a major league experience at the Great American Ball Park - home of the Cincinnati Reds. Or experience the famous tailgating before, during or after a Cincinnati Bengals game.

CINCINNATI BENGALS - (513) 621-3550 or www.bengals.com. (I-75 exit 1A follow the 2nd Street signs) Be part of the jungle. Professional football at Paul Brown Stadium (downtown, riverfront). Join the Bengals Kids Club for great novelty items (August – December).

CINCINNATI REDS - www.cincinnatireds.com. (513) 421-REDS or (877) 647-REDS. (I-75 exit 1A follow the 2nd Street signs). Professional Major League baseball at the Great American Ball Park. First professional baseball team. Several family-friendly ticket days and fun promotions for kids on game days. ($5.00 - $25.00+) (April – September)

CAREW TOWER

Cincinnati - *441 Vine Street (5th and Vine, across from Fountain Square, Downtown, I-75 exit 1C) 45202. Phone: (513) 241-3888. Hours: Monday-Thursday 9:30am-5:30pm, Friday 9:00am-6:00pm, Saturday/Sunday 10:00am - 7:00pm.*

An 1930's Art Deco building that is the tallest building downtown. The building itself is a study in old and new. Modern elevators passing renovated plush office floors transport guests only as high as the 45th floor. A trip to the observation deck requires a ride in a rickety, phone booth-sized elevator to the 48th floor. The Observation deck has a panoramic view. Small admission fee per person ($1.00-2.00).

CINCINNATI ART MUSEUM

Cincinnati - 953 Eden Park Drive 45202. www.cincinnatiartmuseum.org. Phone: (513) 721-ARTS. Hours: Tuesday-Sunday 11:00am-5:00pm. Extended Wednesday evening hours. Closed Thanksgiving, Christmas and New Years. Admission: FREE admission daily except during special exhibits.

Art collection presents 5000 years of visual arts. Favorites include the Syrian Damascus Room, Blue glass chandelier, old musical instruments, Andy Warhol's Pete Rose and the futuristic robot (good size Contemporary Art Section). Family First Saturdays. Museum shop and café.

CINCINNATI FIRE MUSEUM

Cincinnati - 315 West Court Street, near Plum, Downtown (I-75 exit 1C follow signs for 5th Street) 45202. Phone: (513) 621-5553. www.cincyfiremuseum.com. Hours: Tuesday-Friday 10:00am-4:00pm, Weekends Noon-4:00pm. Closed holidays.

Admission: $7.00 adult, $6.00 senior (55+), $5.00 child (2-12).

From the minute you walk in the restored fire station, the kids will be intrigued by the nation's first professional fire department exhibits. Displays chronicle fire fighting history from antique equipment to the cab of a newer fire truck where you can actually pull levers, push buttons, ring bells, operate the siren and flash emergency lights. The history of Cincinnati in frontier days comes to life as the children participate in a "hands-on" bucket brigade and take a turn on an old style hand pumper. Three interactive computers are fun and tell you all about today's firefighting and fire safety. The museum has an emphasis on fire safety with "Safe House" models (touch and demo area) and a video about fire fighting dangers. Before you leave be sure you slide down the 5-foot fire pole or ring the old fire bell. Let's Stop, Drop and Roll. Everyone can do it! This is the most kid-friendly fire museum in the Midwest!

KROHN CONSERVATORY

Cincinnati - *950 Eden Park Drive (I-71 North to the Reading Road exit #2. Turn right at the end of the exit/traffic light onto Eden Park Drive) 45202. Phone: (513) 421-4086. www.cinci-parks.org. Hours: Daily 10:00am-5:00pm.*

A rainforest full of 5000 varieties of exotic desert and tropical plants. The Palm, Tropical, Desert and Orchid houses exhibit permanent displays of exotic plants in natural settings, complete with a 20 foot rainforest waterfall. One of the nation's largest - check out their seasonal displays. FREE, Small admission for special exhibits.

CHRISTMAS OPEN HOUSE

Cincinnati – Krohn Conservatory. Buildings decorated for holidays, Santa visit, entertainment and light refreshments served. Great way to expose younger ones to historical homes that might be boring otherwise. Admission. (mostly first weekend of December)

NATIONAL UNDERGROUND RAILROAD FREEDOM CENTER

Cincinnati - *50 East Freedom Way (Cincinnati waterfront, I-71 exit 2nd street, I-75 exit 1A) 45202. Phone: (513) 333-7500. www.freedomcenter.org. Hours: Tuesday-Sunday 11:00am-5:00pm. Freedom Center Closed During Bengals Home Games. Admission: $12.00 adult, $10.00 senior (60+) and students with ID, $8.00 child (6-12). Miscellaneous: Audio tours, one for adults and another for children, are available free of charge with paid admission.*

Ohio's involvement in guiding slaves to freedom is commemorated in a museum that helps tell the story of the Underground Railroad. The Center is made up of three buildings that symbolize the cornerstones of freedom - it's a warm art museum with an historical twist. A dynamic presentation, the "moving painting" titled "Suite for Freedom" takes visitors on an emotional journey from freedom to un-freedom. Next, move on to the Slave Pen - used to "warehouse" slaves being moved further south for sale. ESCAPE! This child-friendly gallery uses storytelling and hands-on interaction. Probably the only area designed for kids, time can be spent listening to choices slaves must make, then testing YOUR decisions as a computer-interactive slave yourself. Your choices reveal a lot about your character. From Slavery to Freedom takes the visitor on a journey from the slaves' arrival in the New World through the Colonial period to the Civil War. The Concluding Experience area is designed to help each visitor put into personal perspective all that he or she has just experienced.

SW Area

What does freedom mean today? To you? To all of us? Visitors can participate in individual polling based on "what would you do" scenarios. This is serious stuff, be sure your children are prepared to think about their reactions to the material. (The site would be an excellent student post-study of Pre-and-Post Civil War era history). Some pre-study of the Underground Railroad is helpful. The Center leaves an enduring impression on those who "get it."

TAFT MUSEUM OF ART

Cincinnati - 316 Pike Street (Broadway to Fifth to Pike Sts, I-75 exit 1C) 45202. Phone: (513) 241-0343. www.taftmuseum.org. Hours: Tuesday-Friday 11:00am-5:00pm, Saturday 10:00am-5:00pm, Sunday Noon-5:00pm. Admission: $6.00-$8.00 (age 18+). Kids are FREE. The museum is FREE to all on Wednesdays. Educators: Lesson plans online under Education icon. Miscellaneous: Café and gift shop.

See works of European and American painters, Chinese porcelains, Limoges enamels displayed in a federal period mansion. At the greeter's desk on the second floor, pick up one of the Family Gallery Guides or, before you go, download themed Self-Guided Family Tours from their website (ex. Animals, Children). Select Saturdays "Families Create!" programs combine storytelling and games with art-making activities. If you need an action break, Lytle Park is across the street and is a great play space.

CINCINNATI HISTORY MUSEUM

Cincinnati - 1301 Western Avenue, Cincinnati Museum Center (I-75 south exit 2A; I-75 north exit 1G) 45203. www.cincymuseum.org. Phone: (513) 287-7000 or (800) 733-2077. Hours: Monday-Saturday (& Holidays) 10:00am-5:00pm, Sunday 11:00am-6:00pm. Closed Thanksgiving and Christmas. Admission: $6.00-$8.00 per person. Toddler (age 1-2) rates are slightly lower. Combo prices with other museums in the Center are well worth the few extra dollars if you have the whole day to explore. Parking fee. Miscellaneous: Gift Shops - Worth a good look! OmniMax Theatre on premises has several shows daily (a movie fee is charged per person). Educators: look for a wide list of pdf Teachers Guides on current and past exhibits on the online icons: Educators, then Teacher Resources.

As you enter the museum, your eyes will race around the Cincinnati in Motion model of the city (from 1900-1940) with interactive computer booths and most of the transportation moving (planes, trains, cars, etc). Such an easy and fun way to learn about historical buildings in town or, just reminisce or admire the fascinating layout. Next, you'll visit with The Flynns (ring the doorbell first) talking about life at home during World War II. Hop on board a streetcar with the conductor telling news of the war. Moms and grandmothers will have to check out the "Leg Makeup Bar" (clue: there was a stocking shortage during

the war). Now, walk through a life-like forest with shadows and birds wrestling and singing. Then, walk through re-created streets of Cincinnati. Visit the Fifth Street Market and Millcreek Millery - try on hats of the early 1900's and then shop next door at the pretend open air market. The kids can play in a miniature cabin and flat boat, then actually

See a miniature Cincinnati...

board a steamboat and pretend you're the captain. Very authentically presented, clever displays throughout the whole museum. Cincinnati folks should be proud.

DUKE ENERGY CHILDREN'S MUSEUM

Cincinnati - *Cincinnati Museum Center, 1301 Western Avenue (I-75 south exit 2A; I-75 north exit 1G) 45203. www.cincymuseum.org. Phone: (800) 733-2077 or (513) 287-7000. Hours: Monday-Saturday (& Holidays) 10:00am-5:00pm, Sunday 11:00am-6:00pm. Closed Thanksgiving and Christmas. Admission: $6.00-$8.00 per person. Toddler (age 1-2) rates are slightly lower. Combo prices with other museums in the Center are well worth the few extra dollars if you have the whole day to explore. Parking fee. Miscellaneous: Museum stores (great kids gift ideas). Snack Bar.*

Jenny thought the treehouse was way cool....

Start in the Woods, kiddies. The dim lighting adds mystery to the slides, tunnels, rope climbing mazes and walls, and treehouses. The Energy Zone has kids move plastic balls along a conveyor to a gigantic dump bucket. It's actually a gigantic physics experiment in this Zone - lots of

machines and tubes to move balls. Kids At Work lets them make real-life and pretend structures from blocks, pebbles and Legos. They can even use a 12 foot crane to move and lift blocks. Other highlights are the Little Sprouts Farm (age 4 and under), Water Works, Kids Town (pretend town), or Animal Spot (lots of unusual skeletons). Each area is so interactive and so different from the other. Each exhibit had activities for toddlers up

Daniel & Mom sure had fun at the Water Works....

to pre-teens. We liked how most areas required friend's/parent's participation to complete a task. Make a new friend each visit!

MUSEUM OF NATURAL HISTORY AND SCIENCE

Cincinnati - 1301 Western Avenue, Cincinnati Museum Center (I-75 south exit 2A; I-75 north exit 1G) 45203. www.cincymuseum.org. Phone: (513) 287-7000 or (800) 733-2077. Hours: Monday-Saturday (& Holidays) 10:00am-5:00pm, Sunday 11:00am-6:00pm. Closed Thanksgiving and Christmas. Admission: $6.00-$8.00 per person. Toddler (age 1-2) rates are slightly lower. Combo prices with other museums in the Center are well worth the few extra dollars if you have the whole day to explore. Parking fee. Miscellaneous: Gift Shops - Worth a good look! OmniMax Theatre on premises has several shows daily (a movie fee is charged

per person). Educators: look for a wide list of pdf Teachers Guides on current and past exhibits on the online icons: Educators, then Teacher Resources.

Want to know a lot about the Ohio Valley's Natural and Geological history? The Glacier and Cavern simulated areas are both wonderful walk-thru reproductions that are so real, it's almost spooky. Start at the

The caves seemed so real....

Ice Age of fossils and re-created walk-through glaciers. Maybe try to solve the Ice Age mystery or change the landscape of glaciers. The Paleo Lab (within the Ice Cave) is the place to watch actual scientists at work on lots of fossils. On to the simulated Limestone Cavern with underground waterfalls and a live bat colony (behind glass!). (There are two routes - one that is challenging and involves much climbing and navigating, and the other that is wheelchair or stroller accessible). Look for lots of dino skeletons in Dinosaur Hall. Find out "All About You" as you explore inside, outside and beneath your great body. Brush a huge tooth, see under the skin of your hand, pretend in the office of

doctors and dentists, or maybe play pinball as your "food ball" goes through the digestive system. Plan a few hours at this extremely well done museum - we promise it will engage you and you'll learn many new things…easily!

CINCINNATI SYMPHONY ORCHESTRA

Cincinnati - *1241 Elm Street 45210. www.cincinnatisymphony.org. Phone: (513) 381-3300.*

The CSO presents soloists, pops concerts and an artist series in Music Hall. Young People's Concerts introduce students to orchestral music and performance with stimulating prep activities done beforehand. Lollipop Concerts are themed concerts with instrument demos and hands-on activities. CSO RiverBend Music Center hosts Symphony/Pops Orchestra, plus contemporary artists (May-September).

UNITED DAIRY FARMERS

Cincinnati - *3955 Montgomery Road, 45212. Phone: (513) 396-8700 - Ask for Consumer Relations. Admission: FREE. Tours: Mondays and Fridays, 9:30am-1 ½ hours, Ages 6 and up. Maximum 25 persons. Advice: They only book tours on November 1st for January-June of the next year and on May 1st for July-December of the current year. I was also told that you have to start calling at 8:00am on those days because the tours book up for the 6 month time period in just a few hours!!! Certainly something that is not for the impromptu planner, but it's worth the effort! Educators: A simple, cutsie diagram of how ice cream is made is on the Homemade Brand page online.*

> United Dairy Farmers is proud to announce that they only bottle milk from farms that pledge not to use artificial growth hormones.

Who wouldn't love a visit to a giant science factory that makes ice cream? In 1938 Carl H. Lindner Sr. had an idea to start a small dairy in Norwood, Ohio. At a time when almost all milk was home-delivered and paid for on a weekly or monthly basis, Carl Sr. had a new concept: he would process milk and other dairy products and sell them, cash-and-carry, at his own dairy

Early beginnings at United Dairy Farmers

store. Begin your tour, as a group, weighing yourselves on their giant truck scale! See milk being filled in containers (and the large vats where they store raw and treated milk). The plastic bottles are also made on the premises from tiny pellets of plastic melted, blown up and compressed (see it up close). Next, stop in and visit with the Food Scientists in the Flavor

SW Area

Lab (maybe help pick a new flavor). Best of all, watch ice cream packed and frozen (you even get to step inside the deep-freeze room!). Get a free ice cream sundae (flavor of the day - right off the production line) as a souvenir. We have found this to be one of the best organized, interesting and fun factory tours around!

STOWE HOUSE, HARRIET BEECHER

Cincinnati - 2950 Gilbert Avenue (corner of MLKing Drive) (SR 3 and US 22) 45214. Phone: (513) 632-5120. www.ohiohistory.org/places/stowe. Hours: Tuesday-Thursday, Saturday 10:00am-2:00pm (May-Labor Day). Only open Wednesday and Saturday (rest of year). Closed January. Admission: Donations.

The home of the author of "Uncle Tom's Cabin" novel that brought attention to the evils of slavery. Displays describe the Beecher family, the abolitionist movement and the history of African-Americans. Request the video about the story of the book. Mrs. Stowe's journal is available for viewing, as are photo quilts of slave faces. This museum is best visited after some study of the anti-slavery roots along the Ohio River. The videos are long, but helpful.

TAFT NATIONAL HISTORIC SITE, WILLIAM HOWARD

Cincinnati - 2038 Auburn Avenue (I-71S, take Exit 3 (Taft Road). Go 3/4 mile to Auburn Avenue. Turn left and go 1/2 mile to the home) 45219. Phone: (513) 684-3262. www.nps.gov/wiho. Hours: Daily 8:00am-4:00pm. Closed Thanksgiving, Christmas and New Year's. Admission: Donations. Miscellaneous: Check out the orientation video first in the Education Center adjacent. Tours every 30 minutes on the hour and half hour. Educators: Lesson Plans and mini-bios of Taft family members online under the For Teachers tab.

Visit the birthplace and boyhood home of a US President and Chief Justice. Four of the rooms are furnished to reflect Taft's family life 1857-77. Other exhibits depict his public service career. The signature exhibit of the center is an animatronic figure of the President's Son, Charlie Taft. Charlie tells stories about different family members. Children's group tours give kids the opportunity to dress up from a trunk of period hats and over-garments and play with old fashioned toys. This really helps the children understand life for a young person in the mid-1800's.

SW Area

CINCINNATI ZOO AND BOTANICAL GARDENS

Cincinnati - *3400 Vine Street (I-75 to exit 6, Mitchell Ave) 45220. Phone: (513) 281- 4700 or (800) 94-HIPPO. www.cincinnatizoo.org. Hours: Daily 9:00am-6:00pm (Summer); 9:00am-5:00pm (Winter). Admission: $13.00 adult, $9.00 senior (62+), $9.00 child (2-12). Children's Zoo and rides are $2.00-$6.00 additional. Parking Fee $6.50. Look for online specials. Miscellaneous: Safari Restaurant. Concessions. Tram and train rides, 4D Theater, & Carousel (additional fee), Children's Zoo & Animal Nursery. Wildlife Theatre. Stroller rentals. Educators: Self-Guided Scavenger Hunts. Get your students involved in learning while at the Zoo with these standards-based activities. Download and print as many copies as you need (click on Discovery/ Schools/TeacherResources).*

Recognized by Child Magazine as one of the "10 Best Zoos for Kids."

Ranked one of the top 5 zoos in the United States, its highlight is the successes in breeding white Bengal tigers and other rare wild animals. Komodo dragons (10 feet long and 300 lbs!) and endangered Florida Manatees are some of the large, unusual animals there. Visitors can pass into the underwater world of the manatee in a freshwater spring habitat. Cameras positioned above and behind the manatee tank provide a behind-the-scenes experience for visitors. The Lords of the Arctic area features polar bears on land and nose-to-nose through underwater glass panels, too. Dramatic waterfalls and a polar bear cave, with educational interactives complement the exhibit. The zoo added to its furry family the first-ever Mexican wolf pups born in 2007 - now exploring Wolf Woods in the Children's Zoo. And, just recently, a new eye level experience - Giraffe Ridge. This 27,000 square-foot exhibit, complete with an elevated viewing platform, provides an amazing interactive experience, bringing guests eye-to-eye with a herd of giraffes. Their landscaped gardens duplicate the animals' world and the Jungle Trails exhibit even has a tropical rainforest. The first Insectarium (you guessed it!) in the nation is also here.

EASTER CELEBRATION

Cincinnati – *Cincinnati Zoo & Botanical Gardens. Easter Bunny appearance, treat stations, egg hunts, Zoo Blooms, and animal enrichment. Admission. (Easter weekend and/or weekend before)*

FESTIVAL OF LIGHTS

Cincinnati – Cincinnati Zoo & Botanical Gardens. Ice Skating, decorated villages, and Santa. All include hundreds of thousands of lights & holiday / storybook characters. Daily, evenings. Admission. (Thanksgiving - January 1)

CONEY ISLAND

Cincinnati - 6201 Kellogg Avenue (Off I-275 East) 45228. Phone: (513) 232-8230. www.coneyislandpark.com. Hours: Daily: Pool 10:00am-8:00pm, Rides 11:00am-9:00pm (Memorial Weekend-Labor Day). Admission: $11.95 for pool or rides day pass. Discount combo park passes (Ages 4+). Tikes pricing around $4.00-7.00. Half price after 4:00pm. Discount coupon links online. Parking $7.00.

Sunlite, the world's largest re-circulating pool (200' x 401' and holding more than three million gallons of water!) with a huge slide and 6 diving boards, is one of the many fun attractions. Also, Zoom Flume water toboggan, Pipeline Plunge tube water slide, Giant Slide, kiddie rides, classic rides (Scrambler, Ferris Wheel, Tilt-a-whirl, etc) miniature golf, bumper boats, pedal boats and picnic areas.

PARKY'S FARM

Cincinnati - 10073 Daly Road (Winton Woods Park) (Winton Road & Lake Forest Drive) 45231. www.hamiltoncountyparks.org/parks/parkys.htm. Phone: (513) 521-PARK. Hours: Winton Park open daily during daylight hours. Farm open daily (late morning to late afternoon) but activities only open daily during the summer and weekends (including Fridays) in the Spring and Fall.

The park has a 3-mile paved hike-bike trail (bike rental is available), bridle trail and riding center on the south side of Winton Lake. The park also has picnic areas, a 1-mile fitness trail, a boathouse, nine shelters and an 18-hole Frisbee golf course and a regular golf course. At Parky's Farm explore orchards and crops plus farm animals. Pony rides, Wagon Rides and PlayBarn (farm theme play pits with plastic apples and eggs to jump in) cost $2.00 each. Note, some parts of farm are open only in the summer.

COVEDALE CENTER FOR THE PERFORMING ARTS

Cincinnati - 4990 Glenway Avenue (I-75 to Harrison Ave exit. Follow signs to Queen City Ave, take that 2 miles. Left on Sunset Ave. Right on Glenway) 45238. Phone: (513) 241-6550. www.cincinnatilandmarkproductions.com/ccpa/. Hours: Thursday-Saturday 8:00pm, Sunday 2:00pm (mid-April-mid-October). Additional

SW Area

shows on Wednesdays and Sundays on the Majestic. Weekends (November, December seasonal shows).

Contemporary and classic musicals, comedies and dramas. Choose venues from the Showboat Majestic - live riverfront shows (moored at Broadway St landing); Cincinnati Young Peoples Theatre - end of summer drama; or the Covedale Center Performances - including a Christmas Carol. $16.00-$21.00 for tickets.

COCO KEY WATER RESORT

Cincinnati - *Sheraton Cincinnati North, 11320 Chester Road (I75 exit 15) 45246. Phone: (513) 771-2080. www.cocokeyresort.com. Admission: Day passes from Sunday-Friday are $20.00 per person and on Saturdays, holidays and peak times are $25.00 per person (based on availability) for ages 3 and up, with children 2 and under free. Hotel packages at the Sheraton Cincinnati North begin at $169.00 per night and include four day passes. Lodging: The 257 guest rooms, including Club Level, now have the Sheraton Sweet Sleeper^{SM} bed for total relaxation. Other amenities include two pools and a complete Fitness Center. The remodeled Hamilton Hotel, adjacent, has family-friendly rooms with refrigerators and somewhat discounted pricing.*

A nice, moderate sized indoor waterpark that includes water raft rides, a river tube ride, climbing area and dining with an arcade, too. The 50,000 square feet facility, nearly as large as a football field, features décor and atmosphere reminiscent of a Key West vacation with untamed water slides, an interactive play island and whirlpools, where it's always 84 degrees inside. Noted attraction on the property: Dip-in Theatre Children's Pool: Shallow water to float in while enjoying movies and animation on a movie-size projection screen. (Opened early winter 2008)

ALL AMERICAN BIRTHDAY PARTY

Cincinnati – Sawyer Point , downtown. A full day of parades, rides, entertainment and fireworks. (July 4th)

OKTOBERFEST-ZINZINNATI

Cincinnati - Fifth Street, downtown. www.oktoberfest-zinzinnati.com. The nation's largest authentic Oktoberfest featuring seven areas of live entertainment, food and a children's area. FREE. (third weekend in September)

SW Area

BB RIVERBOATS

Cincinnati (Covington, KY) - *Covington Crossing, just over the blue suspension bridge (I-75 exit 192 to Riverboat Row) 45202. Phone: (800) 261-8586. www.bbriverboats.com. Admission: $13.95 and up. Basically, double the cost if meal served. Children nearly half price. Tours: 1 hour sightseeing cruises on the Ohio River. Several times daily (best to call for schedule). Reservations Required (May-October). Concessions on board.*

Docked at the foot of Madison Street see the Modern "Funliner", "Mark Twain" sternwheeler or steamboat "Becky Thatcher". Also theme cruises like Lock and Dam or year-round holiday tours. Many cruises offer additional lunch, brunch and dinner cruise options with live entertainment.

JUNGLE JIM'S INTERNATIONAL MARKET

Cincinnati (Fairfield) - *5440 Dixie Highway (Route 4) (I-75 exit 16 west on I-275 to exit 41 north) 45014. Phone: (513) 674-6000. www.junglejims.com. Hours: Open daily 8:00am-10:00pm.*

A grocery store is an adventure? This store, selling exotic foods is! This Fairfield, Ohio landmark is as popular a supermarket as it is a tourist attraction.

Ohio's Famous Playground for Food Lovers (Foodies) allows customers to shop in four acres of food from all around the world all under one roof. Plastic animals and giant fruits greet you. Once inside, the store is

A replica of the SS Minnow in a supermarket? Be sure to allow lots of time to explore here!

divided into theme areas. Visit Amish Country, The Ocean, Europe, South America, India and the Middle East. Does the Big Cheese ever change? Try some new food like medallions of alligator! Their fish are so fresh, they keep them in holding ponds and tanks in the store until they are ready to be purchased. You can view this tanks and a mezzanine walkway near the indoor ponds. Spicy food is inside a walk-thru firetruck - hot. Food from England lies under a moving display of Robinhood and friends in the Sherwood Forest. Tea and crumpets, anyone? Even Elvis is here and will occasionally sing a tune while you choose pastries.

SW Area

LOVELAND CASTLE

Cincinnati (Loveland) - *12025 Shore Road (2 miles South of Kings Island) 45140. Phone: (513) 683-4686. www.lovelandcastle.com. Hours: Daily 11:00am-5:00pm (April-September). Weekends only (October – March). Admission: $3.00 general admission. Self-guided tour. Higher fee for special events. Tours: Guided tours are weekdays, by appointment (warm weather season). Groups must have 20 or more people. 35-40 minute tours. Miscellaneous: Only authentically built*

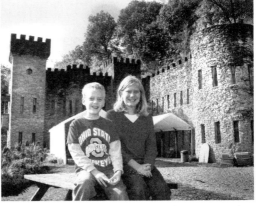

medieval castle in the United States. Call for directions, or for a map that you can print, visit our website. Dads: Any man of high ideas who wishes to help save civilization is invited to become a member of the Knights of the Golden Trail, whose only vows are the Ten Commandments.

This is a real hidden castle and a huge family favorite! Chateau LaRoche was the vision of Harry D.

OK - usually a picture is worth a thousand words, but, even that won't accurately describe Loveland Castle. This is a must see for sure!

Andrews and construction spanned some 50 years beginning in 1929. He actually did 99% of the work himself! The castle is authentic in its rugged structure with battlement towers, a princess chamber, a dungeon, narrow passageways, tower staircases, a "king's" dining room, and tower bedrooms.

You can see the bricks (made from concrete cast in milk cartons) behind Daniel & Jenny

Over 32,000 hand-made (cast in milk cartons donated by neighbors) bricks were used to build parts of the structure (ask to see a sample). Learn a lot about castle building and why the front door has over 2500 nails in it. A real Knight of the Golden Trail (or Lady) will greet you and answer any questions throughout your visit. If you're brainy,

SW Area

try some of the challenging games and puzzles that Harry and his Knights designed. Curious about Harry and his Knights? Look for the 10 Commandments Creed in the Chapel and the video interviews with Harry playing continuously upstairs. If you have time, plan to bring a picnic, they have many tables scattered near the garden or the water below. Don't miss this real adventure that your children and you will love (maybe even play pretend - bring along dress up clothes)!

CINCINNATI NATURE CENTER

Cincinnati (Milford) - *4949 Tealtown Road, 45150. www.cincynature.org. Phone: (513) 831-1711. Hours: Open all year, dawn to dusk. Admission: FREE on Mondays. Weekdays, $3.00. Weekends $5.00.*

This original Cincinnati Nature Center site boasts 18 miles of hiking trails for visitors to explore and enjoy. Educational programs for people of all ages take place in this outdoor classroom. Hike a trail through pristine natural habitat at Rowe Woods, Milford or Long Branch in Goshen. Or, explore the children's garden and farmyard at Gorman Heritage Farm, Evendale (www. gormanheritagefarm.org). Some properties are only open to the public for events.

PUMPKIN MAZE PLAYLAND

Cincinnati (Milford) - Shaw Farm, I-275 & Rte 131 due north. Pumpkin Patches / Hayrides / Corn Mazes / Fall Playland - Admission (average $6.00). Plan on at least two hours playtime. Open weekends, some weekdays (by appointment) and weeknights. Weekday educational tours learning how farm grown products reach your supermarket. www.shawfarms.com. (late September - late October).

RIDE THE DUCKS NEWPORT

Cincinnati (Newport, KY) - *One Aquarium Way (Newport on the Levee, I-275 East to I-471 North. Newport Exit) 41071. http://newportducks.com/. Phone: (859) 815-1439. Admission: $13.00 adult, $10.00 child (2-12). Tours: Summer hours daily 10:00am-8:00pm. Fall/Spring hours generally daily Noon - 5:00pm (subject to weather and groups).*

Quack-Tastic Fun! Ride The Ducks Newport is a 40-minute amphibious sightseeing experience. Travel on land and water in one amazing vehicle. Tour the streets and then SPLASH into the Ohio River. From the water, explore the historic waterfronts of Newport, Covington, and Cincinnati. See the World Peace Bell, Newport Aquarium, Historic Riverside Drive, Great

American Ballpark, Paul Brown Stadium and much more. Your Captain will en-tour-tain you with stories of past and present. Learn about Newport and Ohio history, the Ohio River, its famous personalities and its impact on the state and our nation. Find out about Greater Cincinnati's role in film, song and sports too. Use the famous Wacky Quacker to become a part of the show as you roam the streets. Free with every ride, the Wacky Quacker will grab locals' attention and get the Duck rocking as you roll through the city streets. We always suggest Duck tours for kids to have fun with historical cities and never get bored because they're having too much fun quacking - they never realize they're learning.

HERITAGE VILLAGE MUSEUM

Cincinnati (Sharonville) - *11450 Lebanon Pike, Sharon Woods Park (I-75 exit 16 east to US 42, 1 mile south of I-275 exit 46) 45241. www.heritagevillagecincinnati.org. Phone: (513) 563-9484. Hours: Tuesday-Saturday 10:00am-5:00pm, Sunday 1:00-5:00pm. (May-October). Admission: $5.00 adult, $3.00 child (6-11). Educators: Click on the Teachers Page under Education Programs or rent a History to Go program. Miscellaneous: Dressed interpreters. Bicycle rental, hiking trails. $2.00 entry into Sharon Woods park (per vehicle). Many picnic and shelter areas, mostly wooded for shade. General Store with many pioneer hand-make items and lots of American Girl clothes and books for sale.*

See 18th Century Ohio. Nine actual buildings from Southwest Ohio including: The Elk Lick House - "fancy house", learn about the Gothic Ohio clock and why the "mouse ran up the clock"; the Train Station - with its treasure trunk hands-on pieces to play with; Kemper Log House - look for Isabella's sampler (Little House on the Prairie theme here) and the "Y" staircase; the

kitchen and smokehouse - during festivals they cook here; and the medical office - see Civil War medical and pharmaceutical equipment - amputation city! Their Kids History Camps are wonderfully organized and a great way to "participate" in history.

EASTER EGG HUNTS

Cincinnati (Sharonville) – Heritage Village. Easter Bunny appearance, treat stations, egg hunts, and kids' entertainment and crafts. Admission. (usually held the Saturday before Easter and/or the weekend before)

CIVIL WAR DAYS

Cincinnati (Sharonville) - Heritage Village Museum becomes the ideal backdrop for the public to experience the fascinating civil war adventures in an authentic 19th-Century setting. Demonstrations of military and civilian activities, military drills, inspections, Calvary units and general camp life will open up a forgotten world for visitors, with many hands-on activities for all ages. Admission. (second or third weekend in May)

HARVEST FEST

Cincinnati (Sharonville) - Heritage Village Museum. The weekend is full of heritage games, crafts, activities, entertainment, demonstrations and refreshments. Included in the bountiful Harvest Fest are "pioneer chores", candle dipping, sack races, tug-o-war, scarecrow making, hearth cooking and many other activities. In addition, the Village hosts guided tours of its 19th-century buildings. Admission. (last weekend in September)

HOLLY DAYS

Cincinnati (Sharonville) - Heritage Village Museum starts the season with Holly Days a two weekend event of 1800's celebrations. Guests tour the historic Village and see wonderful decorations in every building and are delighted with the old fashioned tastes of gingerbread, molasses cookies, candy, and bread pudding. One of the historic houses in the Village interprets Hanukah in the mid 1800's where guests taste latkes and other traditional Jewish foods. Music plays through out the village and on several occasions local school groups sing holiday carols. In the Village Train Station guests see the Forest of Christmas Trees, a collection of over 15 trees all decorated by local businesses and friends of the museum. Admission. (first two weekends of December)

SW Area

HOLIDAY IN LIGHTS

Cincinnati (Sharonville) - *Sharon Woods. www.holidayinlights.com. (mid-November thru December)*

HOMEWOOD SUITES BY HILTON CINCINNATI NORTH

Cincinnati (Sharonville) - *2670 E. Kemper Road (I-275 exit 44, Mosteller Road) 45241. Phone: (513) 772-8888. http://homewoodsuites.hilton.com. This all two-room suite property offers a complimentary hot breakfast buffet 7 days a week and a complimentary evening Manager's Reception Monday - Thursday. For your leisure, the hotel offers an outdoor pool, Jacuzzi, sports court, and work out facility on and off site. There are also laundry facilities on-site and a Suite Shop that is open 24 hours. Every spacious suite features enough space for work, study or entertaining, plus all the comforts of home, including a fully equipped kitchen with a full-size refrigerator, coffee maker and microwave oven. Family Fun Packages and good central location make this a good place to base from.*

ENTERTRAINMENT JUNCTION

Cincinnati (West Chester) - *7379 Squire Court (I-75 exit 22 toward Mason) 45069. Phone: (513) 898-8000. www.entertrainmentjunction.com. Hours: Monday-Saturday 10:00am-6:00pm, Sunday Noon-6:00pm. Closed only Easter, Thanksgiving and Christmas. Admission: $12.95 adult, $11.50 senior (65+), $9.95 child (3-12). There is a separate charge of $2.50 for the Kids' Express hand-cranked locomotives (open seasonally June-Labor Day), weather permitting. Seasonal Journey prices run $6.00-$8.00 extra.*

Enter the front doors into an American village square of yesteryear with brick streets and little shops. Billed as the "the world's only Railroad Themed Family Entertainment Center," EnterTrainment Junction offers the largest interactive indoor G-scale layout known, with more than two miles of track and 90 trains, depicting every era of American railroading (called the Train Journey). Start in the early days (pre-Civil War) up to the present. Each train car (over 1,200 of them!) is about the size of a loaf of bread. Even though they're big, they're not all at eye level - some are below and some even high in the air. Actual water flows through canals and rivers into a large lake with a huge waterfall backdrop. Lots of tunnels, small towns, trestles and trains shine with lights. There's also an American Railroading Museum and a 5,000-square-foot play area for kids called "Imagination Junction," that includes a climbing structure

SW Area

and interactive games. Kids Express (summer): Outside, kids become their own train engineers at Kids Express. Youngsters board hand-cranked locomotives and power their way around a 300 foot track.

SEASONAL JOURNEY:

- FUNHOUSE JUNCTION (January - September): old-time amusement park fun house.

- JACK-O-LANTERN JUNCTION (fall): well-lit mazes through an old Victorian village that is slightly haunted. Mirror mazes, clown rooms, chain-link mazes, and a wind tunnel.

- CHRISTMAS AT THE JUNCTION (winter): walk-thru either A Christmas Carol scene or a Journey to the North Pole.

The Junction also offers train displays of all different sizes, as well as exhibits on railroading and model railroading.

Clarksville

PUMPKIN MAZE PLAYLAND

Clarksville - Bonnybrook Farms, 3779 SR 132. Pumpkin Patches/ Hayrides / Corn Mazes / Fall Playland. www.bonnybrookfarms.com. Admission (average $6.00). Plan on at least two hours playtime. Open weekends, some weekdays (by appointment) and weeknights. (late September - late October).

College Corner

HUESTON WOODS STATE PARK

College Corner - *6301 Park Office Road (5 miles North of Oxford off State Route 732) 45003. www.huestonwoodsresort.com. Phone: (513) 523-6381 or (800) 282-7275 reservations.*

A big feature of this park is the Nature Center with programs including their nature crafts, movies, fossils, and fabulous animals (like bobcat, cougar, bunny, snakes, turtles). The Raptor Rehab Center is where they care for injured animals, nursing them back to health (hawks, owls, etc). At the park is also a Rent-a-Camp, biking and rentals, camping, hiking/bridle trails and rentals, boating and rentals, fishing, swimming and winter sports. Kids/Family activities include swimming pool games, candy crafts, guided hikes (fossil hunts) and the ever popular, Bingo games. Evening hikes and bonfire/marshmallow roasts, too. There are cute, cozy, newly remodeled family cottages and a lodge with overnight rooms, indoor / outdoor pools, sauna and fitness areas.

MAPLE SYRUP FESTIVAL

College Corner – *Hueston Woods State Park. Meet at the main beach parking area. Explore the process of maple sugaring from the methods used by Native Americans to the modern methods used today. Pancake breakfast is offered for a small fee. Tour the sugar bush. (first and second weekend in March)*

Corwin

LITTLE MIAMI STATE PARK

Corwin - *(North of Corwin) 45068. Phone: (513) 897-3055. www.dnr.state.oh.us.*

As the river twists and bends, visitors will discover many natural wonders such as steep rocky cliffs, towering sycamores and elegant great blue herons on the wing. Little Miami State Park introduces a new concept to the state park system--a trail corridor. This non-traditional approach focuses on offering numerous recreational pursuits--bicycling, hiking, cross-country skiing, rollerblading, backpacking and horseback riding. The corridor also provides access to canoeing the Little Miami River. Three staging areas (Loveland, Morrow and Corwin) have been located along the developed portion of the park. These include parking lots, restrooms, public phones and trail access points.

Georgetown

GLASS REFACTORY

Georgetown - *9262 Mt. Orab Pike 45121. www.glassrefactory.com. Phone: (888) 291-5690. Admission: FREE. Tours: By appointment, Tuesday-Friday 9:00am-5:00pm. Minimum group size is 8, maximum is 75. Must be at least 6 years old.*

Recycling with a twist…recycling bottles into pieces of art. First collect used glass, melt it and form it into suncatchers. Custom designed molds and some whimsical. Some of their items are sold in the gift shop at places like the National Underground Railroad Freedom Center. Plan to bring $6.00-$10.00 to purchase one at the shop.

SW Area

GRANT BOYHOOD HOME

Georgetown - *219 East Grant Avenue (one block west of SR 125) 45121. Phone: (937) 378-4222. www.ohiohistory.org/places/grantsh. Hours: Wednesday-Sunday Noon-5:00pm (summer). Weekends only (September, October). Admission: $1.00-$3.00 per adult or student. Educators: a bio of Grant is on the link to ohiohistorycentral.org.*

The Grant Boyhood Home in Georgetown was the home of Ulysses S. Grant, 18th president of the United States, from 1823, when Grant was one year old, until 1839, when he left to attend West Point. Ulysses Grant lived in this home longer than any other during his lifetime. Ulysses worked in his father's tannery and, from the ages of about six to thirteen, he attended classes in the little schoolhouse on Water Street. The home was restored and furnished, with one room which is dedicated to Grant and Georgetown memorabilia.

Hamilton

PYRAMID HILL SCULPTURE PARK

Hamilton - *1763 Hamilton-Cleves Road (I-275 to SR 27 to SR 128) 45011. Phone: (513) 868-8336. www.pyramidhill.org. Hours: Monday-Friday 8:00am-5:00pm (until 6:00pm weekends April-October). Monday-Friday 8:00am-5:00pm, Weekends, 10:00am-5:00pm (November-March). Admission: $1.50-$5.00 (age 5+).*

Pyramid Hill is an outdoor museum focusing on monumental pieces of sculpture in an environment of meadows, forests, and various gardens. Their mission includes the eventual establishment of a collection which will demonstrate the complete history of sculpture, making Pyramid Hill the only art park in the world working on the accomplishment. This park currently has 50 titled sculptures. Especially noticeable is "Abracadabra" by internationally famous sculptor, Alexander Liberman. Many passengers flying into Cincinnati can see the 2 ½ story high, bright red contemporary walk-thru sculpture from above. Isn't Rockababy Moon sweet? The Baroque Trajectory arrived the summer of 2002. This piece survived the September 11 attack - it stood just 3 blocks away in New York City!

HOLIDAY LIGHTS ON THE HILL

Hamilton – *Pyramid Hill Sculpture Park. Hundreds of thousands of lights & holiday / storybook characters. Daily, evenings (unless noted). Admission. (Thanksgiving - January 1)*

SW Area

PUMPKIN MAZE PLAYLAND

Hamilton - *Neiderman Farm, 5110 Lesourdsville West Chester Rd. Pumpkin Patches / Hayrides / Corn Mazes / Fall Playland - Admission (average $6.00). Plan on at least two hours playtime. Open weekends, some weekdays (by appointment) and weeknights. www.harvestmoonmaze.com. (late September - late October).*

Harveysburg

OHIO RENAISSANCE FESTIVAL

Harveysburg - *5 miles East of Waynesville on SR-73. www.renfestival.com. (513) 897-7000. The recreation of a 16th century English Village complete with costumed performers, strolling minstrels, may pole dances, full-armored jousting, sword play or feast on giant turkey legs and hearty bread bowls. Two Student Days (Wednesdays) are open special each year: (This is the recommended time to attend with families) Interview Sessions with Queen Elizabeth, Puppet Theatre, Experiment with Historical Games & Rides, Pirate Invasions on the 65-foot Pirate Ship, Combat Demonstrations, Knighthood & Chivalry Discussions, Scottish Dance & Bagpipe Demonstrations, Music Workshops. Admission average $8-15.00 (age 5+). (weekends beginning end of August through mid-October)*

Hillsboro

ROCKY FORK STATE PARK

Hillsboro - 9800 North Shore Drive (6 miles Southeast of Hillsboro off State Route 124) 45133. Phone: (937) 393-4284. www.dnr.state.oh.us.

Unlimited horsepower boating allows for excellent skiing on the lake which also provides catches of bass, muskellunge and walleye. A scenic gorge, dolomite caves and natural wetlands add to the popularity of this recreation area. A 1.5 mile hiking trail takes visitors through cool woodlands, scenic gorges and moist wetlands. A short trail near the campground takes nature lovers to an observation station where excellent birdwatching can be pursued. A two-mile mountain bike trail is also popular with park visitors. 3,464 acres of camping, hiking, boating rentals, and swimming.

THUNDER IN THE HILLS HYDROPLANE RACE

Hillsboro - *Rocky Fork Lake State Park. (937) 393-4284. Hydroplane boat racing, 2nd largest race in the country. FREE. (mid-September)*

SW Area

Kings Mills

KINGS ISLAND & BOOMERANG BAY

Kings Mills - *I-71 to Exit 25A or 24 (24 miles North of Cincinnati) 45034. Phone: (513) 754-5700 or (800) 288-0808. www.visitkingsisland.com. Hours: Daily 10:00am-Dark (Memorial Day-Late August). Weekends Only (April, May, September, October). Park closed for maintenance first two weeks of September. Admission: ~$48.00 general, ~$31.00 child (3-6) and senior (60+). Ticket includes both the amusement park and the waterpark. Discounts available at area hotels, online and at local stores. Check local tourism site. Parking Fee $9.00. Miscellaneous: Three restaurants plus 60 fast food areas. Local favorites like LaRosa's Pizza, Graeter's Ice Cream, Montgomery Inn Ribs and Skyline Chili. Kings Island is now smoke-free (except in designated areas).*

Some of the 80+ featured attractions at King's Island are: BOOMERANG BAY Water Park Resort - The Aussie-themed resort area has more than 50 water activities, including 30 water slides, tropical lagoons, rushing rivers, surfable waves, three family activity areas and careening waterfalls. ACTION ZONE – The Beast (longest wooden coaster), The Crypt (1st indoor coaster to catapult in the dark at high velocity), Thunder Alley (racing car simulator of high speed stock car racing), Backlot Stunt Coaster, Whitewater Rides; the Racer (the Racer is also notable for its appearance in the Cincinnati Kids episode of The Brady Bunch, filmed at the park in 1973), Adventure Express mine ride - journey into ancient temples, proceed thru chambers and strap into a vehicle to make a daring escape. Kings Island has the greatest variety of children's attractions, including four kids' coasters (more than any park in the world), a collection of 20 rides and the fun, live stage shows including: HANNA BARBERA LAND – Scooby Doo's, Cartoon characters. NICK UNIVERSE includes a total of 18 rides and attractions bringing to life Nickelodeon's most popular character celebrities and adventures. Most popular with school age kids. Family rides of all types. Favorite Nick Jr. Characters might visit (i.e. Dora). Amusement Today readers awarded Paramount's Kings Island with the prestigious Golden Ticket Award for Best Kid's Area in the world. Live shows throughout the park, too.

SW Area

Lebanon

LEBANON MASON MONROE RAILROAD

Lebanon - *(two depots: Cincinnati Riverfront - 1901 River Rd (west of downtown) & Lebanon - 198 South Broadway/US 42) 45036. Phone: (513) 398-8584 or (513) 933-8022 info line. www.lebanonrr.com. Departures: Late Morning, Noon, Early Afternoon. Thursday-Sundays (peak) and weekends year-round. Admission: $17.00 adult, $12.00 child (2-12). Special rates for theme train rides for the holidays and Day Out with Thomas. $25.00 plus for excursion trains. Miscellaneous: Station Depot with Gift Shop. The passenger cars do not have restrooms and are not heated or air-conditioned. You are permitted to bring snacks and beverages on the trains. Refreshments are also available for purchase on specific rides.*

LEBANON: The one-hour rides depart from Historic downtown Lebanon and travel along the original CL&N line. Trains operate with a restored 1950s-era GP-7 diesel-electric locomotive, open window commuter coaches built in 1930 and a popular open-air gondola car on the rear of the train allows you to enjoy a panoramic view of the countryside. Besides the holiday trains, they have fun theme train rides like: Civil War, Clifford's Big Red Train, Curious George, Day out with Thomas, Little Engine that Could, Muggles, and Tea Party Mystery Trains. So fun you probably can't just do one!

CINCINNATI: Climb aboard their 1950's / 1960's vintage stainless steel High-Level streamliner coaches and settle back for a nostalgic journey. You'll be treated to a unique High Level experience as you ride up above the surrounding terrain. Most excursions are half or whole day long.

EASTER TRAIN

Lebanon – *Lebanon MM Railroad. Easter Bunny appearance, treat stations, egg hunts, and kids' entertainment and crafts. Admission. (usually held the Saturday before Easter)*

PUMPKIN TRAIN

Lebanon – *Lebanon MM Railroad. Take your little ones on a delightful train ride to the Pumpkin Patch where they can choose their special pumpkin to be transported back to the station on the flatbed car attached to the train. Ride the train to Schappacher Farm where you can pet animals, select a pumpkin and play in the hay before heading back. Small admission fee for ride and for pumpkin. (October weekends)*

SANTA TRAIN

Lebanon – Lebanon MM Railroad. Train trip in decorated coaches with Santa. Songs and treats. Dress warmly. Admission. (Thanksgiving weekend thru weekend before Christmas)

WARREN COUNTY HISTORICAL SOCIETY MUSEUM

Lebanon - 105 South Broadway, 45036. www.wchsmuseum.org. Phone: (937) 932-1817. Hours: Tuesday-Saturday 9:00am-4:00pm, Sunday Noon-4:00pm. Admission: $2.00-$4.00.

The Museum contains artifacts from prehistoric eras to the 1830s and mid-20th century periods. In its Village Green exhibit, antiques are displayed in re-created store fronts. They have the largest collection of Shaker furniture. The Golden Lamb (Ohio's oldest inn) is open for lunch/dinner. Many Presidents have spent the night here. Historical rooms.

PUMPKIN MAZE PLAYLAND

Lebanon - Irons Fruit Farm, 1650 Stubbs Mills Road. Pumpkin Patches / Hayrides / Corn Mazes / Fall Playland - Admission (average $6.00). Plan on at least two hours playtime. Open weekends, some weekdays (by appointment) and weeknights. Applefest in September. www.ironsfruitfarm.com. (late September - late October).

Mason

GREAT WOLF LODGE

Mason - 2501 Great Wolf Drive (I-71 Western Row Rd exit 24) 45040. Phone: (800) 913-9653. www.greatwolf.com. Hours: Waterpark generally open 10:00am-8:00pm off peak days. Open until 10:00pm peak days. Admission: Basically a family stay package (includes waterpark passes) begins at around $219.00 but plan on around $269.00 and up during peak breaks or weekends.

Great Wolf Lodge defies the weather outside with an indoor waterpark experience. It's always a balmy 84 degrees inside the resort's mammoth, 78,000 square-foot indoor waterpark. Bear Track Landing puts the emphasis on fun with 11 waterslides, six pools and a four-story treehouse waterfort. Besides the basics most every other Ohio indoor waterpark has, try the new water roller coaster ride and cannon bowl tube ride or one of six pools: Gigantic wave pool, recreation pool, zero-depth entry children's pool, lazy river, adult whirlpool and family whirlpool. Supervised yet independent kid-friendly fun gives parents time to relax with children in sight.

Great Wolf Lodge provides a comprehensive package of destination lodging amenities, including: 401 all-suite guest rooms; Camp Critter Bar & Grille, a themed family restaurant and bar; The Loose Moose Cottage, a gourmet buffet; Elements Spa featuring Scooops Kid Spa (an ice cream themed spa); MagiQuest game that immerses guests into a world of Renaissance-style fantasy using a techno wand to solve the challenges around the resort; Cub Club children's craft and activity room; an animated Great Clock Tower; Northern Lights Arcade with ticket redemption center; Iron Horse Fitness Room; Bear Claw Café and confectionery, coffee and gift shops.

THE BEACH WATERPARK

Mason - *2590 Waterpark Drive (I-71 Exit 25B - 20 miles North of Cincinnati) 45040. Phone: (513) 398-SWIM or (800) 886-SWIM. www.thebeachwaterpark.com. Hours: Daily opens 10:00am-Closing varies (usually at dark). (Memorial Weekend to mid-September). Admission: $11.00-$28.00 Children – Senior – General. Discounts after 4:00pm. Save lots purchasing general admission tickets online. Parking fee $7.50. Miscellaneous: Food Service. No outside food or drink allowed into the park. Bags are checked.*

Over 40,000 square feet of beach and two million gallons of water and waves await you! As a tropical themed adventure for the whole family and the largest stand alone waterpark in Ohio, The Beach is situated on 35 acres of rolling wooded terrain that provides lots of shade and lush ambiance. Real live palm trees, real white ocean sand, real waterfalls and crashing waves help set the scene and Reggae music and sand volleyball reinforce the tropical island experience. Favorites include the Pearl leisure heated tropical spa pool, Aztec Adventure watercoaster, Thunder Beach Wave Pool and the Lazy Miami River inner tube ride. The young children's water area has Splash Mountain with warm water and Jolly Mon non-water areas!

HOLIDAY FEST

Mason - The Beach Waterpark. A festive holiday paradise featuring the largest outdoor ice skating rink under the stars, old fashion carriage rides, the area's largest outdoor miniature train display, and twinkling holiday lights. The little ones will have lots to see and do with the North Pole Petting Corral, Santa Stable pony rides, and the Candy Cane Maze. This holiday display is complete with a live Nativity and the chance to visit with Santa. Admission. (Thanksgiving weekend thru New Years Eve)

Middletown

MIDDFEST INTERNATIONAL

Middletown - Donham Plaza, downtown. www.middfestinternational.org. (513) 425-7707. Exhibits, music, authentic ethnic dances & menus from many countries. Youth Park. International sports and games, ethnic craft demos, food prep and customs. (October weekend)

LIGHT UP

Middletown - Smith Park, downtown off Rte. 73 / Rte. 4. Hundreds of thousands of lights & holiday / storybook characters. Drive thru. Daily, evenings. www.visitmiddletown.org. Admission. (Thanksgiving - January 1)

Okeana

GOVERNOR BEBB PRESERVE

Okeana - 1979 Bebb Park Lane (follow SR 129 (Hamilton-Scipio Road) about 8 miles. Turn left on California Road then right on Cincinnati-Brookville Road) 45053. Phone: (513) 867-5835 or (877) PARK-FUN. www.butlercountymetroparks.org. Hours: Saturday and Sunday 1:00-5:00pm (summer). Park open daily from 8:00am-dark.

Visit the small 1812 village with the restored log cabin (birthplace of William Bebb - born in 1802). He was the governor of Ohio from 1846 - 48 and a trial lawyer noted for his emotional zeal. There is an 1850's covered bridge, picnic sites, a group picnic shelter, playgrounds, nature trails, restrooms and an on-site park ranger. Rustic family campsites, youth group campsites and a reservable cabin are also available. Good to visit during special events.

Oregonia

SW Area

FORT ANCIENT

Oregonia - 6123 State Route 350 and Middleboro Road (I-71 to Rt. 123 to State Route 350) 45054. www.ohiohistory.org/places/ftancien. Phone: (513) 932-4421 or (800) 283-8904. Hours: Wednesday-Saturday 10:00am-5:00pm, Sunday Noon-5:00pm (April-October). Admission: $8.00 adult, $4.00 student (all ages).

The Museum at Fort Ancient contains 9000 sq. ft. of exhibits, including many interactive units, focusing on 15,000 years of American Indian history in the Ohio Valley. Ohio's entire Indian heritage is displayed from prehistoric to modern times. The 100 acre field is where graves and artifacts were found and is also home to the second largest earthwork in the nation (constructed by Hopewell Indians between 300 BC - 600 AD). Great to visit during Indian Celebration weekends, Children's Day (games and chores) or Night Hiker evenings. Hiking trails.

Oxford

MCGUFFEY MUSEUM

Oxford - *Spring & Oak Sts. (Miami University campus area) 45056. Phone: (513) 529-2232 or (513) 529-1809 campus tours. www.units.muohio.edu/mcguffeymuseum/. Hours: Tuesday-Sunday 1:00-5:00pm (Except Campus holidays and breaks). Weekends 1:00pm-4:00pm. Campus tours are at your leisure during University hours of operation. Admission: FREE. Miscellaneous: Points of interest around campus are: Gardens, Anthropology & Zoology Museums (Upham Hall), Geology Museum (Shideler Hall on Patterson), the Library and the Chapel.*

See an original collection of McGuffey Readers (lesson books on the three R's and morality, i.e. brotherly love, honesty and hard work). The First Eclectic Readers, published in 1836, started the series of books that was to educate five generations of Americans by 1920. They are still in print and still used today. The home, (built in the early 1830's) is where William Holmes McGuffey wrote his readers while preparing class work for children. On display is Professor McGuffey's lectern and traveling 3-part secretary/bookcase. Check out his eight-sided desk! Recently, they've added some activities for kids ages 3-12 (or so) - reproduction 19th-century costumes (for boys and girls), a butter-making activity in the Kitchen, readers to look at in the Library, and a reproduction stereoscope and cards to view in the Parlor. (yeah! we love when museums add more "hands-on" history).

Pleasant Plain

STONELICK STATE PARK

Pleasant Plain - *2895 Lake Drive (1 mile South of Edenton off State Route 727) 45162. Phone: (513) 625-7544.. www.dnr.state.oh.us.*

An interesting feature of the Stonelick landscape is the significance of sweet gum trees. Normally, sweet gum is a subordinate tree but co-dominates the woodlands of Stonelick with beech and maple. Also, colonies of dense flying star, purple fringeless orchid and Virginia mountain mint - all uncommon wildflowers in Ohio - can be found in the park. 5+ miles of hiking trails provide opportunities for exercise and nature study. Hiking trails are also open to mountain bikes. A 500-foot public beach is located on the lake's south shore. 1,258 acres of camping, hiking trails, boating, fishing, swimming & winter sports.

Point Pleasant

GRANT BIRTHPLACE

Point Pleasant - *219 East Grant Avenue (off US 52) 45157. Phone: (513) 553-4911 or (800) 283-8932. www.ohiohistory.org/places/grantbir. Admission: $1.50-$2.00 per adult or student. Tours: Wednesday – Saturday 9:30am – 5:00pm, Sunday Noon-5pm (April-October). Closed for lunch each day (except Sunday). 5th grade and above.*

Civil War General and 18th President's birthplace cottage with period furniture. This restored one-story, three-room cottage, which was built in 1817, was next to the tannery where Grant's father worked. At one time the birthplace made an extensive tour of the United States on a railroad flatcar and was also temporarily displayed on the Ohio State fairgrounds. The small white home has no heat and is sparsely lit – daytime in comfortable weather is best.

Ripley

RANKIN HOUSE

Ripley - *6152 Rankin Road, Rankin Hill (Northeast off US 52, Race Street or Rankin Road) 45167. www.ohiohistory.org/places/rankin. Phone: (937) 392-1627 or (800) 752-2705. Hours: Wednesday-Saturday 10:00am-5:00pm, Sunday Noon-5:00pm (early May - mid-December). Admission: $1.00-$3.00 per adult or student. Educators: Lesson plans focused on Choice to help or not is on the link to ohiohistoryteachers.org.*

This restored home of Reverend John Rankin (early Ohio abolitionist) was part of the Underground Railroad and home to Eliza, a character in "Uncle Tom's Cabin", who found refuge off the Ohio River. A lighted candle in an upstairs window of the Rankin House signaled slaves that it was safe to proceed on the route to freedom. They sheltered (along with neighbors) more than 2,000 slaves escaping to freedom. In this modest home, there were as many as 12 escapees hidden at one time. Winding roads lead to the remote cabin hidden in a clearing in the woods.

Trenton

PUMPKIN MAZE PLAYLAND

Trenton - Barn N Bunk Farm Market, SR 73 & Wayne-Madison Road. Pumpkin Patches / Hayrides / Corn Mazes / Fall Playland - Admission (average $6.00). Plan on at least two hours playtime. Open weekends, some weekdays (by appointment) and weeknights. www.barnnbunk.com. (late September - late October).

Waynesville

CAESAR CREEK STATE PARK

Waynesville - 8570 East State Route 73 (State Route 73, 6 miles West of I-71, near Waynesville) 45068. Phone: (513) 897-3055.. www.dnr.state.oh.us/parks/.

The park's excellent fossil finds give testimony to the life of this long vanished body of water. The Caesar Creek area was named for a black slave captured by the Shawnee on a raid along the Ohio River. The Shawnee adopted Caesar and gave him this valley as his hunting ground. Caesar lived in this area during the time Blue Jacket was war chief and was said to have gone on many raids with him. Caesar Creek's clear waters and 1,300-foot beach offer excellent swimming opportunities. A five-mile mountain bike trail is located between Harveysburg Road and Center Road. The park's nature center houses interesting displays of the cultural and natural history of the area. Naturalist programs are offered year round. The pioneer village (open seasonally for special events) features 15 historic buildings depicting life in the early 1800s. Bridle trails. 10,771 acres of camping, hiking trails, boating, fishing and winter sports.

MAPLE SYRUP WEEKEND

Waynesville – Caesar Creek State Park. Syrup making demos. Pancake dinners/ breakfasts. Sugarbush tours by foot on a woodland walk and learn how trees are drilled to collect sap for making syrup. (third weekend in February)

Wilmington

COWAN LAKE STATE PARK

Wilmington - *1750 Osborn Road (5 miles South of Wilmington off US 68) 45177. Phone: (937) 289-2105. www.dnr.state.oh.us.*

The limestone near Cowan and other parts of the exposed arch are some of the most famous fossil hunting fields in the world. (Collection of fossils requires a permit from the Chief). American Lotus, a brilliant water lily, is abundant in the lake's shallow areas. It is unusual to find such a large colony of lotus on an inland lake. The plant's leaves grow up to two feet in diameter supporting large yellow flowers. Swimming, fishing, sailing and canoeing are popular on the lake. Meandering trails through mature woodlands compliment the natural features of this scenic park. Nature programs. Bike Rental. 1,775 acres of camping, boating and rentals, winter sports and family cabins.

BANANA SPLIT FESTIVAL

Wilmington - *Memorial Park, SR 3 / US 22, downtown. www.bananasplitfestival.com. Celebrate the birthplace of the banana split (first made at Hazzard's Drug Store in 1907). If you love a good old-fashioned festival, set to the tune of the fabulous 50s and 60s, then you've come to the right place. Just think drive-in movies, poodle skirts, sock hops, Dick Clark's American Bandstand, hula hoops, classic cars, and roadside diners. The highlight is the "build your own" banana split booth. (second weekend in June)*

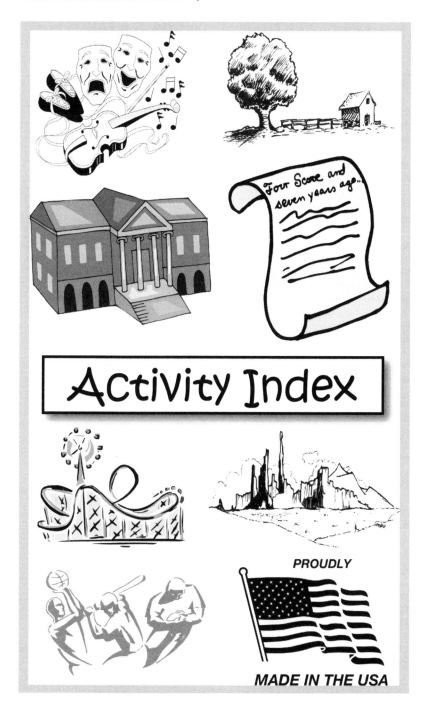

Activity Index

OUTDOOR EXPLORING *(cont.)*

OUTDOOR EXPLORING *(cont.)*

OUTDOOR EXPLORING *(cont.)*

SW Pleasant Plain, *Stonelick State Park*, 285

SW Waynesville, *Caesar Creek State Park*, 287

SW Wilmington, *Cowan Lake State Park*, 288

SEASONAL & SPECIAL EVENTS

C Buckeye Lake, *Cranberry Bog Annual Open House*, 6

C Circleville, *Circleville Pumpkin Show*, 7

C Columbus, *Holiday Tours on Capitol Square*, 10

C Columbus, *Holidays at the Conservatory*, 11

C Columbus, *Dickens of a Christmas*, 13

C Columbus, *Festival Latino*, 19

C Columbus, *Red, White And Boom*, 19

C Columbus, *Ohio State Fair*, 19

C Columbus, *Greek Festival*, 20

C Columbus, *All American Quarterhorse Congress*, 20

C Columbus, *Columbus International Festival*, 20

C Columbus, *First Night Columbus*, 20

C Columbus (Dublin), *Irish Festival*, 20

C Columbus (Hilliard), *Franklin County Fair*, 21

C Columbus (Powell), *Eggs, Paws, & Claws*, 23

C Columbus (Powell), *Wildlight Wonderland*, 23

C Columbus (Reynoldsburg), *Tomato Festival*, 23

C Columbus (Worthington), *Christmas Open House*, 25

C Delaware, *Alum Creek Holiday Fantasy Of Lights*, 26

C Delaware, *Maple Syrup Festival*, 28

C Delaware, *Harvest Festival*, 28

C Delaware, *Little Brown Jug & All Horse Parade*, 28

C Grove City, *Fall Fun Days*, 29

C Hebron, *Pumpkin Maze Playland (s)*, 31

C Marion, *Popcorn Festival*, 34

C Marion, *Marion County Fair*, 34

C Marion, *Apple Festival*, 35

SEASONAL & SPECIAL EVENTS *(cont.)*

C Marion, *Christmas By Candlelight*, 35

C Marion, *Popcorn Pop-N-Drop*, 35

C Milford Center, *The Maize At Little Darby Creek*, 35

C Mt. Vernon, *Knox County Fair*, 37

C Newark, *Luminary Tour*, 38

C Ostrander, *Pumpkin Maze Playland*, 39

C Sugar Grove, *Pumpkin Maze Playland*, 39

C Utica, *Ice Cream Festival*, 40

C Utica, *Harvest Festival*, 40

C Utica, *Pumpkin Maze Playland*, 40

CE Barnesville, *Barnesville Pumpkin Festival*, 45

CE Berlin, *Christmas In Berlin*, 48

CE Bolivar, *Siege of Fort Laurens Lantern Tour*, 50

CE Canal Fulton, *Olde Canal Days*, 53

CE Canal Fulton, *Yankee Peddler Festival*, 53

CE Canton, *Professional Football Hall Of Fame Festival*, 56

CE Canton, *Christmas Open House*, 57

CE Canton, *Italian American Festival*, 57

CE Carrollton, *Holiday Lights*, 60

CE Columbiana, *Pumpkin Maze Playland*, 60

CE Coshocton, *Apple Butter Stirrin' Festival*, 61

CE Coshocton, *Christmas Candlelightings*, 61

CE Coshocton, *Hot Air Balloon Festival*, 62

CE Dennison, *Railroad Festival*, 64

CE Dennison, *Polar Express*, 64

CE Dover, *Victorian Home Open House, J.E. Reeves*, 65

CE East Liverpool, *Tri-State Pottery Festival*, 66

CE Gnadenhutten, *Pioneer Days*, 68

CE Hartville, *Pumpkin Maze Playland*, 69

CE Millersburg, *Old Fashioned Apple Butter Stirring*, 72

CE Millersburg, *Holidays at the Mansion*, 72

CE Orrville, *Jumpin Pumpkin Special*, 77

CE Shreve, *Apple Festival*, 77

CE Steubenville, *Fort Steuben Festival*, 79

CE Sugarcreek, *Ohio Swiss Festival*, 79

SEASONAL & SPECIAL
EVENTS *(cont.)*

SEASONAL & SPECIAL
EVENTS *(cont.)*

SEASONAL & SPECIAL
EVENTS *(cont.)*

NE Cleveland (Berea), *Irish Cultural Festival*, 189
NE Cleveland (Brookpark), *I-X Center Indoor Amusement Park*, 189
NE Cleveland (Brookpark), *Cleveland Christmas Connection*, 189
NE Cuyahoga Falls, *Blossom Holiday Lighting Festival*, 190
NE Geneva, *Great Lakes Medieval Faire*, 191
NE Hinckley, *Buzzard Day*, 191
NE Jefferson, *Civil War Train Raid*, 192
NE Jefferson, *Wild West Weekend*, 192
NE Jefferson, *Kids Pumpkin Train*, 192
NE Jefferson, *Train Rides With Santa*, 193
NE Jefferson, *Children's Old-Fashioned Williamsburg Christmas & Walk*, 193
NE Jefferson, *Ashtabula County Covered Bridge Festival*, 194
NE Kirtland, *Maple Sugaring Weekend*, 195
NE Kirtland, *Village Peddler & Pumpkin Harvest Weekends*, 195
NE Kirtland, *Country Lights*, 195
NE Medina, *Ice Festival*, 196
NE Mentor, *Presidents Day at the Garfield National Memorial Site*, 198
NE Mentor, *Christmas Open House*, 198
NE Middlefield, *Pumpkin Maze Playland*, 198
NE Newbury, *Sled Dog Classic*, 200
NE Peninsula, *Maple Sugar Express*, 202
NE Peninsula, *Easter Bunny Express*, 202
NE Peninsula, *Day Out With Thomas the Tank Engine*, 202
NE Peninsula, *Pumpkin Train*, 202
NE Peninsula, *Holiday Express, Christmas Tree Adventure, or Polar Express*, 202
NE Twinsburg, *Twins Days Festival*, 203
NE Youngstown, *First Night Youngstown*, 207
NW Archbold, *Dairy Days*, 213
NW Archbold, *Old Fashioned 4th of July At Sauder Village*, 213
NW Archbold, *Apple Butter Making Week*, 214
NW Archbold, *Holiday Lantern Tours*, 214

SEASONAL & SPECIAL
EVENTS *(cont.)*

NW Attica, *Oak Ridge Festival*, 214
NW Bluffton, *Bluffton Blaze Of Lights*, 214
NW Defiance, *Black Swamp Steam & Gas Show*, 217
NW Defiance, *Johnny Appleseed Fest*, 217
NW Findlay, *Tracks to the Past*, 219
NW Findlay, *Pumpkin Train*, 220
NW Findlay, *Santa Train*, 220
NW Lima, *Apple Festival*, 222
NW Toledo, *Lights Before Christmas*, 224
NW Toledo, *Lagrange Street Polish Festival*, 225
NW Toledo (Maumee), *Children's Wonderland*, 226
NW Toledo (Perrysburg), *1813 Independence Celebration*, 227
NW Toledo (Perrysburg), *Fort Meigs Holiday Open House*, 228
NW Van Wert, *Kernel Coopers Corn Maze*, 228
S Chillicothe, *Feast Of The Flowering Moon*, 240
S Chillicothe, *Apple Festival*, 240
S Logan, *Maple Sugaring in the Hills*, 243
S Logan, *Hocking Fall Color Tour*, 243
S Logan, *Washboard Music Festival*, 243
S Marietta, *Ohio River Sternwheel Festival*, 246
S Marietta, *Red, White And Blues*, 247
S Marietta, *Pumpkin Maze Playland*, 247
S McArthur, *Holiday Lights*, 248
S Nelsonville, *Easter Egg Hunts*, 249
S Nelsonville, *Santa Train*, 249
S Nelsonville, *Paul Bunyan Show*, 249
S Rio Grande, *Farm Festival*, 251
SW Cincinnati, *Christmas Open House*, 261
SW Cincinnati, *Easter Celebration*, 267
SW Cincinnati, *Festival of Lights*, 268
SW Cincinnati, *All American Birthday Party*, 269
SW Cincinnati, *Oktoberfest-Zinzinnati*, 269
SW Cincinnati (Milford), *Pumpkin Maze Playland*, 272
SW Cincinnati (Sharonville), *Easter Egg Hunts*, 274
SW Cincinnati (Sharonville), *Civil War Days*, 274

SUGGESTED LODGING & DINING *(cont.)*

CE Wooster, *Amish Door Restaurant*, 81
CE Wooster, *Melvins*, 82
NC Loudonville, *Landoll's Mohican Castle Resort*, 131
NC Mansfield, *Spruce Hill Inn/Cottages*, 135
NE Ashtabula, *Covered Bridge Pizza*, 169
NE Brunswick, *Mapleside Farms Restaurant*, 174
NE Newbury, *Punderson Manor House Resort*, 199
NE Warren, *Most Magnificent Mcdonalds In America*, 204
NW Toledo, *Tony Packo's Café*, 223
S Chillicothe, *Sumburger Restaurant*, 239
SW Cincinnati (Sharonville), *Homewood Suites By Hilton Cincinnati North*, 275

THE ARTS

C Columbus, *Columbus Children's Theatre*, 10
C Columbus, *Balletmet*, 13
C Columbus, *Columbus Museum of Art*, 13
C Columbus, *Columbus Symphony Orchestra*, 14
C Columbus, *Davis Discovery Center*, 15
C Lithopolis, *Wagnalls Memorial Library*, 32
CE Berlin, *Behalt, Amish & Mennonite Heritage Center*, 46
CE Cambridge, *Living Word Passion Play*, 50
CE Canton, *Canton Symphony Orchestra*, 54
CE Canton, *Players Guild Theatre*, 54
CE Wilmot, *Amish Door Dinner Theatre*, 80
CW Dayton, *Dayton Philharmonic Orchestra*, 94
CW Dayton, *Dayton Art Institute*, 95
CW West Liberty, *Mad River Theater Works*, 113
NC Lakeside, *Lakeside*, 130
NC Mansfield, *Biblewalk*, 136
NE Akron, *Akron Symphony Orchestra*, 167
NE Akron, *Weathervane Playhouse*, 167
NE Cleveland, *Cleveland Museum of Art*, 177

THE ARTS *(cont.)*

NE Cleveland, *Cleveland Orchestra*, 179
NE Cleveland, *Cleveland Playhouse*, 179
NE Youngstown, *Butler Institute Of American Art*, 206
NE Youngstown, *Youngstown Symphony*, 207
NW Findlay, *Mazza Collection Museum*, 219
NW Toledo, *Toledo Museum Of Art*, 225
NW Toledo, *Toledo Symphony Orchestra*, 225
S Bainbridge, *Magic Waters Theatre*, 234
S Portsmouth, *Portsmouth Murals*, 250
SW Cincinnati, *Cincinnati Art Museum*, 260
SW Cincinnati, *Taft Museum Of Art*, 262
SW Cincinnati, *Cincinnati Symphony Orchestra*, 265
SW Cincinnati, *Covedale Center For The Performing Arts*, 268
SW Hamilton, *Pyramid Hill Sculpture Park*, 278

TOURS

C Columbus, *Ohio State University Museums*, 8
C Columbus, *Al's Delicious Popcorn (The Popcorn Outlet)*, 17
C Columbus, *Graeter's Ice Cream Factory*, 17
C Columbus, *Anthony Thomas Candy Company*, 18
C Columbus, *Schakolad Chocolate Factory*, 19
C Columbus (Worthington), *American Whistle Corporation*, 25
C Hebron, *Zanesville & Western Scenic Railroad*, 30
C Utica, *Velvet Ice Cream: Ye Olde Mill Ice Cream Museum*, 40
CE Barnesville, *Dickson Cattle Company*, 45
CE Berlin, *Schrock's Amish Farm And Village*, 47
CE Berlin, *Wendell August Forge Gift Tour*, 48
CE Cambridge, *Boyd's Crystal Art Glass Company*, 50
CE Cambridge, *Mosser Glass*, 51
CE Canal Fulton, *St Helena III Canal Boat*, 53

TOURS *(cont.)*

TOURS *(cont.)*

Travel Journal & Notes:

Travel Journal & Notes: